SEASIDE™

Pastels & Pickets

SEASIDE™
Pastels & Pickets

Published by Seaside Town Council, Inc.

Copyright © 1994 Seaside Town Council, Inc.
P.O. Box 4957
Seaside, Florida 32459
1-904-231-1551

Library of Congress Catalog Number: 94-72067
ISBN: 0-87197-410-X

Edited, Designed and Manufactured by
Favorite Recipes® Press
P.O. Box 305142
Nashville, Tennessee 37230
1-800-358-0560

Editorial Manager: Mary Jane Blount
Project Manager: Mary Cummings
Editorial Staff: Jane Hinshaw, Linda Jones,
Carolyn King, Elizabeth Miller
Debbie Van Mol, Mary Wilson
Production Designer: Pam Newsome
Typographers: Jessie Anglin, Sara Anglin

Manufactured in the United States of America
First Printing: 1994 10,000 copies

ABOUT OUR TOWN...

Once upon a time...(or so the best of stories always begin), . . . there was only the gentle surf . . . with its spectacular clear emerald green water . . . tall dunes of soft sugar-white sand . . . sea oats waving on the breeze, weathered pines and scrub oaks . . . small rays dancing in graceful formation along the shore and ghost crabs playing an endless game of musical chairs . . . to their own music . . . .

. . . From such a setting emerged our small eighty-acre community of Seaside, . . . located in the Florida Panhandle on the Gulf of Mexico . . . . The land was inherited from his grandfather by Robert Davis, developer and visionary in the plan of Seaside. He was inspired by his own childhood summers spent on these same waters, and by car trips with wife, Daryl, searching for the best small town prototypes.

In the mid nineteen seventies, Davis conferred with Miami architects, Andres Duany and Elizabeth Plater-Zyberk, a husband-wife team who have since gained worldwide prominence for their efforts in planning suburbia. A town square concept, promoting pedestrian traffic and bicycles in lieu of automobiles, was chosen as the design directive for Seaside, together with a remarkably stringent building code embracing demand for fine-quality construction, materials, and aesthetics of classic proportion. It is a mix of residential and commercial, shops and restaurants, markets and main street.

Prominent notoriety points to recognition of Seaside by Prince Charles in his book, *A Vision of Britain*, calling the community "extraordinary" and points out that "it's beginning to influence architectural thinking all over the United States." *Time* magazine has cited Seaside as among the top winners for best design of the decade. In addition, The American Institute of Architects named Seaside's master plan as one of the top United States architectural achievements of the last ten years.

Seaside was conceived extolling the virtues of "Small Town, USA" . . . a return to reflections on personal quality time and the importance of people . . . family, friends, and their enjoyment. Even our town motto says this: "the new town, . . . the old ways." And work has a way of getting done "on Seaside time" (as the locals refer to it). The first house was constructed in 1981, with land presently about two-thirds built-out . . . and on true "Seaside time," there is no particular hurry to finish . . . .

There is an ever-present ambiance here, . . . the architecture, the brick streets, porch swings gently swaying, an array of white picket fences, and color, ... always color everywhere and changing with the light! Our Seaside Town Council and Homeowners invite you to "stroll" through our cookbook and enjoy our "Seaside . . . *PASTELS & PICKETS!*

ABOUT OUR BOOK...

PASTELS & PICKETS had its beginnings steeped in the tradition of great Southern small towns, to the end that people and good times almost always are inseparable from great food!

This cookbook has been almost four years in planning . . . with its original objectives being to promote community spirit and interaction among Homeowners, and to provide a means of revenue production. Proceeds from the sale of this book will be returned to the community through the Seaside Town Council benefiting both directed charities and the Seaside community as a whole.

The name suggests the delightfully obvious features in Seaside . . . Colorful Pastels of houses, water, and sky . . . and Picket Fences and so many designs . . . The 'Over the Fence' comments are the bits of small talk people often exchanged in small towns as they talked . . . The Color Swatches, (over Ingredients), suggest paint brushes, a never-ending part of Seaside!

Our Homeowners are from all over the United States and some foreign countries, and yet very few actually live at Seaside. As a result, we have gathered a unique collection of recipes, reflecting great diversity of the USA and other global destinations.

PASTELS & PICKETS is a result of the time, effort, and dedication of the following COOKBOOK COMMITTEE MEMBERS . . . and their families, too! SPECIAL THANKS:

Joan Anderson	Bill Ginn
Betty Mustachio	Melanie Hansbrough
Rosemary Scoggins	Marilyn Cataldie

Carolyn Pendleton, Chairperson

to . . . DON GAETZ, . . . for his Foreword . . . "A Welcoming Aperitif," and his ability to capture the essence of our community with such verbal style and charisma!
to . . . ALL HOMEOWNERS, . . . who provided not only great recipes, but great ideas and comments and support throughout the whole planning process!
to . . . JAY THOMAS . . . for . . . PHOTOGRAPHY OF SEASIDE: . . . exquisite scenes capturing the essence of our community. Jay is a commercial photographer based in Atlanta, Georgia, a native Georgian, and University of Georgia graduate.
to . . . SEASIDE TOWN COUNCIL MEMBERS & PRESIDENTS . . . Don Gaetz, Bill Wright, and Woods Weathersby . . . for wisdom, direction, and support of the Cookbook idea.
to . . . SEASIDE TOWN MANAGER . . . Connie McFarland...for help when it was needed with any aspect!

and

to . . . FAVORITE RECIPES® PRESS . . . Mary Cummings, Dave Kempf, and their brilliant staff for making it all happen!!!

TABLE OF CONTENTS

A Welcoming Aperitif — 8

Appetizers & Beverages — 10

Soups & Stews — 32

Salads & Dressings — 48

Bread & Breakfast — 64

Pasta Plus & More — 82

Vegetables & Side Dishes — 98

Beef & Veal / Pork & Lamb — 114

Poultry Main Dishes — 128

Fish & Shellfish — 142

Just Desserts — 156

Rainy Days & Sunburns — 182

Seaside Restaurant Sampler — 196

The Art of Food — 212

Nutritional Profiles — 224

Contributors — 232

Cottages — 233

Index — 234

Order Information — 239

A Welcoming Aperitif

If Seaside were a culinary creation, it wouldn't be puréed soup. Although Seaside is celebrated for its integrated architectural character and is governed by a tightly designed town plan, the ingredients of our community are each intrinsic and unique and defy being boiled down to simplistic stock. That's because, to the extent Seaside is or ever will be a town, our community's value is not in its code but in its people.

Yes, we are a gathering place for architects and planners, but even they don't always agree. In fact, it's better when they don't. Walk into our town, look past the pastel chimera, and study the individual homes. They strain against conformity and defy generalizations. Thomas Jefferson's classicism lives in some kind of eclectic harmony even with Walter Chatham and Robert Stern. That's because Seasiders are as different as they are alike, and where they choose to spend their best days reflects tastes that range across beauty, utility, fantasy, and homeliness.

You'll meet our citizens in these pages. Business tycoons and coffee house artisans, shopkeepers and ship owners, authors and illustrators and homecoming queens, professors and politicians and performers. And the rest of us. You'll get to know how truly original they are by the foods and concoctions that define the aromas of their sunrise breakfasts and the tastes that linger with sunset suppers by the Gulf.

This is an invitation to join them in their kitchens or on their porches and share what they choose to sup and sip on during Seaside times, those times they think of as the most memorable and familial. Some of these recipes are the heirlooms of great old Southern families.

Others are offerings from the other side of the world, where some of our citizens live when they're not here. Still others are the secrets—now shared here—of the terrific eateries of our Emerald Coast. The variety is remarkable. You should ravish up and down the continuum of delights.

No, Seaside and its people aren't a purée. If anything, Seaside is a bouillabaisse. Each ingredient succulent in its own right, each individual contribution intriguing, each aspect a tangy spice or a gentle herb. But the magic of good cooking, like the magic of Seaside, is that the lovingly simmered result is greater and always more wonderful than the mere sum of its interesting parts.

Don Gaetz
First Chairman
Seaside Town Council

Appetizers & Beverages

Allison Cottage • American Dream • Anderson Cottage • Annisto
James Cottage • Beach Walk • Bella Vista • Belvedere • Benedictu
• Blue Note • Boswell Cottage • Briar Patch • Brickwalk • Bridgepo
e • Callaway Cottage • Cape May • Carey Cottage • Caribbean • Ca
Chelsea • Clark Cottage • Colony • Colors • Compass Rose • oqu
tage • Dahlg
stle • ollhous
cher • r • Du
Eclips h Cotta
e • Flo Cottag
t's Roo • Gray
anor • Harv
• Hodg House
ine • J idosco
t Editi Cottag
ine L e • Lu
rtha G cLaugh
mmer M e • Mo
vana ge • Ou
es 'n Cream • Pelican Perch • Periwinkle • Persimmon • Per asio
razy • Portera Cottage • Postcard • Precious • Propinquity • Pugli

..."O Oysters, come and walk with us!" / The Walrus did beseech,
"A pleasant walk, a pleasant talk, / Along the briny beach;...
Lewis Carroll

cky's • Roanoke • Robin's Nest • Roger's Lighthouse • Romanc
andcastle • Sandi Shore • Sandia • Sandpail • Sandpiper • Savann
e • Sea for Two • Sea View • Sealink • Seaquel • Seaspell • Seasta
Sea • Skinny Dip • Smith Cottage • Somewhere In Time • South

Appetizers

Apricot Pecan Spread, 13

Baked Brie, 13

Asparagus Roll-Ups, 14

Cheddar Chili Squares, 14

Cheese Strips, 15

Balsamic Chicken Wings, 15

Sea Time Finger Sandwiches, 16

Chicken Wings, 16

Crab Grass, 17

Green Olives and Ham Canapés, 17

Ham and Cheese Rolls, 18

Barbecued Appetizer Meatballs, 18

Spiced Oyster Crackers, 19

Boiled Peanuts, 19

Easy Shrimp Butter, 20

Sun-Dried Tomato Pâté, 20

Sausage Mushrooms, 21

Tortilla Roll-Ups, 21

Artichoke Dip, 21

Baked Beef Dip, 22

Black-Eyed Pea Dip, 22

Bleu Cheese Dip, 23

Green Chili and Tomato Dip, 23

Microwave Crab Dip, 24

Hummus, 24

Salsa Dip, 25

Shoe Peg Corn Dip, 25

Mexican Taco Dip, 26

Spinach Dip, 26

Vidalia Onion Dip, 27

Beverages

Champagne Punch, 27

Christmas Eve Punch, 28

Christmas Eve Eggnog, 28

Kentucky Eggnog Spike, 29

Sangria, 29

Blonde Sangria, 30

Instant Spiced Tea, 30

Beach Cooler, 31

Wassail, 31

APRICOT PECAN SPREAD

- Combine kefir cheese, cream cheese, apricots and pecans in bowl; mix well.
- Serve with assorted crackers.
- Glazed Australian apricots are available at specialty stores.
- Yield: 16 servings.

  Over the Fence: The glazed Australian apricots are very important. You can use regular dried apricots and the result will be good; the item from Down Under makes it great.

Ingredients

8 ounces kefir cheese, at room temperature

8 ounces cream cheese, softened

4 to 6 large glazed Australian apricots, at room temperature, chopped

1/2 cup chopped pecans

"GULF MANOR" BAKED BRIE

- Preheat oven to 375 degrees.
- Spread crescent roll dough in single sheet; do not separate into sections.
- Place Brie in center of dough. Sprinkle top and side with brown sugar.
- Wrap Brie in dough to cover. Place on ungreased baking sheet.
- Bake for 15 minutes or until brown. Serve warm with assorted crackers.
- Yield: 6 servings.

Ingredients

1 (8-count) can crescent rolls

1 (8-ounce) wheel of Brie

1/2 cup packed light brown sugar

ASPARAGUS ROLL-UPS

Ingredients

1 (16-ounce) loaf white bread

8 ounces ham

3/4 cup pecans

1/2 cup butter

8 ounces cream
cheese, softened

2 tablespoons mayonnaise

Salt and pepper to taste

Chopped fresh parsley to taste

1 (16-ounce) can
asparagus, drained

- Preheat oven to 350 degrees.
- Trim crust from bread; roll to flatten.
- Chop ham and pecans in food processor. Remove mixture to bowl.
- Process butter, cream cheese, mayonnaise, salt, pepper and parsley in food processor until smooth. Add ham and pecan mixture. Process just until blended.
- Spread cream cheese mixture on bread slices. Place 1 asparagus spear on each bread slice; roll to enclose. Place in baking dish. Chill in refrigerator.
- Bake until brown. Serve whole or sliced.
- Yield: 20 servings.

CHEDDAR CHILI SQUARES

Ingredients

1 (4-ounce) can chopped
green chilies, drained

1 pound sharp Cheddar
cheese, shredded

4 eggs

1/4 cup milk

- Preheat oven to 350 degrees.
- Line bottom of 9x9-inch baking dish with chilies. Sprinkle with cheese.
- Beat eggs and milk in bowl. Pour over cheese.
- Bake for 45 minutes. Cut into squares.
- Yield: 16 servings.

CHEESE STRIPS

Great hot or cold! Serve with a glass of wine.

- Combine bacon, cheese, onion, almonds, mayonnaise, Worcestershire sauce, salt and pepper in bowl; mix well.
- Spread bacon mixture on bread slices; cut into 1½-inch strips. Place on baking sheet. Freeze until firm.
- Preheat oven to 400 degrees.
- Bake for 10 minutes.
- Yield: 25 servings.

Ingredients

6 slices crisp-fried
bacon, crumbled

8 ounces sharp Cheddar
cheese, shredded

2 to 3 tablespoons chopped onion

¾ cup chopped almonds

¾ cup mayonnaise

2 teaspoons
Worcestershire sauce

Salt and pepper to taste

1 (24-ounce) loaf thinly sliced
bread, crusts trimmed

"NEWNUM-QUEEN" BALSAMIC CHICKEN WINGS

An easy recipe for dinner after a day at the beach.

- Rinse chicken and pat dry.
- Combine chicken, vinegar and scallions in bowl, tossing to coat. Marinate, covered, in refrigerator for 6 hours to overnight, stirring occasionally.
- Preheat oven to 450 degrees.
- Let chicken stand until room temperature; drain. Place on baking sheet.
- Bake for 25 minutes or until crisp and brown or grill over medium-hot coals for 8 to 10 minutes per side.
- Serve hot or at room temperature.
- Yield: 12 servings.

Ingredients

2 pounds chicken wings

⅔ cup balsamic vinegar

3 large scallions, thinly sliced

SEA TIME FINGER SANDWICHES

A delicious filling that resembles chicken salad.

- Combine pecans, egg, olives, onion, mayonnaise, celery seeds, salt and pepper in bowl; mix well. Chill, covered, for 3 hours.
- Spread mixture on 8 slices bread; top with remaining bread slices. Cut sandwiches into thirds.
- Yield: 24 servings.

Ingredients

1 cup finely chopped pecans
1 hard-boiled egg, finely chopped
1 (2-ounce) jar Spanish olives
with pimento, finely chopped
1 small onion, finely chopped
1 cup mayonnaise
1 teaspoon celery seeds
Salt and pepper to taste
16 slices sandwich bread,
crusts trimmed

"FLAMINGO" CHICKEN WINGS

- Preheat oven to 350 degrees.
- Rinse chicken and pat dry. Separate at joints; discard tips. Place in 9x13-inch baking dish.
- Pour mixture of teriyaki sauce, soy sauce, garlic powder and ginger over chicken.
- Bake for 1½ hours, turning chicken every 30 minutes. Serve warm.
- Yield: 12 servings.

Ingredients

2 pounds chicken wings
½ cup teriyaki sauce
½ cup soy sauce
⅛ teaspoon garlic powder
Ginger to taste

Over the Fence: At Flamingo Cottage, Olive Nut Stuffed Celery is a snap. Combine 3 ounces softened cream cheese, ¼ cup chopped salted peanuts and ¼ cup finely chopped olives. Spread into six 9-inch celery sticks and cut into 1-inch pieces.

CRAB GRASS

- Preheat oven to 350 degrees.
- Squeeze moisture from spinach.
- Sauté onion in butter in large skillet. Stir in spinach. Add crab meat and Parmesan cheese; mix well. Spoon into baking dish.
- Bake for 20 minutes. Serve with wheat thins or assorted crackers.
- Yield: 16 servings.

Ingredients

1 (10-ounce) package frozen chopped spinach, cooked, drained

1/2 medium onion, chopped

1/4 cup butter

1 pound lump crab meat, flaked

1 cup grated Parmesan cheese

"WILDER" GREEN OLIVES AND HAM CANAPES

- Combine cream cheese, salt and pepper in microwave-safe bowl; mix well. Microwave until softened; stir.
- Spread 1/2 of the ham slices with cream cheese mixture; top with remaining slices. Cut into squares.
- Arrange olives and ham squares on wooden picks.
- Yield: 16 servings.

Over the Fence: Very eye-catching. Your guests will think you spent hours stacking these little layers.

Ingredients

8 ounces light cream cheese, softened

Salt and pepper to taste

1 (8-ounce) package thinly sliced ham

1 (7-ounce) jar stuffed green olives, drained

"ALLISON COTTAGE" HAM AND CHEESE ROLLS

Ingredients

1 cup butter, softened

1 small onion, chopped

3 tablespoons mustard

1 tablespoon poppy seeds

Tabasco sauce to taste

1 teaspoon Worcestershire sauce

2 (12-count) packages
Parker House rolls

1 (8-ounce) package
thinly sliced ham

4 ounces Swiss cheese,
thinly sliced

- Preheat oven to 325 degrees.
- Combine butter, onion, mustard, poppy seeds, Tabasco sauce and Worcestershire sauce in bowl; mix well.
- Split rolls horizontally; do not separate. Spread cut sides with butter mixture.
- Place ham and cheese slices on 1 cut side; top with remaining rolls.
- Bake for 15 minutes; cut into individual rolls.
- Yield: 24 servings.

BARBECUED APPETIZER MEATBALLS

Ingredients

1½ pounds ground chuck

1½ teaspoons
Worcestershire sauce

1 (5-ounce) can evaporated milk

1 envelope onion soup mix

2 cups catsup

1 cup packed brown sugar

1 tablespoon
Worcestershire sauce

- Preheat oven to 350 degrees.
- Combine ground chuck, 1½ teaspoons Worcestershire sauce, evaporated milk and soup mix in bowl; mix well. Shape into 1-inch balls. Place on baking sheet.
- Bake for 30 minutes or until brown; drain.
- Combine catsup, brown sugar and 1 tablespoon Worcestershire sauce in saucepan; mix well. Cook until blended, stirring occasionally. Add meatballs. Cook just until heated through, stirring occasionally.
- Yield: 30 servings.

"ROBINS" SPICED OYSTER CRACKERS

- Combine dressing mix, dillweed and garlic salt in bowl; mix well. Pour crackers over mixture.
- Drizzle oil over crackers, stirring to mix.
- Yield: 32 servings.

Ingredients

1 envelope ranch
salad dressing mix

2 tablespoons dillweed

1/2 teaspoon garlic salt

1 (16-ounce) package
oyster crackers

3/4 cup (or less) oil

"MELROSE" BOILED PEANUTS

*Luverne, Alabama, has the world's largest
peanut boil every Labor Day weekend.*

- Rinse peanuts. Place peanuts and enough water to cover in stockpot. Season with salt.
- Boil until peanuts are tender-crisp; drain.
- Yield: variable.

Over the Fence: *The key to good boiled peanuts is the kind of peanuts you buy. They must be green peanuts which are only available in the late summer to early fall. When eating boiled peanuts, crack the shell with your teeth and suck the juice out. Then open the shell and eat the nut inside.*

Ingredients

Peanuts

Water

Salt to taste

"DREAM CHASER"
EASY SHRIMP BUTTER

Ingredients

2 (5-ounce) cans shrimp,
  finely chopped
1 tablespoon minced onion
Juice of 1 lemon
1/4 cup mayonnaise
3/4 cup butter, softened
8 ounces cream cheese, softened
1/4 teaspoon garlic powder

- Combine shrimp, onion, lemon juice, mayonnaise, butter, cream cheese and garlic powder in mixer bowl. Beat until combined.
- Serve with assorted crackers.
- Yield: 16 servings.

SUN-DRIED TOMATO PÂTÉ

Ingredients

1 (3-ounce) package
  sun-dried tomatoes
Salt to taste
1 clove of garlic
10 to 20 calamata or
Greek black olives, pitted
1/2 teaspoon oregano
Olive oil to taste

Serve this spread with an assortment of cheeses and a nice wine at sunset at Seaside.

- Combine sun-dried tomatoes, salt and enough water to cover in saucepan. Simmer for 10 minutes. Let stand until cool. Drain.
- Combine tomatoes, garlic, olives and oregano in food processor container. Process until smooth. Add olive oil as needed for desired consistency.
- Yield: 10 servings.

Over the Fence: *The easiest way to pit olives is to place them on a cutting board, place the broad side of a chef's knife blade on top and hit it with your fist—the same way in which you would crush a clove of garlic.*

SAUSAGE MUSHROOMS

- Brown sausage in skillet, stirring until crumbly; drain.
- Combine sausage and cream cheese in bowl; mix well. Spoon mixture into mushroom caps. Place on baking sheet; sprinkle with Parmesan cheese.
- Preheat broiler.
- Broil for 3 to 4 minutes or until brown.
- Yield: 30 servings.

Ingredients

1 pound hot sausage
8 ounces cream cheese, softened
30 large mushroom caps
1/2 cup grated Parmesan cheese

TORTILLA ROLL-UPS

- Combine cream cheese, chilies and olives in bowl; mix well. Spread over tortillas; roll to enclose filling.
- Chill, wrapped in plastic wrap, overnight. Cut into 1/2-inch slices. Serve with picante sauce.
- Yield: 90 servings.

Ingredients

32 ounces cream cheese, softened
3 (4-ounce) cans chopped green chilies
1 (2-ounce) can chopped black olives
10 large flour tortillas

"MCLAUGHLIN COTTAGE" ARTICHOKE DIP

- Preheat oven to 350 degrees.
- Combine chopped artichokes, mayonnaise, lemon juice, Tabasco sauce and Parmesan cheese in bowl; mix well. Spoon into baking dish.
- Bake for 10 minutes or until bubbly.
- Serve with tortilla chips.
- Yield: 16 servings.

Ingredients

1 (16-ounce) can artichoke hearts, drained, chopped
1 cup mayonnaise
1 tablespoon lemon juice
Tabasco sauce to taste
1 cup grated Parmesan cheese

BAKED BEEF DIP

- Preheat oven to 350 degrees.
- Melt butter in skillet. Stir in pecans and salt. Cook until pecans are brown, stirring constantly.
- Combine cream cheese, milk, dried beef, onion flakes, pepper, horseradish and sour cream in bowl; mix well. Spoon into baking dish. Sprinkle with pecans.
- Bake for 20 minutes. Serve with assorted crackers.
- Yield: 12 servings.

Ingredients

2 tablespoons butter

1/2 cup coarsely chopped pecans

1/2 teaspoon salt

8 ounces cream cheese, softened

2 tablespoons milk

1 (2 1/2-ounce) jar dried beef, chopped

1 1/2 tablespoons onion flakes

1/4 teaspoon pepper

1 teaspoon horseradish

1/2 cup sour cream

BLACK-EYED PEA DIP

Serve as a dip or as an accompaniment to grilled meat, fish or chicken.

- Combine black-eyed peas, green peppers, onion, green onions, jalapeño peppers, pimentos, garlic salt, pepper and salad dressing in bowl; mix well.
- Serve with tortilla chips.
- Yield: 25 servings.

Ingredients

4 (16-ounce) cans black-eyed peas

2 cups chopped green bell peppers

1/2 cup chopped onion

1 cup chopped green onions

1/2 cup chopped jalapeño peppers

2 (4-ounce) jars pimentos, drained, chopped

1 tablespoon garlic salt

Pepper to taste

1/2 to 1 cup light Italian salad dressing

BLEU CHEESE DIP

- Beat cream cheese in mixer bowl until light and fluffy. Stir in bleu cheese, evaporated milk, green pepper, olives, garlic salt and celery salt.
- Chill, covered, for 3 to 4 hours.
- Let stand at room temperature for 30 minutes before serving. Sprinkle with paprika.
- Serve with fresh vegetables.
- Yield: 16 servings.

Ingredients

8 ounces cream cheese, softened
4 ounces bleu cheese, crumbled
1/4 cup evaporated milk
1/3 cup chopped green bell pepper
3 tablespoons chopped pimento-stuffed green olives
1/4 teaspoon garlic salt
1/4 teaspoon celery salt
Paprika to taste

GREEN CHILI AND TOMATO DIP

- Combine undrained green chilies, ripe olives, tomatoes, salt, green onions, garlic powder, pepper, cider vinegar and oil in bowl; mix well.
- Chill, covered, until serving time.
- Serve with tortilla chips.
- Yield: 8 servings.

Ingredients

1 (4-ounce) can chopped green chilies
1 (4-ounce) can chopped black olives, drained
2 large tomatoes, chopped
1/2 teaspoon salt
3 or 4 green onions with tops, chopped
1 teaspoon garlic powder
1/2 teaspoon pepper
1 1/3 tablespoons cider vinegar
1 tablespoon oil

Over the Fence: Easy-does-it at Just Peachy Cottage where Clam Dip is a specialty. Combine 16 ounces softened cream cheese, 2 cans minced clams, 2 tablespoons each mayonnaise and parsley flakes, 1/4 cup chopped onion, 1 tablespoon Worcestershire sauce, a squeeze of lemon and a dash of Tabasco sauce and salt.

"TOASTY SUNSET" MICROWAVE CRAB DIP

Ingredients

6 tablespoons butter
1/4 cup finely chopped onion
1 clove of garlic, minced
1 tablespoon chopped
fresh parsley
8 ounces cream cheese, chopped
1 to 2 teaspoons
Worcestershire sauce
1/4 teaspoon Tabasco sauce
1/8 teaspoon salt
12 ounces crab meat

- Microwave butter in microwave-safe dish on High for 45 seconds or until melted. Stir in onion, garlic and parsley.

- Microwave, covered, on High for 2 1/2 to 3 1/2 minutes or until onion is tender. Add cream cheese. Microwave on High for 30 to 60 seconds or until creamy, stirring once.

- Stir in Worcestershire sauce, Tabasco sauce and salt. Fold in crab meat. Microwave on High for 1/2 to 2 1/2 minutes or until heated through, stirring once.

- Serve with melba rounds or assorted crackers.

- Yield: 8 servings.

"HORN COTTAGE" HUMMUS

Ingredients

1 (19-ounce) can chickpeas
1/4 to 1/2 cup sesame tahini
1 clove of garlic
1 teaspoon tamari
2 teaspoons (or more)
lemon juice
1 green onion, chopped
Parsley sprigs
Salt and black pepper to taste
Lemon pepper to taste

This recipe is of Middle East origin. It is rich in usable, high-quality protein and calcium and can be made as mild or as spicy as you desire.

- Combine chickpeas, tahini, garlic, tamari, lemon juice, green onion, parsley sprigs, salt, black pepper and lemon pepper in food processor container. Process until coarse paste forms. Adjust seasonings.

- Serve with fresh vegetables or toasted pita wedges.

- Yield: 12 servings.

"POSTCARD" SALSA DIP

- Chop and drain tomatoes. Chop green onions finely.
- Combine tomatoes, green onions, relish, sliced olives, garlic salt, olive oil and vinegar in bowl; mix well.
- Serve with tortilla chips.
- Yield: 10 servings.

Ingredients

4 or 5 tomatoes

3 or 4 green onions

1 can jalapeño pepper relish

1 (2-ounce) can sliced black olives, drained

1 teaspoon garlic salt

2 tablespoons olive oil

1 1/2 tablespoons cider vinegar

SHOE PEG CORN DIP

- Cut circle in top of loaf.
- Scoop out center of loaf carefully to form shell. Cut bread from center into cubes.
- Combine butter and cream cheese in saucepan. Cook until smooth, stirring constantly. Stir in chilies and corn. Cook just until heated through, stirring constantly.
- Spoon corn mixture into bread shell. Serve dip with bread cubes.
- Yield: 12 servings.

Ingredients

1 round loaf French bread

1/2 cup butter

8 ounces cream cheese

2 (4-ounce) cans chopped green chilies, drained

1 (11-ounce) can Shoe Peg corn, drained

"SUNRISE" MEXICAN TACO DIP

Ingredients

1 avocado, mashed

1 cup sour cream

2 to 4 green onions, chopped

1 (8-ounce) jar taco sauce

1 (8-ounce) package shredded
Monterey Jack cheese

1 (4-ounce) can sliced
black olives

*Layered in a glass serving bowl, this dip is visually
inviting and is a wonderful snack variation.*

- Layer avocado, sour cream, green onions, taco sauce,
shredded cheese and black olives in order listed in glass
serving bowl.
- Serve with tortilla chips or taco chips.
- May substitute salsa for taco sauce.
- Yield: 12 servings.

"SHANGRI-LA" SPINACH DIP

Ingredients

1 (10-ounce) package frozen
chopped spinach, thawed

1 cup sour cream

1 cup mayonnaise

1 small onion, chopped

1 (8-ounce) can water
chestnuts, drained, chopped

1 envelope vegetable soup mix

- Squeeze moisture from spinach.
- Combine spinach, sour cream, mayonnaise, onion, water
chestnuts and soup mix in bowl; mix well.
- Chill, covered, in refrigerator overnight.
- Serve with assorted crackers or fresh vegetables.
- Yield: 16 servings.

*Over the Fence: At Dunseth Cottage, Pizza Dip
welcomes hungry guests. Spread 8 ounces softened
cream cheese in ovenproof dish. Top with pizza
sauce, shredded mozzarella cheese, sliced pepperoni,
sliced green olives and grated Parmesan cheese.
Bake at 325 degrees for 15 minutes and serve with
crackers or chips.*

VIDALIA ONION DIP

- Bring water, vinegar, sugar and dry mustard to a boil in saucepan, stirring occasionally. Pour over onions in bowl. Chill, covered, overnight.
- Drain onions, discarding liquid. Stir in mayonnaise and celery seeds. Serve with saltine crackers.
- Yield: 8 servings.

Ingredients

2 cups water

1/2 cup vinegar

1 cup sugar

1/4 teaspoon dry mustard

4 large Vidalia onions, sliced, cut into quarters

1/2 cup mayonnaise

1/4 teaspoon celery seeds

"PERSIMMON" CHAMPAGNE PUNCH

- Chill wine, juice and Champagne well.
- Combine wine, juice and lemonade concentrate in punch bowl; mix well.
- Add Champagne just before serving; mix gently. Add ice ring if desired.
- Yield: 25 servings.

Ingredients

3 (750-milliliter) bottles of dry white wine

2 (46-ounce) bottles of pineapple-grapefruit juice

2 (26-ounce) bottles of Champagne

2 (6-ounce) cans frozen lemonade concentrate

Over the Fence: Microwave Reuben Spread for a fast cocktail snack. Combine 6 ounces chopped corned beef, 3 cups shredded Swiss cheese, 16 ounces sauerkraut, drained, and 1/2 cup Thousand Island salad dressing. Heat and serve on cocktail rye bread or crackers.

"BRIAR PATCH" CHRISTMAS EVE PUNCH

Ingredients

2 cups orange juice

2/3 cup lemon juice

1 (32-ounce) bottle of light cranberry juice cocktail

1 (46-ounce) can unsweetened pineapple juice

1 quart diet ginger ale

- Chill all ingredients.
- Combine orange juice and lemon juice in punch bowl. Add cranberry juice and pineapple juice; mix well.
- Mix in ginger ale gradually at serving time. Add ice ring if desired.
- Yield: 30 servings.

Over the Fence: We always serve this at our annual Mother-Daughter Christmas Cookie Swap. I measure the orange juice and lemon juice mixture in jars so I can refill the punch bowl by adding whole bottles of ingredients. I add an ice ring or block made of orange juice, orange slices, lemon slices and strawberries.

"PHILLIPS COTTAGE" CHRISTMAS EVE EGGNOG

Ingredients

12 egg yolks

1 1/2 cups sugar

1 cup bourbon

1 quart whipping cream

6 egg whites

- Beat egg yolks in mixer bowl. Add sugar; beat until thick and smooth. Add whiskey gradually.
- Beat whipping cream in mixer bowl until soft peaks form. Beat egg whites in mixer bowl until stiff.
- Fold whipped cream and stiffly beaten egg whites into egg yolk mixture. Chill for several hours.
- Yield: 16 servings.

"PEACHES 'N CREAM" KENTUCKY EGGNOG SPIKE

- Combine bourbon, rum and brandy in 1-quart bottle. Cut vanilla bean into halves lengthwise. Scrape seeds into bottle; add pod to bottle.
- Crack whole nutmeg into 4 or 5 pieces. Add to bottle with cinnamon sticks and cloves; seal bottle.
- Let stand in cool dark place for 1 week to 3 months.
- Yield: 32 (2-tablespoon) servings.

Over the Fence: *We find this to be a perfect gift for those who indulge in holiday eggnog. Include instructions for adding several tablespoons to a cup of eggnog.*

Ingredients

2 cups bourbon
1 cup dark rum
1 cup brandy
1 vanilla bean
1 whole nutmeg
2 large cinnamon sticks
7 whole cloves

"TIDE'S INN" SANGRIA

- Combine vodka, brandy, wine, sugar dissolved in a small amount of water, lemon juice, vanilla, cinnamon sticks and lemon slices in pitcher; mix well. Chill in refrigerator.
- Add 7-Up at serving time; mix gently.
- Yield: 6 servings.

Over the Fence: *A family friend from Spain gave this recipe to us and we find it a wonderful enhancement to paella or Mexican food.*

Ingredients

1 ounce vodka
2 ounces brandy
1 fifth of Cella Lambrusco
5 tablespoons sugar
Juice of 3 lemons
1 teaspoon vanilla extract
2 cinnamon sticks
1 lemon, thinly sliced
1/2 (12-ounce) can 7-Up

BLONDE SANGRIA

Ingredients

1 fifth of white wine
1 cup pineapple juice
1/3 cup orange juice
3 tablespoons lemon juice
1 tablespoon lime juice
1/4 to 1/2 cup sugar
1 (7-ounce) bottle of club soda

- Combine wine, pineapple juice, orange juice, lemon juice, lime juice and sugar in pitcher; mix well to dissolve sugar.
- Add club soda just before serving; mix gently.
- Yield: 6 servings.

"JUST PEACHY" INSTANT SPICED TEA

Ingredients

2 cups orange instant breakfast drink mix
4 cups sugar
1/2 cup instant tea mix with lemon
1 teaspoon ground cloves
1/2 teaspoon ground cinnamon

The pungent aroma of spiced tea and a nippy coastal day make an unbeatable combination.

- Mix orange drink mix, sugar, instant tea mix, cloves and cinnamon in bowl. Spoon into airtight container.
- Dissolve 2 to 4 teaspoons of the mixture in 1 cup boiling water for each serving.
- Yield: 50 to 100 servings.

Over the Fence: *Make several batches when you have time, and give as gifts in decorative airtight containers.*

"ABOUT TIME" BEACH COOLER

*A very refreshing and almost calorie-free
drik for the beach at Seaside.*

- Squeeze lemon and lime slices over ice in 2 large plastic glasses. Add diet soda, ginger ale and vinegar; mix well.
- Yield: 2 servings.

Ingredients

1/2 lemon, sliced

1/2 lime, sliced

2 (12-ounce) cans diet Slice

1 (13-ounce) can diet ginger ale

1 tablespoon apple cider vinegar

"PICTURE BOOK" WASSAIL

Serve during the Thanksgiving and Christmas holidays.

- Tie cinnamon and cloves in cheesecloth bag. Combine with 2 cups water and sugar in 10-quart stockpot or heatproof container.
- Bring to a boil. Boil for 5 minutes. Remove spice bag. Add orange juice, lemon juice, grapefruit juice, apple cider and 2 cups water. Bring to a boil.
- Add 1 cherry to each cup. Ladle wassail into cups.
- Yield: 12 servings.

Ingredients

2 cinnamon sticks

16 whole cloves

2 cups water

1 cup sugar

3/4 cup unsweetened orange juice

1/4 cup lemon juice

1/2 cup grapefruit juice

2 cups apple cider

2 cups water

12 maraschino cherries

Soups & Stews

illman Cottage • Stringer Cottage • Sundance • Sundaze • Sunnysi
ottage • Thanksgiving • The Beach House • The Conservatory • Th
nset • Tommy T • Topisaw • Tower Breeze • Toye • Treetops • Tri
anda • Villa Whimsey • Vista del Mar • Wakeham Cottage • Watersi
dward • Woodlawn • Wright By the Beach • Zebulon • eidma

...Make haste, your morning task resign;
Come forth and feel the sun....
William Wordsworth

• Marietta's Cottage • Marisol • Martha Green • McChesney Cottag
ries • Midsummer Night's Dream • Mirador • Mis B'Haven • Mod
• Nightshade • Nirvana • Olson Cottage • On the Veranda • Ondin
Peach Delight • Peaches 'n Cream • Pelican Perch • Periwinkle

Soups & Stews

Chilled Avocado Soup, 35

Gazpacho, 35

French Market Soup, 36

Wharton Cheese Soup, 37

Firehouse Chili, 37

Great San Luis Green Chile Soup, 38

Chinese Hot and Sour Soup, 39

Cucumber Soup, 39

Great Lakes Corn Chowder, 40

Carrot Vichyssoise, 41

Crab Bisque, 41

Jalapeño Potato Soup, 42

Taco Soup, 42

Tortilla Soup, 43

Tortellini Spinach Soup, 44

Portuguese Vegetable Soup, 44

Turkey Vegetable Soup, 45

Crenshaw County Camp Stew, 46

French Stew, 47

CHILLED AVOCADO SOUP

- Reserve several tablespoons chopped green onion stems for garnish.
- Combine avocados, garlic, remaining green onions, cilantro, jalapeño pepper and Tabasco sauce in blender container. Process until smooth. Add 3 cups sour cream. Process until blended.
- Stir in buttermilk and chicken broth. Season with salt.
- Chill, covered, in refrigerator.
- Ladle into soup bowls. Top each with a scant tablespoon of the remaining 1/2 cup sour cream. Sprinkle with reserved chopped green onion stems.
- Yield: 10 servings.

Ingredients

4 green onions, chopped

4 medium avocados

1 clove of garlic, minced

5 tablespoons chopped
fresh cilantro

1 tablespoon undrained sliced
pickled jalapeño pepper

1/2 teaspoon Tabasco sauce

31/2 cups sour cream

1 cup buttermilk

8 cups chicken broth, chilled

Salt to taste

"BLUE BELLE" GAZPACHO

- Cut tomatoes, onion and green pepper into quarters. Peel, seed and chop cucumber.
- Combine tomatoes, onion, green pepper, cucumber, parsley, chives, garlic, carrots, wine vinegar, oil, consommé, peppers and salt in blender container. Process until of desired consistency.
- Chill, covered, overnight. Ladle into soup bowls.
- Yield: 8 servings.

Ingredients

4 large tomatoes

1 each onion, green bell
pepper and cucumber

3 tablespoons chopped parsley

2 tablespoons chopped chives

1 clove of garlic

2 carrots, cut into halves

1/3 cup wine vinegar

1/4 cup vegetable oil

2 (10-ounce) cans consommé

1/2 teaspoon each cayenne
pepper and black pepper

1 teaspoon salt

FRENCH MARKET SOUP

Soup Mix Ingredients

1 pound dried navy beans
1 pound dried pinto beans
1 pound dried Great
Northern beans
1 pound dried green split peas
1 pound dried yellow split peas
1 pound dried black-eyed peas
1 pound dried lentils
1 pound dried baby limas
1 pound dried large limas
1 pound dried black beans
1 pound dried red beans
1 pound dried soybeans
1 pound pearl barley
1 pound dried garbanzo beans

Soup Ingredients

2 cups French Market Soup Mix
2 quarts water
1 ham hock
1¼ teaspoons salt
¼ teaspoon pepper
1 (16-ounce) can whole
tomatoes, coarsely chopped
1 large onion, chopped
1 clove of garlic, minced
1 chili pepper, coarsely chopped
¼ cup lemon juice

Great to give as Christmas gifts to teachers and friends.

- Combine all ingredients for the mix in bowl; mix well. Divide into fourteen 2-cup packages. Give as gifts with the recipe for French Market Soup.

- To make the soup, sort and rinse beans. Place in stockpot. Add enough water to cover 2 inches above beans. Soak overnight; drain.

- Add water, ham hock, salt and pepper; mix well.

- Bring to a boil; reduce heat. Simmer, covered, for 1½ hours or until beans are tender, stirring occasionally.

- Stir in undrained tomatoes, onion, garlic, chili pepper and lemon juice. Simmer for 30 minutes, stirring occasionally.

- Remove ham hock from soup. Remove meat from bone; chop meat. Return meat to soup, stirring until mixed.

- Ladle into soup bowls.

- May substitute 1 pound Polish sausage or venison sausage for ham hock. May substitute 1 seeded and chopped jalapeño pepper for chili pepper.

- Yield: 10 servings.

WHARTON CHEESE SOUP

A great easy cheese soup!

- Chop green onions and celery. Sauté with carrots in butter in saucepan. Stir in broth. Simmer for 30 minutes, stirring occasionally.
- Add soup and cheese; mix well. Simmer for 15 minutes, stirring occasionally. Season with salt and pepper.
- Ladle into soup bowls.
- Yield: 9 servings.

Ingredients

3 green onions
3 stalks celery with leaves
2 carrots, grated
1/4 cup butter
2 (10-ounce) cans chicken broth
3 (10-ounce) cans potato soup
2 cups shredded Cheddar cheese
Salt and pepper to taste

FIREHOUSE CHILI

- Brown ground beef in olive oil in skillet, stirring until ground beef is crumbly. Stir in onion and garlic. Cook until onion is tender, stirring constantly; drain.
- Combine ground beef mixture with salt, cayenne pepper, cumin, oregano and chili powder in stockpot; mix well. Add chopped tomatoes, tomato sauce and kidney beans; mix well. Heat to simmering. Adjust seasonings.
- Simmer for 30 minutes, stirring occasionally. Simmer, covered, for 1 1/2 hours, stirring occasionally. Ladle into soup bowls.
- May add tomato juice if needed for desired consistency.
- Yield: 12 servings.

Ingredients

3 pounds lean ground beef
1 tablespoon olive oil
1 large onion, chopped
2 cloves of garlic, crushed
1/2 teaspoon salt
Cayenne pepper to taste
1/2 teaspoon cumin
1/2 teaspoon oregano
2 tablespoons chili powder
1 (10-ounce) can
tomatoes and chilies
1 (16-ounce) can plum tomatoes
2 (8-ounce) cans tomato sauce
2 (16-ounce) cans
red kidney beans

GREAT SAN LUIS GREEN CHILE SOUP

Ingredients

6 medium Anaheim chiles

1 large red bell pepper

1 jalapeño pepper

2 ounces salt pork, chopped

8 ounces boned chicken
breast, thinly sliced

8 ounces pork butt steak,
thinly sliced

1 medium onion, chopped

6 tablespoons butter

1/2 cup flour

1 1/2 teaspoons chili powder

1 teaspoon ground cumin

1 small clove of garlic, minced

3/4 cup tomato sauce

2 quarts chicken broth, heated

1/2 cup chopped peeled
tomato, seeded

1 tablespoon minced
fresh cilantro

1 avocado, peeled, sliced

1/2 cup sour cream

- Place Anaheim chiles, red pepper and jalapeño pepper on rack in broiler pan. Roast under broiler until skins blister, turning to char on all sides. Place peppers in plastic bag for 10 minutes. Peel and chop; set aside.

- Cook salt pork in skillet until fat is rendered. Remove salt pork with slotted spoon to drain on paper towels.

- Sauté sliced chicken and sliced pork in pan drippings in skillet until brown. Drain; set aside.

- Sauté onion in butter in large saucepan until tender. Stir in flour. Cook until golden brown, stirring constantly. Remove from heat.

- Stir in chili powder, cumin, garlic and tomato sauce. Whisk in chicken broth. Heat to simmering, stirring constantly.

- Add chopped roasted peppers, salt pork and sautéed chicken and pork; mix well. Cook until heated through, stirring frequently.

- Stir in tomato and cilantro. Cook until heated through, stirring frequently.

- Ladle into soup bowls. Top with sliced avocado and sour cream. Serve with warm flour tortillas.

- May be prepared a day in advance.

- Yield: 8 servings.

CHINESE HOT AND SOUR SOUP

*Cooked scallops or shrimp may be added
for a heartier version of this delicious soup.*

- Soften mushrooms in warm water in bowl; drain. Remove stems; slice caps.
- Bring mushrooms, ham, bamboo shoots, soy sauce and chicken stock to a boil in large saucepan; reduce heat. Simmer for 3 minutes, stirring occasionally. Season with salt and white pepper.
- Stir in bean curd and wine vinegar. Bring to a boil. Add mixture of cornstarch and 3 tablespoons cold water; mix well.
- Stir in mixture of Tabasco sauce and hot chili oil. Cook until slightly thickened, stirring constantly.
- Stir in egg gently. Remove from heat; stir in sesame oil. Season with MSG if desired.
- Ladle into soup bowls; sprinkle with green onions.
- Yield: 4 servings.

Ingredients

1 teaspoon chopped dried
cloud ear mushroom

4 dried black oriental
mushrooms

1/2 cup finely chopped ham

1/2 cup slivered bamboo shoots

1 tablespoon soy sauce

4 cups chicken stock

Salt and freshly ground
white pepper to taste

1 cup finely sliced bean curd

3 tablespoons red wine vinegar

2 tablespoons cornstarch

1/2 to 1 teaspoon mixture of
Tabasco sauce and hot chili oil

1 egg, slightly beaten

1 tablespoon sesame oil

6 green onions, finely chopped

"SANDCASTLE" CUCUMBER SOUP

A great beach recipe because it is so simple to prepare.

- Combine green onions, cucumbers and green pepper in food processor container. Process until smooth.
- Add soup, chicken broth, lemon juice and sugar. Process until blended. Chill, covered, in refrigerator.
- Stir in sour cream. Ladle into soup bowls.
- Yield: 6 servings.

Ingredients

3 each green onions and
cucumbers, chopped

1 green bell pepper, chopped

2 (10-ounce) cans each celery
soup and chicken broth

1 tablespoon lemon juice

1 tablespoon sugar

1 cup sour cream

GREAT LAKES CORN CHOWDER

This is absolutely the BEST corn chowder recipe yet! The fresh peppers and corn are essential to turn this one out in style.

Ingredients

6 medium ears of corn

6 slices bacon, cut into 1/2-inch pieces

1 small onion, finely chopped

1 small green bell pepper, finely chopped

1 jalapeño pepper, seeded, chopped

1 stalk celery, finely chopped

3 medium tomatoes, peeled, seeded, finely chopped

1 pound potatoes, peeled, chopped

1 teaspoon salt

1/8 teaspoon allspice

Sugar to taste

1 bay leaf

2 cups light cream, at room temperature

1 cup milk

Freshly ground pepper to taste

Chopped fresh parsley

- Cut tops of corn kernels into bowl with sharp knife. Scrape ears with back of knife to remove juice; set aside.

- Fry bacon in skillet over medium-high heat for 10 minutes or until crisp. Drain, reserving 3 tablespoons drippings. Crumble bacon and set aside.

- Sauté onion in reserved drippings in skillet for 4 to 5 minutes or until golden brown. Stir in green pepper, jalapeño pepper and celery. Cook for 2 minutes or just until vegetables are tender.

- Add tomatoes, potatoes, salt, allspice, sugar, bay leaf and corn; mix well. Cook over medium heat just until mixture begins to boil, stirring frequently; reduce heat.

- Simmer, covered, for 35 to 45 minutes or until potatoes are tender, stirring occasionally.

- Stir in light cream and milk.

- Cook just until mixture begins to boil, stirring frequently. Remove from heat. Discard bay leaf; season with pepper.

- Ladle into soup bowls; sprinkle with crumbled bacon. Garnish with parsley.

- Yield: 6 servings.

CARROT VICHYSSOISE "FANTASIA"

This beautifully colored soup is from Four Seasons Restaurant in New York. It can be served hot or cold.

- Bring chicken stock, potatoes, carrots and leek to a boil in saucepan. Simmer for 25 minutes or until vegetables are tender, stirring occasionally. Purée in blender.
- Pour puréed mixture into bowl. Stir in cream, salt, white pepper and nutmeg. Chill, covered, in refrigerator.
- Ladle into soup bowls. Garnish with shredded carrot.
- Yield: 4 servings.

Ingredients

3 cups chicken stock
2 cups chopped peeled potatoes
1 1/4 cups sliced carrots
1 leek bulb, sliced
1 cup cream
1 teaspoon salt
White pepper and nutmeg to taste
Shredded carrot

"ABOUT TIME" CRAB BISQUE

This bisque is a welcome treat for a family with loved ones in the hospital or a perfect entrée for a football party. But best of all, it is perfect to have after watching a Seaside sunset in November.

- Combine butter and flour in saucepan. Cook over medium heat until smooth, stirring constantly.
- Stir in tomato paste, onion, celery, green onions, garlic, green pepper and parsley. Cook until vegetables are tender, stirring constantly.
- Add chicken stock; mix well. Stir in Worcestershire sauce, bay leaves, thyme, salt, white pepper, cayenne pepper and catsup gently. Fold in drained and flaked crab meat.
- Simmer for 45 minutes, stirring frequently. Discard bay leaves.
- Ladle into soup bowls.
- May freeze bisque for 1 month if fresh crab meat is used.
- Yield: 10 servings.

Ingredients

1 cup melted butter
1 cup flour
1/4 cup tomato paste
2 cups chopped onion
1 1/2 cups chopped celery
1 cup chopped green onions
6 cloves of garlic, finely chopped
1 cup chopped green bell pepper
1/4 cup chopped fresh parsley
2 1/2 quarts chicken stock
2 tablespoons Worcestershire sauce
2 bay leaves
1 1/2 teaspoons each thyme and salt
1/4 teaspoon white pepper
Cayenne pepper to taste
1 teaspoon catsup
1 1/2 pounds crab meat

"SUNDAZE" JALAPEÑO POTATO SOUP

Ingredients

5 pounds russet potatoes

1 medium onion, chopped

1/4 cup butter

8 cups chicken broth

1 teaspoon cumin

1/4 to 1/2 cup coarsely chopped
pickled jalapeño peppers

Pinch of baking soda

4 cups evaporated milk

Salt and pepper to taste

1/2 cup sour cream

4 green onions, chopped

- Peel and chop potatoes.
- Sauté onion in butter in stockpot until tender. Add potatoes, chicken broth and cumin; mix well. Cook, covered, until potatoes are tender, stirring occasionally.
- Stir in undrained jalapeño peppers, baking soda and evaporated milk. Mash potato mixture coarsely with potato masher. Season with salt and pepper. Simmer for 15 minutes, stirring occasionally.
- Ladle into soup bowls. Top with sour cream; sprinkle with green onions.
- Yield: 16 servings.

"BRIAR PATCH" TACO SOUP

*An incredibly easy "dump" soup. This recipe is one
that should be shared with a special friend!*

- Brown ground beef with onion in large saucepan, stirring until ground beef is crumbly; drain. Stir in pinto beans, hominy, stewed tomatoes, tomatoes and green chilies, taco seasoning mix and salad dressing mix.
- Simmer for 25 to 30 minutes or until of desired consistency.
- Ladle into soup bowls. Sprinkle with cheese; top with salsa. Serve with tortilla chips.
- Yield: 12 servings.

Ingredients

2 pounds ground beef

1 small onion, chopped

2 (16-ounce) cans pinto beans
with jalapeño peppers

2 (16-ounce) cans hominy

2 (16-ounce) cans stewed tomatoes

1 (10-ounce) can tomatoes and
green chilies

1 envelope taco seasoning mix

1 envelope Ranch dressing mix

1/2 cup shredded Cheddar cheese

1/2 cup salsa

"Gulf Manor" Tortilla Soup

Serve this healthy soup as a first or main course.

- Arrange tomatoes and onion in single layer on oiled baking sheet. Roast under broiler for 20 minutes, turning several times. Cool.

- Combine roasted tomatoes and onion with garlic in blender container. Process until puréed.

- Rinse chicken. Bring water and beef broth to a boil in stockpot. Add chicken parts. Bring to a boil; reduce heat. Stir in puréed mixture, basil, cumin, chili powder, pepper and oregano.

- Simmer for 1 1/2 to 2 hours or until chicken is tender. Remove chicken to platter. Cool. Shred chicken, discarding skin and bones. Return chicken to stockpot.

- Add carrots and celery to stockpot. Cook for 4 minutes, stirring occasionally. Add zucchini. Cook for 3 minutes, stirring occasionally. Stir in spinach. Cook until tender-crisp, stirring occasionally. Stir in tomato sauce.

- Ladle into soup bowls. Top with cheese and avocado strips. Serve with tortilla chips or French bread.

- Yield: 12 servings.

Ingredients

4 large tomatoes, cut
into quarters

1 large onion, cut into quarters

1 tablespoon oil

4 cloves of garlic

4 pounds chicken pieces

10 cups water

1 (10-ounce) can beef broth

3 tablespoons basil

3 to 4 teaspoons cumin

1 to 2 teaspoons chili powder

1 1/2 teaspoons pepper

1 teaspoon oregano

3 carrots, julienned

3 stalks celery, thinly sliced

2 zucchini, julienned

30 leaves fresh spinach,
cut into strips

3/4 cup tomato sauce

3 cups shredded
mozzarella cheese

2 avocados, cut into strips

"SEASTAR" TORTELLINI SPINACH SOUP

Ingredients

4 to 5 (10-ounce) cans
low-sodium chicken broth
1 cup thinly sliced carrots
1 medium onion, chopped
3/4 teaspoon oregano, crushed
1 teaspoon chopped garlic
1 (12-ounce) package frozen
cheese-filled tortellini
1 (10-ounce) package frozen
leaf spinach, thawed
1/4 cup shredded mozzarella cheese

- Bring chicken broth, carrots, onion, oregano and garlic to a boil in stockpot. Add tortellini.
- Boil for 4 to 5 minutes or until tortellini are almost tender, stirring occasionally; reduce heat.
- Stir in spinach. Simmer for 2 to 3 minutes or until tortellini are tender, stirring occasionally.
- Ladle into soup bowls; sprinkle with cheese. Serve with bagels or breadsticks.
- Yield: 6 servings.

PORTUGUESE VEGETABLE SOUP

Ingredients

1 pound Italian sausage
8 ounces ground beef
2 cups chopped onions
3 cloves of garlic, minced
1/2 head cabbage, shredded
1 (16-ounce) can tomatoes
2 teaspoons salt
1/4 teaspoon pepper
4 ounces cooked ham, chopped
2 quarts beef broth
1 teaspoon each thyme and basil
1 cup crushed coil capellini

Kids call this "sgetti" soup. It's a mainstay of the school lunch program.

- Brown sausage and ground beef in heavy saucepan, stirring until crumbly; drain.
- Stir in onions, garlic and cabbage. Cook until vegetables are tender-crisp, stirring constantly. Add tomatoes, salt, pepper, ham and broth; mix well.
- Simmer, covered, for 20 minutes, stirring occasionally. Stir in thyme, basil and capellini.
- Boil for 2 minutes, stirring occasionally.
- Ladle into soup bowls.
- Yield: 8 servings.

"PEACHES 'N CREAM" TURKEY VEGETABLE SOUP

Great way to use leftover turkey.

- Sauté onions in butter in large saucepan over medium-high heat for 10 minutes or until tender. Stir in flour and curry powder. Cook for 2 to 3 minutes or until thickened, stirring constantly.

- Add broth, potatoes, carrots, celery, parsley and sage; mix well.

- Bring to a boil; reduce heat. Simmer, covered, for 10 minutes. Stir in turkey, half and half and spinach.

- Simmer, covered, for 7 minutes or until heated through, stirring frequently. Season with salt and pepper.

- Ladle into soup bowls.

- Yield: 6 servings.

~

Over the Fence: *On a lazy winter day at the beach, simmer a hearty soup in the slow cooker and pop ingredients for bread into the bread machine. The house will smell delicious all day, and you'll have a wonderful supper with no effort.*

Ingredients

2 medium onions, chopped

1/4 cup butter

2 tablespoons flour

1 teaspoon curry powder

3 cups chicken broth

1 cup chopped potatoes

1/2 cup thinly sliced carrots

1/2 cup sliced celery

2 tablespoons chopped fresh parsley

1/2 teaspoon sage

2 cups chopped cooked turkey

1 1/2 cups half and half

1 (10-ounce) package frozen chopped spinach

Salt and freshly ground pepper to taste

"WOODLAWN COTTAGE" CRENSHAW COUNTY CAMP STEW

Ingredients

1 pound chicken breasts
1 pound pork chops
1 pound beef stew meat
1 large onion, chopped
2 or 3 large potatoes,
   peeled, chopped
Juice of 1/2 lemon
1 (28-ounce) can tomatoes
1/2 (14-ounce) bottle of catsup
3 tablespoons
   Worcestershire sauce
Seasoned salt to taste
Liquid smoke to taste
Tiger sauce to taste

Just the thing for a chilly fall day.

- Rinse chicken.
- Combine chicken, pork chops and beef with enough water to cover in stockpot. Cook for 3 hours or until tender.
- Add onion, potatoes, lemon juice, tomatoes, catsup, Worcestershire sauce, seasoned salt, liquid smoke and tiger sauce.
- Simmer for 1 hour or until vegetables are tender.
- Ladle into soup bowls.
- Yield: 12 servings.

Over the Fence: Camp Stew has been a tradition in Crenshaw County for many years. For homecoming in Luverne, Alabama, each class would contribute an ingredient and room mothers would cook the stew over a fire in big black pots. It was served in the lunchroom with crackers, bread, homemade cake, Pepsi Cola and Sun Drop.

~

Over the Fence: Camp Stew could easily be prepared by combining all ingredients in large baking dish. Bake, tightly covered, at 250 degrees for 8 to 10 hours.

"Greenpeace" French Stew

- Preheat oven to 350 degrees.
- Fry bacon in Dutch oven until crisp. Drain, reserving pan drippings. Crumble bacon.
- Coat beef with mixture of flour, salt and pepper. Brown in reserved drippings in Dutch oven.
- Add red wine, parsley flakes, garlic, beef broth and thyme; mix well. Bake, covered, for 45 to 60 minutes or just until beef is almost tender. Stir in potatoes, onions, carrots and mushrooms.
- Bake, covered, for 1 hour.
- Ladle into soup bowls. Top with crumbled bacon and chopped parsley.
- Serve with tossed salad and French bread.
- Yield: 6 servings.

Over the Fence: I realized soon after I introduced my husband to this recipe, I could get anything I wanted if I made this dish.

~

Over the Fence: Use wine from the bottle you plan to drink with dinner in dishes calling for wine as an ingredient to give the meal a subtle consistency.

Ingredients

6 slices bacon

1 pound beef stew meat

1/2 cup flour

1 teaspoon salt

1 teaspoon pepper

1 cup dry red wine

2 tablespoons parsley flakes

1 clove of garlic, minced

1 to 1 1/2 (10-ounce) cans beef broth

1 1/2 teaspoons thyme

4 potatoes, cut into quarters

3 onions, cut into quarters

3 carrots, sliced lengthwise

10 whole mushrooms

1/4 cup chopped fresh parsley

rsimmon • Persuasion • Peterson Cottage • Picture Book • Pitter Pa
Propinquity • Puglin • Rainbow • RemBach • Renaissance • Ren
ghthouse • Romance • Rooftops • Rose Cottage • Ryan's Castle • S
ndpiper • Savannah Rose • Savannah Sands • Sawyer Cottage • So
aspell • Seastar • Seawynds • Serendipity • Shangri-La • Shell See
ne • Southern Comfort • Southern Splendor • Spinnaker • Stanzia
ndaze • Sunnyside • Sunset • Sunset Dream
e Conservatory • This Is the Life • Tide's Inn • Tiger Paw • Tilling-
ye • Treetops • Trio • Tropical Holiday • Tupelo Honey • Tupelo T
akeham Cottage • Waterside • Wayback • Weber Cottage • Wilder Co
ach • Zebulon • Zeidman Cottage • Zurn Cottage • A Summer Place
erican Dream • Anderson Cottage • Anniston • April 16th • Ashle
ach Walk • Bella Vista • Belvedere • Benedictus • Beside the Wat
swell Cottage • Briar Patch • Brickwalk • Bridgeport • Briermor by
ttage • Cape May • Carey Cottage • Caribbean • Carpe Diem • Carr
ark Cottage • Colony • Colors • Compass Rose • Coquina • Coral Co
'Scape • Cubbie Hole • Curphey Cottage • Dahlgren Cottage • Da
ttage • DeoGratis • Desire • DoLittle House • Dollhouse • Dolphin
eam Chaser • Dream On • Dreamsicle • Dreamweaver • Duet • Du
lipse • Ecstasea • Eden • Elegance • Enchantment • English Cottag
ridays • For Keeps • Forsythe Cottage • Frascogna Cottage • Fru

Salads & Dressings

...Who countest the steps of the Sun,
Seeking after that sweet golden clime
Where the traveler's journey is done;... William Blake

ost • GoodnightMoon • Gorlin Cottage • Grayton One • Grayton Two
lfview • Gull Cottage • Haardt Cottage • Hampton • Harvest Home •
ttage • Home Alone • Honalee • Hoover Cottage • House of Cards
sper • Jennifer's Castle • Josephine's • Jubilee • Kaleidoscope

easure Principal • Plum Crazy • Portera Cottage • Postcard • Precio
s • Rhett's Revenge • Ricky's • Roanoke • Robin's Nest • Roge
ottage • Salad Days • Sandcastle • Sandi Shore • Sandia • Sandpa
age • Scruggs Cottage • Sea for Two • Sea View • Sealink • Seaque
sters Three By The Sea • Skinny Dip • Smith Cottage • omewhere
ge • Starry   e • Sundanc
ime • Taupe   Beach House
ea • Time O   Tower Breez
ower • Up   Vista del Ma
Windler Cot   • Wright By t
t Time • Aca   llison Cottag
You Like It   ames Cottag
 Bit-O-Heav   n • Blue Note
• Brigadoo   tage • Callaw
use • Casa   am • ChelSe
rn Cottage •   ottage • Cred
en • Dargus   Castle • De
omino • Do   ream Catche
age • Dune   aster Cottag
n • Eyer Cot   tcher Cottag
Bandersnate   way II • Gian
 Cottage •   e • Gulf Mano
 Cottage • H   ouse • Hodg
n! • Idlewi   South • Irvine Cottage • Isaacs Cottage y • Jasmin
 Cottage • Key West • Kitchens Cottage • Krier • La. House •

Salads & Dressings

Salad with Sugared Almonds and Orange Vinaigrette, 51

Apricot Salad, 52

Tossed Club Salad, 52

Salad with Artichokes and Hearts of Palm, 53

Cauliflower Salad, 54

Pecan and Chicken Salad, 54

California Salad, 55

Sesame and Almond Slaw, 56

Summer Coleslaw, 56

Mobile Bay Salad, 57

Florida Salad, 57

Potato Salad, 58

Artichoke and Rice Salad, 58

Yellow Rice Salad, 59

Wild Rice Salad, 59

Shrimp Salad, 60

Spinach Salad, 60

Spinach Salad with Chutney Dressing, 61

Herbed Tomatoes, 62

Cool Tomato Salad, 62

Green Salad with Tarragon Bleu Cheese Dressing, 63

"DREAM CHASER" SALAD WITH SUGARED ALMONDS AND ORANGE VINAIGRETTE

- Preheat oven to 325 degrees.

- Beat egg white at high speed in mixer bowl until foamy. Add sugar 1 tablespoon at a time, beating until stiff peaks form. Fold in almonds. Spread in margarine in 9x9-inch baking pan.

- Bake for 20 to 25 minutes or until dry, stirring every 5 minutes. Cool completely.

- Combine lettuces, oranges, strawberries and green onion in salad bowl.

- Whisk olive oil, vinegar, orange juice, orange rind, poppy seeds, salt and pepper in bowl until smooth.

- Add almonds and vinaigrette to salad; toss gently to coat well.

- Yield: 6 servings.

Salad Ingredients

1 egg white

1/4 cup sugar

1 cup sliced almonds

2 tablespoons melted margarine

1 head Bibb lettuce, torn

1 head leaf lettuce, torn

1 (11-ounce) can mandarin oranges, drained

10 fresh strawberries, thinly sliced

1 green onion, chopped

Vinaigrette Ingredients

3/4 cup olive oil

1/4 cup red wine vinegar

1 tablespoon orange juice

1 teaspoon grated orange rind

1/2 teaspoon poppy seeds

1/8 teaspoon salt

1/8 teaspoon pepper

"ROBINS" APRICOT SALAD

A favorite with the kids.

- Drain some of the juice from pineapple; place partially drained pineapple in saucepan. Heat until bubbly.
- Add gelatin gradually, stirring to dissolve completely. Cool mixture.
- Add buttermilk and whipped topping; mix well. Spread in shallow dish; sprinkle with pecans. Chill until firm.
- Yield: 12 servings.

Ingredients

1 (20-ounce) can crushed pineapple

1 (6-ounce) package apricot gelatin

2 cups buttermilk

12 ounces whipped topping

1/2 cup chopped pecans

TOSSED CLUB SALAD "MCCLOY"

The dressing makes the salad taste just like a club sandwich.

- Combine mayonnaise, Worcestershire sauce, capers, salt and seasoned pepper in small bowl; mix well.
- Combine spinach, bacon, chicken, tomatoes and croutons in salad bowl; toss lightly. Add dressing; toss just before serving.
- Yield: 6 servings.

Ingredients

3/4 cup mayonnaise

1 tablespoon Worcestershire sauce

1 tablespoon capers

1 teaspoon salt

1 teaspoon seasoned pepper

4 to 6 cups torn fresh spinach

8 ounces bacon, crisp-fried, crumbled

3 cups chopped cooked chicken

2 tomatoes, peeled, chopped

1 1/2 cups seasoned croutons

"Sandpiper" Salad with Artichokes and Hearts of Palm

- Combine onion, sugar, vinegar, catsup, oil, Worcestershire sauce and lemon juice in bowl; whisk until smooth.
- Chill until serving time.
- Combine spinach, hearts of palm, artichoke hearts, bacon, green onions, tomatoes and eggs in salad bowl. Chill in refrigerator.
- Add dressing; toss to coat well.
- Yield: 8 servings.

~

Over the Fence: *For an easy Creamy Bleu Cheese Dressing to serve over any green salad, blend 4 ounces bleu cheese with 2 cups mayonnaise, ½ cup sour cream, ¼ cup vinegar, 1 mashed clove of garlic and 1 teaspoon sugar in mixer bowl. Beat until smooth and fold in 4 ounces crumbled bleu cheese.*

Dressing Ingredients

1 medium onion, minced

¾ cup sugar

½ cup vinegar

⅓ cup catsup

⅓ cup salad oil

2 tablespoons Worcestershire sauce

2 teaspoons lemon juice

Salad Ingredients

1 pound spinach, torn

1 (16-ounce) can hearts of palm, drained, thinly sliced

1 (16-ounce) can artichoke hearts, drained, sliced

6 slices bacon, crisp-fried, crumbled

4 green onions, chopped

3 tomatoes, cut into wedges

2 hard-boiled eggs, chopped

"LOWE COTTAGE" CAULIFLOWER SALAD

Ingredients

1 head lettuce, torn
Flowerets of 1 head cauliflower
1 large onion, thinly sliced
1 pound bacon,
crisp-fried, crumbled
2 cups mayonnaise
1/4 cup sugar
1/2 cup freshly grated
Parmesan cheese

- Layer lettuce, cauliflower, onion and bacon in salad bowl. Spread mixture of mayonnaise and sugar over top, sealing to edge of bowl. Sprinkle with cheese.
- Chill, tightly covered, overnight. Toss at serving time.
- Yield: 8 servings.

Over the Fence: This does not keep well after it is tossed, so do not plan for leftovers. At our house, it is a favorite to be enjoyed only seldom because of its high fat content.

"SPINNAKER" PECAN AND CHICKEN SALAD

Ingredients

1/2 cup pecan halves
4 cups chopped cooked chicken
2 cups finely chopped celery
1 (4-ounce) jar whole
mushrooms, drained
4 slices bacon,
crisp-fried, crumbled
1 cup mayonnaise
1 cup sour cream
2 tablespoons lemon juice
1 1/2 teaspoons salt

- Preheat oven to 350 degrees.
- Spread pecans on baking sheet. Toast for 15 minutes, stirring frequently.
- Combine chicken, celery, mushrooms, bacon and pecans in large bowl. Add mixture of mayonnaise, sour cream, lemon juice and salt; toss lightly.
- Chill until serving time. Serve in lettuce cups.
- Yield: 6 servings.

Over the Fence: We bring the salad ingredients to Seaside for easy assembly just before serving.

CALIFORNIA SALAD

This is the world's best salad.

- Combine oil, vinegar, lemon juice, Worcestershire sauce, sugar, paprika, dry mustard, salt and pepper in bowl; mix well.

- Place 1 wooden pick in each garlic half; add to dressing. Chill until serving time.

- Combine iceberg lettuce, romaine lettuce, watercress, chicken, bacon, tomatoes, eggs, chives, bleu cheese and hearts of palm in salad bowl.

- Sprinkle avocado with lemon juice. Add to salad. Remove garlic and wooden picks from dressing.

- Add dressing to salad; toss gently to coat well. Sprinkle with croutons.

- May add red leaf lettuce, julienned red bell pepper, spinach and Parmesan cheese if desired.

- Yield: 12 servings.

~

Over the Fence: *Make your own tarragon vinegar to use in salad dressings such as the one above or to give as gifts. Simply pack fresh tarragon in hot sterilized jar. Heat white wine vinegar and pour over herbs. Let stand for 4 to 6 weeks. Strain twice. Decant into decorative sterilized jars. Place sprigs of fresh tarragon in jars; seal.*

Dressing Ingredients

1/2 cup salad oil

1/4 cup tarragon vinegar

2 tablespoons lemon juice

1/2 teaspoon Worcestershire sauce

1/2 teaspoon sugar

1/2 teaspoon paprika

1/2 teaspoon dry mustard

1 teaspoon salt

1/4 teaspoon pepper

1 clove of garlic, cut into halves, or 1/4 teaspoon garlic powder

Salad Ingredients

1 head iceberg lettuce, torn

1 head romaine lettuce, torn

1/2 bunch watercress

2 cups chopped cooked chicken breast

6 slices bacon, crisp-fried, crumbled

6 cherry tomatoes, cut into halves

2 hard-boiled eggs, chopped

2 tablespoons chopped chives

3 ounces bleu cheese, crumbled

1 (16-ounce) can hearts of palm, sliced

1 avocado, chopped

Juice of 1/2 lemon

1 cup toasted croutons

"NARNIA" SESAME AND ALMOND SLAW

Ingredients

1 cup vegetable oil

7 tablespoons rice vinegar

1/4 cup sugar

2 teaspoons salt

1 teaspoon pepper

1 head cabbage, chopped

4 green onions, chopped

2 packages ramen noodles

1/2 cup each slivered almonds and sesame seeds, toasted

- Combine oil, vinegar, sugar, salt and pepper in jar with lid; shake to mix well. Chill until serving time.
- Combine cabbage and green onions in large bowl; mix well. Chill in refrigerator.
- Shake dressing again. Add to cabbage mixture with crumbled noodles, almonds and sesame seeds; toss to mix well. Serve immediately.
- Yield: 10 servings.

"BLUE BELLE" SUMMER COLESLAW

Ingredients

1 cup sugar

2 teaspoons dry mustard

2 teaspoons celery seeds

2 teaspoons salt

1/2 cup white vinegar

1/2 cup balsamic vinegar

1/2 cup salad oil

1 head cabbage, shredded

1 each red and green bell pepper, chopped

1 medium sweet onion, chopped

3 carrots, chopped

- Mix sugar, dry mustard, celery seeds and salt in saucepan; mix well. Add vinegars and oil; mix well.
- Bring to a boil, stirring to dissolve sugar completely.
- Combine cabbage, bell peppers, onion and carrots in large bowl; mix well. Add dressing; toss to coat well.
- Marinate, covered, in refrigerator for 1 to 2 days.
- Yield: 12 servings.

Over the Fence: After creating this variation for a friend who doesn't like mayonnaise, we found we preferred it to "standard" coleslaw.

"C'Scape" Mobile Bay Salad

- Layer half the onion, crab meat and remaining onion in salad bowl; sprinkle with salt and pepper.
- Mix oil, vinegar and ice water in small bowl. Pour over layers.
- Chill, covered, for 2 to 12 hours. Stir before serving. Serve with Carrs crackers.
- Yield: 4 servings.

Over the Fence: We prepare this wonderful salad as soon as we arrive at Seaside.

Ingredients

1 medium mild onion, finely chopped

1 pound lump crab meat

Salt and pepper to taste

1/2 cup vegetable oil

6 tablespoons cider vinegar

1/2 cup ice water

"Fantasia" Florida Salad

- Combine almonds and 2 tablespoons sugar in skillet. Heat until almonds are glazed; set aside.
- Combine oil, vinegar, 1 tablespoon sugar, parsley, poppy seeds, salt, Tabasco sauce and pepper in bowl; mix well.
- Combine lettuce, celery, green onions, grapefruit and avocado in salad bowl. Add dressing and almonds; toss to mix well.
- May substitute mandarin oranges for the grapefruit and avocado.
- Yield: 8 servings.

Ingredients

1/2 cup slivered almonds

2 tablespoons sugar

1/4 cup vegetable oil

2 tablespoons balsamic vinegar

1 tablespoon sugar

1 tablespoon chopped parsley

1 teaspoon poppy seeds

1/2 teaspoon salt

Tabasco sauce and pepper to taste

1 small head lettuce, chopped

3/4 cup chopped celery

4 green onions, chopped

Sections of 2 grapefruit

1 avocado, sliced

"SANDCASTLE" POTATO SALAD

Ingredients

4 pounds red new potatoes

4 Vidalia onions or purple onions, sliced into rings

Salt and pepper to taste

1½ cups mayonnaise

¼ cup vegetable oil

½ cup cider vinegar

Chopped parsley to taste

- Cook unpeeled potatoes in water to cover in saucepan until tender; drain. Cool completely. Slice potatoes.
- Alternate layers of potatoes and onions in serving bowl, sprinkling each layer with salt and pepper.
- Combine mayonnaise, oil, vinegar, parsley, salt and pepper in bowl; whisk until smooth. Pour over layers.
- Marinate, covered, in refrigerator overnight. Toss gently before serving.
- Yield: 12 servings.

ARTICHOKE AND RICE SALAD

Ingredients

1 (6-ounce) package chicken-flavored Rice-A-Roni

2 (6-ounce) jars marinated artichoke hearts

⅓ cup mayonnaise

Curry powder to taste

2 green onions, chopped

½ green bell pepper, chopped

½ small zucchini, finely chopped

½ yellow squash, finely chopped

½ carrot, finely chopped

- Cook Rice-A-Roni using package directions. Cool to room temperature.
- Drain artichoke hearts, reserving marinade from 1 jar. Combine reserved liquid with mayonnaise and curry powder in bowl; mix well.
- Slice artichokes into halves. Combine with rice, green onions, green pepper, zucchini, yellow squash and carrot in salad bowl; mix well.
- Add dressing; mix well. Chill for up to 2 days before serving.
- May substitute finely chopped celery for green pepper.
- Yield: 8 servings.

"MAGNOLIA COTTAGE" YELLOW RICE SALAD

- Cook rice using package directions.
- Combine rice, undrained artichoke hearts, pimento and water chestnuts in salad bowl. Stir in peas.
- May add 1 tablespoon mayonnaise if desired.
- Yield: 8 servings.

Ingredients

1 (7-ounce) package saffron rice

1 (6-ounce) jar marinated artichoke hearts

1 (2-ounce) jar sliced pimento, drained

1 (7-ounce) jar sliced water chestnuts, drained

1/2 to 1 (10-ounce) package frozen tiny green peas, thawed

"DREAMWEAVER" WILD RICE SALAD

A great summer salad that is a little different.

- Cook rice using package directions.
- Combine with onion, peas, tomatoes, artichoke hearts, parsley, salt and pepper in salad bowl; mix well.
- Add salad dressing; toss to coat well. Serve at room temperature.
- May substitute French salad dressing for Russian salad dressing.
- Yield: 6 servings.

Ingredients

1 (7-ounce) package long grain and wild rice mix

1/2 cup chopped Vidalia onion or other mild sweet onion

1 (10-ounce) package frozen peas, thawed

12 cherry tomatoes, cut into halves

1 (14-ounce) can artichoke hearts, drained, cut into quarters

Chopped parsley to taste

Salt and pepper to taste

1 (8-ounce) bottle of Russian salad dressing

"SUNDAZE" SHRIMP SALAD

Ingredients

1 (7-ounce) package long
grain and wild rice mix

1½ pounds peeled shrimp, cooked

8 ounces mushrooms, cut
into halves

1 bunch green onions, chopped

2 cups mayonnaise

3 tablespoons celery seeds

4 drops of Tabasco sauce

Salt and pepper to taste

- Cook rice using package directions. Allow to cool.
- Cut shrimp into halves.
- Combine with rice, mushrooms, green onions and mayonnaise in bowl; mix well.
- Add celery seeds, Tabasco sauce, salt and pepper; mix well.
- Chill until serving time.
- Yield: 12 servings.

"TIDE'S INN" SPINACH SALAD

Ingredients

2 (12-ounce) packages fresh
spinach, torn

1 head Boston or
iceberg lettuce, torn

1 pound bacon,
crisp-fried, crumbled

2 (8-ounce) cans mandarin
oranges, chilled, drained

1 cup olive oil

⅓ cup tarragon vinegar

1 egg

1 small white onion, chopped

Several drops of Tabasco sauce

1 teaspoon salt

Serve this salad with a chicken casserole.

- Combine spinach, lettuce, bacon and mandarin oranges in salad bowl.
- Process olive oil, vinegar, egg, onion, Tabasco sauce and salt in blender until smooth.
- Add dressing to salad; toss to coat well.
- Yield: 12 servings.

SPINACH SALAD WITH CHUTNEY DRESSING

We prepare the ingredients for this salad the day before and store them in plastic bags separately in the refrigerator.

- Combine vinegar, chutney, garlic, mustard, sugar, oil, salt and pepper in bowl. Mix until smooth and thick.
- Let stand at room temperature for 30 minutes. Adjust seasonings.
- Combine spinach, mushrooms, water chestnuts, bacon, bean sprouts, cheese and onions in salad bowl.
- Add dressing; toss to coat well.
- Yield: 6 servings.

Over the Fence: *Red Dressing is great with spinach salad. Combine ½ cup salad oil, ¼ cup each catsup and vinegar, ½ cup sugar, 2 tablespoons honey and 1 teaspoon each Worcestershire sauce and onion salt in jar with lid. Shake until mixed.*

Dressing Ingredients

¼ cup wine vinegar

2 to 3 tablespoons chutney

1 clove of garlic, crushed

2 tablespoons coarsely ground French mustard or Creole mustard

2 teaspoons sugar

⅓ to ½ cup vegetable oil

Salt and freshly ground pepper to taste

Salad Ingredients

1 pound fresh spinach, torn

6 mushrooms, sliced

1 cup sliced water chestnuts

6 slices bacon, crisp-fried, crumbled

¾ cup fresh bean sprouts

½ cup shredded Gruyère cheese

¼ cup thinly sliced red onions

"BRIAR PATCH" HERBED TOMATOES

Ingredients

6 large ripe tomatoes, sliced

Several leaves of fresh thyme
and marjoram or 1 teaspoon
each dried thyme and marjoram

1/4 cup finely chopped parsley

1/4 cup chopped chives
or green onion tops

1/2 teaspoon salt

1/4 teaspoon coarsely
ground pepper

1/3 cup salad oil

1/4 cup tarragon vinegar

Also great on sandwiches or burgers.

- Layer tomato slices in deep bowl, sprinkling each layer with thyme, marjoram, parsley, chives, salt and pepper.
- Combine oil and vinegar in small bowl. Pour over layers. Chill until serving time.
- May drain and reserve dressing to pass with tomatoes.
- Yield: 12 servings.

Over the Fence: *Try serving these herbed tomatoes on sandwiches of sourdough bread, thin chicken or London broil slices, pesto, avocado and lettuce.*

"CREOLE COTTAGE" COOL TOMATO SALAD

Ingredients

4 large tomatoes, sliced

1 head Boston lettuce, torn

1/4 cup sliced black olives

1/2 cup crumbled feta cheese

1/4 cup chopped fresh parsley

1/2 cup French vinaigrette

La Martinique is a good true French vinaigrette.

- Arrange tomato slices on lettuce-lined serving plate; sprinkle with olives.
- Sprinkle with cheese and parsley. Drizzle with vinaigrette. Marinate in refrigerator for 20 minutes.
- Yield: 8 servings.

GREEN SALAD WITH "NEWNUM'S OWN" TARRAGON BLEU CHEESE DRESSING

The dressing for this salad is unique.

- Combine cream and vinegar in bowl; stir for 1 minute or until thickened.

- Crumble bleu cheese coarsely into cream. Whisk in milk, mayonnaise, mustard, tarragon, salt and pepper.

- Chill for up to 2 days. Add a small amount of milk if needed for desired consistency.

- Combine lettuces, watercress and tomatoes in bowl; mix well. Spoon salad onto 12 salad plates. Drizzle with bleu cheese dressing.

- Yield: 12 servings.

Dressing Ingredients

1/2 cup whipping cream

1 1/2 tablespoons tarragon wine vinegar

6 ounces Saga bleu cheese, at room temperature

1/4 cup (or more) milk

1/4 cup mayonnaise

1 tablespoon grainy mustard

1/2 teaspoon tarragon

1/4 teaspoon salt

Freshly ground pepper to taste

Salad Ingredients

1 medium head romaine lettuce, torn

1 medium head curly leaf lettuce, torn

2 bunches watercress or arugula

1 pint each red and yellow cherry tomatoes, cut into halves

tion • Latitude • LeBlanc Cottage • Leeward • Lehman Cottage • Leo
ge • Lonesome Dove • Lost Goggles • Lowe Cottage • Lucas Cot
en • McChesney Cottage • McCollister Cottage • McLaughlin Co
ador • Mis B'Haven • Modica Cottage • Moore Fun • Nancy's Fancy
n the Veranda • Ondine • Orth Cottage • Outer Banks • Overboard!
ch • Periwinkle • Persimmon • Peterson • Peterson Cottage • Pic
stcard • Precious • Tranquility • Pugh • Quimby • RumBach • Ren
oger's Lighthouse • Romance • Rooftops • Rose Cottage • Ryan's
ndpail • Sandpiper • Savannah Rose • Savannah Sands • Sawyer Co
quel • Seaspell • Seastar • Seawynds • Serendipity • Shangri-La
mewhere In Time • Southern Comfort • Southern Splendor • Spinna
ndance • Sundaze • Sunnyside Up • Sunrise • Sunrise Wishes • Sun
use • The Conservatory • This Is the Life • Tide's Inn • Tiger Paw
eze • Toye • Treetops • Trio • Tropical Holiday • Tupelo Honey • Tup
akeham Cottage • Waterside • Wayback • Weber Cottage • Wilder
Beach • Zebulon • Zeidman Cottage • Zurn Cottage • A Summer
tage • American Dream • Anderson Cottage • Anniston • April 16
tage • Beach Walk • Bella Vista • Belvedere • Benedictus • Beside
e • Boswell Cottage • Briar Patch • Brickwalk • Bridgeport • Brier
laway Cottage • Cape May • Carey Cottage • Caribbean • Carpe Di
elSea • Clark Cottage • Colony • Colors • Compass Rose • Coqu

Bread & Breakfast

tage • Creole • C'Scape • Cubbie Hole • Curphey Cottage • Dahlgre
stle • Delor Cottage • DeoGratis • Desire • DoLittle House • Dollhou
cher • Dream Chaser • Dream On • Dreamsicle • Dreamweaver
tage • Eclipse • Ecstasea • Eden • Elegance • Enchantment • Engli

...With brightest sunshine round me spread
Of spring's unclouded weather,
In this sequestered nook how sweet...! William Wordsworth

Bread

Beer Bread, 67

Banana Bread, 67

Chili Cheese Bread, 68

Grandmother's Famous Cranberry
Bread, 68

Poppy Seed Bread, 69

Cuban Bread, 69

Pumpkin Spice Bread, 70

Spoon Bread, 70

Strawberry Bread, 71

Three-Two-One Bread Plus, 71

Stone-Ground Wheat Bread, 72

Beignets, 72

Biscuits, 73

Priory Biscuits, 73

New Orleans-Style French Toast, 74

Monkey Bread, 74

German Apple Pancakes, 75

Special Popovers, 75

Cinnamon Rolls, 76

Overnight Pecan Rolls, 77

Breakfast

Artichoke Brunch Pie, 77

South-of-the-Border Omelet, 78

Breakfast Sausage Casserole, 78

Cheesy Sausage Quiche, 79

Spinach Pie, 79

Yesterday's Eggs, 80

Baked Cheesy Apples, 80

Baked Apricots, 81

Rice Pudding, 81

Sunrise Surprise, 81

"McLaughlin Cottage" Beer Bread

- Preheat oven to 350 degrees.
- Combine flour, sugar and beer in bowl; mix well. Spoon into greased loaf pan.
- Bake for 45 minutes. Spread top with butter. Bake for 15 minutes longer.
- Remove to wire rack to cool.
- Yield: 12 servings.

Ingredients

3 cups self-rising flour
3 tablespoons sugar
1 (12-ounce) can beer
2 tablespoons butter

"C'Scape" Banana Bread

A very easy and dependable bread. The lemon juice gives the bread a special flavor. Serve it with cream cheese.

- Preheat oven to 350 degrees.
- Cream margarine and sugar in mixer bowl until light and fluffy. Beat in eggs 1 at a time.
- Add flour, baking soda and salt; mix well. Stir in lemon juice and bananas. Spoon into greased loaf pan.
- Bake for 40 to 50 minutes or until loaf pulls from sides of pan.
- Remove to wire rack to cool.
- May add 1/4 cup chopped nuts if desired.
- Yield: 12 servings.

Ingredients

1/2 cup margarine, softened
1 cup sugar
2 eggs
1 1/2 cups flour
1 teaspoon baking soda
Salt to taste
1 teaspoon lemon juice
3 very ripe bananas, mashed

"BEACH WALK" CHILI CHEESE BREAD

Ingredients

1 loaf French bread

2 cups shredded sharp
Cheddar cheese

1/4 cup chopped green chilies

1/2 cup mayonnaise

1 teaspoon chili powder

1 teaspoon cumin seeds

- Preheat grill.
- Slice bread diagonally, slicing to but not through bottom.
- Combine remaining ingredients in bowl. Spread over cut surfaces of bread. Wrap in foil. Grill over medium-low coals for 15 to 20 minutes, turning occasionally.
- May bake, with foil open, at 350 degrees until heated through.
- Yield: 8 servings.

Over the Fence: This is a good example of the casual outdoor cooking that is typical of meals at Seaside, where we enjoy the beauty of the town and the fresh Gulf air.

GRANDMOTHER'S FAMOUS CRANBERRY BREAD

Ingredients

2 cups sifted flour

1 cup sugar

1 1/2 teaspoons baking powder

1/2 teaspoon baking soda

1 teaspoon salt

1/4 cup butter

1 egg, beaten

1 teaspoon grated orange rind

3/4 cup orange juice

1 1/2 cups golden raisins

1 1/2 cups fresh or frozen
cranberries, chopped

Just substitute additional cranberries for the raisins in this recipe for an all cranberry bread.

- Preheat oven to 350 degrees.
- Sift flour, sugar, baking powder, baking soda and salt into large bowl. Cut in butter until crumbly.
- Add egg, orange rind and orange juice all at once; mix just until moistened. Fold in raisins and cranberries. Spoon into greased 5x9-inch loaf pan.
- Bake for 1 hour and 10 minutes or until wooden pick inserted in center comes out clean. Remove to wire rack to cool.
- Yield: 12 servings.

Over the Fence: This is a good recipe for kids to make—with just a little help from mom.

"SOUTHERN SPLENDOR" POPPY SEED BREAD

- Preheat oven to 325 degrees.
- Combine flour, 2½ cups sugar, baking powder, poppy seeds and salt in bowl. Add eggs, oil, milk and 1½ teaspoons flavorings; mix well. Batter will be thin.
- Spoon into 2 greased and floured loaf pans. Bake for 1 hour. Remove to wire rack to cool.
- Blend orange juice, ¾ cup sugar and ½ teaspoon almond extract in small bowl; mix well. Drizzle over cool loaves.
- Yield: 16 servings.

Over the Fence: *We think that this bread makes great gifts for friends, neighbors and teachers.*

Ingredients

3 cups flour

2½ cups sugar

1½ teaspoons baking powder

1 to 3 tablespoons poppy seeds

1½ teaspoons salt

3 eggs

1½ cups oil

1½ cups milk

1½ teaspoons each butter, almond and vanilla extract

¼ cup orange juice

¾ cup (scant) sugar

½ teaspoon almond extract

CUBAN BREAD

- Dissolve yeast in warm water in bowl. Stir in salt and sugar. Beat in enough flour 1 cup at a time to make a fairly stiff dough.
- Shape dough into ball. Place in greased bowl, turning to coat surface. Let stand, covered with towel, in 80- to 85-degree place until doubled in bulk.
- Shape into 2 long or round loaves on lightly floured surface. Place on baking sheet sprinkled with cornmeal. Let rest for 5 minutes. Slash tops of loaves in 2 or 3 places; brush with water.
- Place loaves in cold oven. Place a pan of boiling water on rack under loaves. Set oven temperature at 400 degrees. Bake for 40 to 45 minutes or until crusty brown.
- Yield: 24 servings.

Ingredients

1 envelope dry yeast

2 cups lukewarm water

1¼ tablespoons salt

1 tablespoon sugar

6 to 7 cups flour

1 tablespoon cornmeal

"TIDE'S INN" PUMPKIN SPICE BREAD

A great Christmas gift!

- Preheat oven to 350 degrees.

- Combine eggs, sugar, butter, pumpkin, oil and vanilla in mixer bowl; beat until smooth.

- Add flour, baking powder, baking soda, cloves, cinnamon, nutmeg and salt; mix well. Fold in pecans. Spoon into 2 greased and floured loaf pans.

- Bake for 1 hour. Cool in pans for 20 minutes. Remove to wire rack to cool completely.

- May bake in bundt pan or tube pan if preferred.

- Yield: 24 servings.

Ingredients

3 eggs
3 cups sugar
1 cup butter, softened
1 (16-ounce) can pumpkin
1 cup vegetable oil
1 teaspoon vanilla extract
3 cups flour
1 teaspoon baking powder
1/2 teaspoon baking soda
1/2 teaspoon ground cloves
1 teaspoon cinnamon
1 teaspoon nutmeg
1/2 teaspoon salt
1 cup chopped pecans

"DREAM CHASER" SPOON BREAD

- Preheat oven to 400 degrees.

- Mix cornmeal, salt and milk in heavy saucepan. Bring to a boil, stirring constantly. Cook for 5 minutes or until very thick, stirring constantly. Add butter; remove from heat. Cool to lukewarm, stirring occasionally.

- Beat egg whites in mixer bowl until stiff but not dry. Beat eggs yolks in bowl slightly. Stir egg yolks into batter. Fold in egg whites.

- Spoon into preheated oiled 1 1/2-quart baking dish. Bake for 35 minutes or until firm and light brown. Serve immediately.

- Yield: 8 servings.

Ingredients

1 cup yellow cornmeal
1 teaspoon salt
3 cups milk
2 tablespoons butter
4 eggs, separated

"STARRY NIGHT" STRAWBERRY BREAD

Tastes great with cream cheese!

- Preheat oven to 325 degrees.
- Combine oil and eggs in mixer bowl; beat until thick and lemon-colored. Add strawberries; mix well.
- Mix flour, baking soda, sugar, cinnamon and salt together. Add to strawberry mixture; mix well. Stir in pecans.
- Spoon into 2 greased and lightly floured 5x9-inch loaf pans. Bake for 1¼ hours or until loaves test done.
- Remove to wire rack to cool.
- Yield: 24 servings.

Ingredients

1¼ cups canola oil
4 eggs
1 quart fresh strawberries, sliced
3 cups flour
1 teaspoon baking soda
1½ cups sugar
1½ teaspoons cinnamon
1 teaspoon salt
1½ cups chopped pecans

"SEASTAR" THREE-TWO-ONE BREAD PLUS

The "plus" in this bread is the cheese.

- Preheat oven to 350 degrees.
- Combine flour, sugar and beer in mixer bowl. Beat for 1 minute. Stir in cheese. Spoon into greased loaf pan.
- Bake for 1 hour and 5 minutes to 1 hour and 15 minutes or until loaf tests done.
- Remove to wire rack to cool.
- Yield: 12 servings.

Ingredients

3 cups self-rising flour
2 tablespoons sugar
1 (12-ounce) can beer,
at room temperature
1 cup shredded
mozzarella cheese

STONE-GROUND WHEAT BREAD

Ingredients

1 envelope dry yeast

1¹/4 cups warm (105- to
115-degree) water

2 cups stone-ground whole
wheat flour

1 cup plus 2 tablespoons
bread flour

2 tablespoons unsalted
butter, softened

2 tablespoons brown sugar

2 teaspoons salt

1 tablespoon melted butter

- Dissolve yeast in warm water in large bowl. Stir in 1 cup whole wheat flour, ¹/2 cup bread flour, 2 tablespoons butter, brown sugar and salt. Beat at medium speed for 2 minutes.

- Add remaining 1 cup whole wheat flour and ¹/2 cup plus 2 tablespoons bread flour. Beat for 1¹/2 minutes.

- Let rise, covered with plastic wrap, in warm place for 1 hour or until doubled in bulk.

- Beat dough for 30 strokes with wooden spoon. Spoon into greased 4x8-inch loaf pan. Let rise, covered, for 45 minutes or until doubled in bulk.

- Preheat oven to 375 degrees. Bake bread for 45 to 50 minutes or until loaf sounds hollow when tapped. Brush top with melted butter. Remove to wire rack to cool.

- May add ¹/2 cup oats or substitute ¹/4 cup wheat berries, plumped in boiling water, for ¹/4 cup of whole wheat flour.

- Yield: 8 servings.

BEIGNETS "FANTASIA"

Ingredients

¹/2 cup butter

1 cup water

2 teaspoons sugar

1 cup flour

2 eggs

1 egg yolk

Oil for deep frying

¹/4 cup confectioners' sugar

- Combine butter, water and sugar in heavy saucepan. Bring to a boil. Add flour all at once, stirring constantly. Cook until mixture leaves side of saucepan, stirring constantly.

- Spoon mixture into bowl; cool slightly. Beat in eggs and egg yolk 1 at a time.

- Preheat oil to 375 degrees. Drop batter by spoonfuls the size of a small egg into hot oil. Deep-fry until golden brown.

- Sprinkle with confectioners' sugar.

- Yield: 8 servings.

"ABOUT TIME" BISCUITS

- Preheat oven to 425 degrees.
- Combine flour and whipping cream in bowl; mix to form smooth dough.
- Roll dough 1/2 to 3/4 inch thick on lightly floured surface. Cut with 2-inch biscuit cutter; place 1 inch apart on baking sheet.
- Bake for 10 minutes or just until golden brown.
- May freeze biscuits on baking sheet and store in food storage bag until ready to bake.
- Yield: 42 small biscuits.

Ingredients

1 1/2 cups self-rising flour
1 cup whipping cream

"ACADIA" PRIORY BISCUITS

- Preheat oven to 350 degrees.
- Mix oats, flour, sugar, baking soda and salt in bowl. Add butter, hot water, syrup and vanilla; mix well.
- Drop by teaspoonfuls onto greased baking sheet. Bake for 10 minutes or until light brown. Remove to wire rack to cool. Store cooled biscuits in airtight container.
- May substitute corn syrup for the golden syrup.
- Yield: 48 biscuits.

Over the Fence: This recipe is from some Welsh hiking friends. The biscuits are just as good on the beach, boat or ski slope as they were on hikes in Wales.

Ingredients

2 cups rolled oats
3/4 cup flour
1 cup sugar
1/2 teaspoon baking soda
1/2 teaspoon salt
1/2 cup butter
2 tablespoons hot water
1 tablespoon Tate and Lyle golden syrup
1/2 teaspoon vanilla extract

New Orleans-style French Toast

Ingredients

1 (12-ounce) can
evaporated milk

1 cup sugar

4 eggs

1 teaspoon almond extract

1 tablespoon Amaretto
and Cognac

1 loaf French bread

1/4 cup confectioners' sugar

- Combine evaporated milk, sugar, eggs, almond extract and Amaretto and Cognac in bowl. Beat for 100 strokes with wire whisk.

- Slice bread 3/4 inch thick. Dip each slice into egg mixture and drain off excess.

- Preheat griddle sprayed with nonstick cooking spray. Bake bread on both sides until golden brown. Drain on paper towel. Sprinkle with confectioners' sugar.

- Yield: 12 servings.

Over the Fence: This is a regular item for breakfast at the Dolphin Inn. It goes well with the fruit sauce on page 203.

"Allison Cottage" Monkey Bread

Ingredients

4 cans Hungry Jack biscuits

1 cup sugar

1 1/2 tablespoons cinnamon

1/2 cup (or more) chopped pecans

1 cup packed brown sugar

1/2 cup margarine

Make this on Thanksgiving and Christmas mornings to enjoy before the turkey is done.

- Preheat oven to 350 degrees.

- Cut each biscuit into quarters. Shake 5 or 6 at a time in mixture of sugar and cinnamon in bag, coating well.

- Layer biscuits and pecans in greased tube pan until all ingredients are used.

- Combine brown sugar and margarine in saucepan. Cook until margarine melts and brown sugar dissolves, stirring to blend well. Drizzle over layers in prepared pan.

- Bake for 35 to 45 minutes or until golden brown. Let stand in pan for 15 minutes. Invert onto serving plate.

- Yield: 16 servings.

"TUPELO HONEY" GERMAN APPLE PANCAKES

- Sprinkle apples with 1 tablespoon sugar and cinnamon in bowl. Let stand until juicy.
- Combine eggs, milk, flour, 1 teaspoon sugar, vanilla and salt in blender container; process until smooth.
- Heat 1 tablespoon of the oil in small skillet. Spoon half the batter into skillet; top with 1/4 of the apple mixture. Bake until bottom of pancake is firm. Turn pancake and top with 1/4 of the apple mixture. Bake for several minutes longer. Remove to plate to keep warm.
- Repeat process with remaining batter and apple mixture.
- Yield: 2 servings.

Over the Fence: This recipe was the specialty of my dad when I was growing up in Jackson, Mississippi. Now it is the favorite of my six-year-old daughter.

Ingredients

2 large Granny Smith apples
1 tablespoon sugar
2 tablespoons cinnamon
4 eggs
2 tablespoons milk
1 tablespoon flour
1 teaspoon sugar
1 teaspoon vanilla extract
Salt to taste
2 tablespoons vegetable oil

"BAGBY-JAMES" SPECIAL POPOVERS

- Preheat oven to 450 degrees. Grease alternate cups in muffin tins to allow room for popovers to expand.
- Whisk eggs in mixer bowl or beat with rotary beater until foamy and lemon-colored. Add milk; whisk just until smooth. Add flour and salt all at once; whisk until foamy and smooth. Pour into greased muffin cups.
- Bake for 15 minutes. Reduce oven temperature to 350 degrees. Bake for 30 minutes longer. Remove from muffin cups with sharp knife. Serve immediately.
- Do not open oven door when popovers are baking. May double recipe.
- Yield: 10 servings.

Ingredients

3 eggs
1 1/4 cups milk, at room temperature
1 1/4 cups flour
Salt to taste

"BRIAR PATCH" CINNAMON ROLLS

Ingredients

1/2 cup milk

1 tablespoon shortening

1 tablespoon dry yeast

1/2 cup lukewarm (105- to 115-degree) water

1/2 cup milk

1/4 cup sugar

1 tablespoon salt

4 cups (about) flour

1 egg white, stiffly beaten

1 cup packed brown sugar

1 cup coconut

1/2 cup chopped pecans

1 1/2 tablespoons cinnamon

1 cup packed brown sugar

1/2 cup water

2 1/2 tablespoons butter

1 cup confectioners' sugar

1/4 cup water

- Scald 1/2 cup milk in small saucepan. Stir in shortening until melted. Dissolve yeast in lukewarm water in cup.

- Combine remaining 1/2 cup milk, sugar and salt in large bowl. Add scalded milk mixture. Add 2 cups of the flour gradually, beating constantly. Stir in yeast. Beat in 1/2 cup flour. Fold in stiffly beaten egg white gently. Add remaining 1 1/2 cups flour, mixing until dough pulls from side of bowl.

- Place dough in greased bowl, turning to coat surface. Let rise, covered, in warm place for 45 to 60 minutes or until doubled in bulk.

- Roll into very thin rectangle on floured surface. Sprinkle with mixture of 1 cup brown sugar, coconut, pecans and cinnamon. Roll dough to enclose filling, pressing edge to seal. Place seam side down on work surface; cut into 1-inch slices.

- Combine 1 cup brown sugar, 1/2 cup water and butter in saucepan. Bring to a boil, stirring to blend well. Pour into lightly greased 10x15-inch baking pan. Place rolls cut side down in syrup. Let rise, covered, for 40 minutes or until doubled in bulk.

- Preheat oven to 350 degrees. Bake rolls for 25 to 30 minutes or until golden brown.

- Mix confectioners' sugar and remaining 1/4 cup water in bowl. Drizzle over hot rolls. Serve warm.

- May roll dough 1/4 inch thick for larger rolls and bake longer.

- Yield: 120 bite-sized rolls.

"ADAGIO"
OVERNIGHT PECAN ROLLS

- Arrange frozen roll dough in greased bundt pan; drizzle with melted margarine.
- Mix pudding mix, brown sugar, pecans and cinnamon in small bowl. Sprinkle over rolls.
- Let rise, covered, overnight.
- Preheat oven to 325 degrees.
- Bake rolls for 25 to 30 minutes or until golden brown. Invert onto serving plate while warm.
- Do not use instant pudding mix in this recipe.
- Yield: 12 servings.

Ingredients

1 (16-ounce) package
frozen roll dough

1/2 cup melted margarine

1 (4-ounce) package vanilla
pudding and pie filling mix

1/2 cup packed brown sugar

1/4 cup chopped pecans

2 teaspoons cinnamon

ARTICHOKE BRUNCH PIE

- Preheat oven to 350 degrees.
- Bake pie shell just until very light brown.
- Sauté green onion tops in butter in skillet; remove from heat. Add flour, artichokes, eggs and cream; mix well. Stir in pepper cheese and 3/4 cup Cheddar cheese.
- Spoon into pie shell. Bake for 35 minutes. Sprinkle with remaining 1/4 cup Cheddar cheese. Bake for 10 minutes longer or until center is set.
- Yield: 6 servings.

Over the Fence: *At About Time Cottage, we serve this to guests with fresh fruit and Champagne. It can even be baked the day before and reheated.*

Ingredients

1 unbaked (9-inch) pie shell

1/3 cup chopped green onion tops

1 tablespoon butter

1 tablespoon flour

1 (14-ounce) can artichoke
hearts, drained, chopped

2 eggs, beaten

3/4 cup light cream

1 cup shredded hot pepper cheese

1 cup shredded Cheddar cheese

SOUTH-OF-THE-BORDER OMELET

Ingredients

1/4 cup chopped green bell pepper

1/4 cup chopped onion

Salt and pepper to taste

2 tablespoons butter

1/2 cup mild salsa

1 tablespoon butter

3 eggs, at room temperature,
slightly beaten

2 slices American cheese

- Sauté green pepper and onion with salt and pepper in 2 tablespoons butter in 8-inch sauté pan until onion is tender. Stir in salsa. Cook for 1 minute longer; set aside.

- Melt 1 tablespoon butter in 8-inch sauté pan. Add eggs; stir several times. Reduce heat to medium.

- Cook eggs just until soft-set. Add salsa mixture just before eggs are done to taste. Top with cheese; fold omelet over to enclose filling. Serve on heated platter.

- Yield: 2 servings.

"JUST PEACHY" BREAKFAST SAUSAGE CASSEROLE

Ingredients

6 slices bread

2 tablespoons butter, softened

1 pound pork sausage

1 1/2 cups shredded longhorn
cheese

6 eggs, beaten

2 cups half and half

1 teaspoon salt

- Trim crusts from bread. Spread bread with butter. Arrange in 9x13-inch baking pan sprayed with nonstick cooking spray.

- Brown sausage in skillet, stirring until crumbly; drain. Spread over bread; sprinkle with cheese.

- Combine eggs, half and half and salt in bowl; mix well. Pour over layers. Chill, covered, overnight.

- Preheat oven to 350 degrees. Let casserole stand at room temperature for 15 minutes.

- Bake casserole for 45 minutes or until set.

- Yield: 8 servings.

"WILDER" CHEESY SAUSAGE QUICHE

Serve with grits casserole, fruit and a sweet bread.

- Brown sausage in skillet, stirring until crumbly; drain. Add milk, eggs, bread, cheese, dry mustard and salt; mix well.
- Spoon into greased 9x13-inch baking dish. Chill, covered, overnight.
- Preheat oven to 350 degrees. Bake casserole for 1 hour.
- Yield: 10 servings.

Over the Fence: *Traditionally, we freeze one or more casseroles and fit them all into one cooler for our trip to the beach. The casseroles thaw overnight and are ready for a wonderful breakfast on the first day at Seaside.*

Ingredients

2 pounds mild pork sausage
3 cups milk
9 eggs, beaten
5 slices bread, cut into 1-inch cubes
2 cups shredded Cheddar cheese
1 1/2 teaspoons dry mustard
1 teaspoon salt

"LAST EDITION" SPINACH PIE

Quick and easy!

- Preheat oven to 400 degrees.
- Combine sausage, spinach soufflé, eggs, milk, onion, mushrooms and cheese in bowl; mix well.
- Spoon mixture into pie shell. Bake for 25 to 30 minutes or until set.
- May substitute crumbled Italian sausage for turkey sausage.
- Yield: 6 servings.

Ingredients

3/4 cup cooked turkey sausage
1 (10-ounce) package frozen spinach soufflé, thawed
2 eggs
3 tablespoons milk
2 teaspoons chopped onion
1/2 cup sliced mushrooms
3/4 cup shredded Swiss cheese
1 unbaked (9-inch) pie shell

YESTERDAY'S EGGS

Ingredients

4 slices bacon

1/2 cup margarine

1/2 cup flour

1 quart milk

8 ounces dried beef, chopped

2 (4-ounce) cans
mushrooms, drained

16 large eggs

1 cup evaporated milk

1/4 teaspoon salt

1/4 cup margarine

- Fry bacon in skillet until crisp; drain and crumble bacon, reserving drippings.
- Melt 1/2 cup margarine in reserved bacon drippings in skillet. Stir in flour. Add milk. Cook until thickened, stirring constantly. Add dried beef and mushrooms.
- Beat eggs with evaporated milk and salt in bowl. Add to 1/4 cup melted margarine in skillet. Cook until eggs are soft-set, stirring frequently.
- Alternate eggs and beef mixture in two 9x13-inch baking dishes until all ingredients are used, ending with eggs. Sprinkle with bacon. Chill, covered, in refrigerator.
- Preheat oven to 300 degrees. Bake casseroles for 1 hour.
- Yield: 20 servings.

"ROMANCE" BAKED CHEESY APPLES

Ingredients

2 (16-ounce) cans sliced apples

1/2 cup melted butter

2 cups shredded Velveeta cheese

3/4 cup flour

1 cup sugar

- Preheat oven to 350 degrees.
- Drain apples and spread in 8x8-inch baking dish.
- Combine butter, cheese, flour and sugar in bowl; mix well. Spread over apples.
- Bake for 30 minutes or until golden brown and crusty.
- Yield: 9 servings.

BAKED APRICOTS

This is great with quail and cheese grits!

- Preheat oven to 300 degrees.
- Alternate layers of apricots, brown sugar and crackers in baking dish until all ingredients are used, dotting cracker layers with butter.
- Bake for 1 hour.
- Yield: 10 servings.

Ingredients

2 (29-ounce) cans apricots, drained

1 (16-ounce) package light brown sugar

1 (12-ounce) package butter crackers, crushed

1 cup butter, sliced

"MOORE FUN" RICE PUDDING

A thin milky pudding that is a breakfast favorite.

- Combine rice, sugar and milk in double boiler. Cook over medium heat for 1½ to 2 hours or until rice is tender and mixture begins to thicken; remove from heat.
- Add vanilla and raisins. Spoon into bowl. Sprinkle with cinnamon. Chill, covered, until serving time.
- Yield: 10 servings.

Ingredients

1½ cups rice

½ cup sugar

5 cups milk

¼ teaspoon vanilla extract

¾ cup raisins

Cinnamon to taste

"BLUE BELLE" SUNRISE SURPRISE

Good and good for you; this breakfast tastes like dessert.

- Combine yogurt, cereal and honey in bowl; mix well. Chill, covered, overnight.
- Yield: 2 servings.

Ingredients

2 cups plain nonfat yogurt

1½ cups Quaker all-natural cereal with dates

½ cup honey

...tottage • Floridays • For Keeps • Forsythe Cottage • Frascogna Cott
ant's Roost • GoodnightMoon • Gorlin Cottage • Grayton One • Gray
nor • Gulfview • Gull Cottage • Haardt Cottage • Hampton • Harvest
dges Cottage • Home Alone • Honalee • Hoover Cottage • House
smine • Jasper • Jennifer's Castle • Josephine's • Jubilee • Kaleido
st Edition • Latitude • LeBlanc Cottage • Leeward • Lehman Cotta
ndpine Lodge • Love the Dove • Lost Goggles • Cottage •
rtha Green • McChesney Cottage • McCollister Cottage • McLaugh
Mirador • Mis B'Haven • Modica Cottage • Moore Fun • Nancy's F
ttage • On the Veranda • Ondine • Orth Cottage • Outer Banks • Ov
lican Perch • Periwinkle • Persimmon • Persuasion • Peterson Cot
ttage • Postcard • Precious • Propinquity • Puglin • Rainbow • Re
bin's Nest • Roger's Lighthouse • Romance • Rooftops • Rose Cotta
andia • Sandpail • Sandpiper • Savannah Rose • Savannah Sands •
alink • Seaquel • Seaspell • Seastar • Seawynds • Serendipity • Sha
omewhere In Time • Southern Comfort • Southern Splendor • Spinn
ndance • Sundaze • Sunnyside Up • Sunrise • Sunrise Wishes • Sun
use • The Conservatory • This Is the Life • Tide's Inn • Tiger Paw
eeze • Toye • Treetops • Trio • Tropical Holiday • Tupelo Honey • Tu
Vakeham Cottage • Waterside • Wayback • Weber Cottage • Wilder
e Beach • Zebulon • Zeidman Cottage • Zurn Cottage • A Summe

Pasta Plus & More

*...Have ye leisure, comfort, calm,
Shelter, food, love's gentle balm?*
Percy Bysshe Shelley

ttage • American Dream • Anderson Cottage • Anniston • April 1
ttage • Beach Walk • Bella Vista • Belvedere • Benedictus • Beside
te • Boswell Cottage • Briar Patch • Brickwalk • Bridgeport • Brie
llaway Cottage • Cape May • Carey Cottage • Caribbean • Carpe

rumious Bandersnatch • Gadsden • Gatewalk • Gazebo • Getaway
o • Green Cottage • Green Gables • Greenpeace • Guest Cottage • G
Hayford Cottage • Heavenly Days • Helvie Cottage • His Greenhous
s • Hurrah! • Idlewild South • Irvine Cottage • Isaacs Cottage • Iv
Kennedy Cottage • Key West • Kitchens Cottage • Kric • La. Hous
onardo da   Dipper • Lit
ottage • Mag   tage • Marisc
ge • Mellow   Night's Drea
arnia • Nat   Nirvana • Ols
! • Park Pla   hes 'n Crean
cture Book   Crazy • Porte
Renaissanc   y's • Roanoke
an's Castle   e • Sandi Sho
Cottage • S   wo • Sea View
Shell Seeke   Smith Cotta
tanziale Co   inger Cottag
ams • Suntin   ng • The Bea
on-the-Sea   opisaw • Tow
ker Tower •   • Vista del M
• Windler   wn • Wright
• About Tim   llegro • Allis

nley • As Yo   Bagby-Jam
terside • Bi   Moon • Bl
the Sea • Brigadoon • B's Nest • Burnett Cottage • C an Cottage
rriage House • Casa del Mar • Casablanca • Charleston • Chatha

Pasta Plus & More

Landing Catch, 85

Catch of the Day Salad, 85

Bowtie Salad, 86

Linguine with Tomatoes, Basil
and Brie, 87

Cheesy Italian Macaroni, 88

Sea Shell Macaroni Casserole, 88

Lasagna, 89

Pesto Pizza, 89

Linguine with Pesto Sauce, 90

Pasta and Chicken Salad, 91

Rotini and Spinach Salad, 91

Angel Hair Pasta, 92

Red Sauce, 93

Sausage and Spaghetti, 94

Spaghetti with Chicken and Sausage, 95

Seafood Pasta, 95

Japanese Sesame Noodles, 96

Pasta-Stuffed Zucchini, 96

Filled Noodles, 97

"SUNDAZE" LANDING CATCH

- Combine vermicelli and chicken broth with enough water to cover in saucepan. Cook using package directions; drain.

- Sauté green onions, onions and garlic in butter in saucepan until onions are tender. Stir in celery. Add flaked crab meat, crayfish and shrimp; mix well. Cook for 10 minutes, stirring occasionally.

- Stir in oysters, soup, salt and pepper. Cook until oysters curl, stirring frequently.

- Arrange vermicelli in a ring on serving platter. Fill center with seafood mixture.

- Yield: 6 servings.

Ingredients

1 (16-ounce) package vermicelli

2 (10-ounce) cans chicken broth

5 green onions, chopped

2 onions, grated

1 clove of garlic, minced

1/2 cup butter

1 cup chopped celery

1 pound each crab meat, cleaned crayfish and peeled shrimp

24 oysters

2 (10-ounce) cans cream of mushroom soup

Salt and pepper to taste

CATCH OF THE DAY SALAD

Take this dish on a picnic, to a potluck dinner or to a tailgate party.

- Prepare tortellini using package directions. Drain; rinse with cold water. Toss with 1 tablespoon oil in bowl.

- Cook zucchini and snow peas in small amount of water in saucepan until tender-crisp. Drain; rinse with cold water. Toss with tortellini.

- Add green onions, olives, tomatoes, cheese and shrimp; mix well. Pour mixture of 1/3 cup olive oil, 2 tablespoons water, wine vinegar and salad dressing mix over mixture, tossing to coat.

- Chill, covered, overnight.

- Yield: 6 servings.

Ingredients

7 ounces cheese tortellini

1 tablespoon vegetable oil

1 medium zucchini, thinly sliced

4 ounces snow peas, cut into thirds

2 medium green onions, chopped

1/3 cup sliced black olives

1 cup cherry tomato halves

1/4 cup grated Parmesan cheese

1 pound cooked peeled shrimp

1/3 cup olive oil

1/3 to 1/2 cup white wine vinegar

1 envelope Ranch dressing mix

"POSTCARD" BOWTIE SALAD

Dressing Ingredients

3/4 cup La Martinique True
French Vinaigrette
Freshly ground black pepper
Red pepper flakes to taste
Salt to taste

Pasta Ingredients

1 (16-ounce) package
bowtie pasta
4 quarts water
2 tablespoons olive oil
1 tablespoon fresh lemon juice
1/2 red bell pepper, chopped
1 1/2 cups firmly packed
chopped fresh basil
2 cups chopped plum tomatoes
3/4 cup grated Parmesan cheese
Fresh basil leaves

Vary the vegetables according to availability. Adjust the Parmesan cheese, dressing and red pepper flakes according to taste. Be creative!

- Combine French vinaigrette, black pepper, red pepper flakes and salt in covered container, shaking to blend.

- Cook pasta in 4 quarts boiling water in saucepan until *al dente*; drain. Toss with olive oil and lemon juice in bowl. Cool to room temperature, stirring occasionally.

- Stir in red pepper, basil, plum tomatoes and cheese.

- Add dressing, stirring to coat. Garnish with basil leaves.

- Add any of your choice of the optional ingredients (see Over the Fence); toss lightly.

- Yield: 8 servings.

Over the Fence: *Use any or all of these optional ingredients: steamed green beans, cut into 1-inch pieces; garden green peas; steamed broccoli flowerettes; sliced steamed carrots; sliced steamed summer squash; cooked shrimp; or sliced summer sausage.*

LINGUINE WITH TOMATOES, BASIL AND BRIE

PASTA PLUS & MORE 87

Great served with grilled fish or meat and a salad.

- Combine tomatoes, Brie, basil, garlic, ½ cup olive oil, chicken broth, white wine, ½ teaspoon salt, pepper, zucchini and eggplant in large bowl; mix well.

- Let stand, covered, at room temperature for 2 hours.

- Bring 6 quarts water to a boil in large saucepan. Add 1 tablespoon olive oil and 2 teaspoons salt; mix well. Add linguine. Boil for 8 to 10 minutes or until tender; drain.

- Toss linguine with sauce in bowl. Serve with freshly grated Parmesan cheese.

- Yield: 6 servings.

~

Over the Fence: *Remember that fresh pasta requires less cooking time than dried pasta and that pasta which is to be added to a dish that will be baked should be undercooked as pasta will continue cooking during baking.*

Sauce Ingredients

4 large tomatoes, chopped

1 pound Brie, rind removed, torn into bite-sized pieces

1 cup firmly packed basil leaves, cut into strips

3 cloves of garlic, finely minced

½ cup extra-virgin olive oil

¼ cup chicken broth

¼ cup white wine

½ teaspoon salt

½ teaspoon freshly ground pepper

2 zucchini, sliced, broiled

1 eggplant, cut into bite-sized pieces, broiled

Pasta Ingredients

6 quarts water

1 tablespoon olive oil

2 teaspoons salt

1½ pounds linguine

½ cup freshly grated Parmesan cheese

CHEESY ITALIAN MACARONI

Ingredients

1 (16-ounce) package ziti

7 tablespoons melted
unsalted butter

5 tablespoons unbleached flour

3 1/2 cups milk

7 ounces Gorgonzola cheese

6 ounces Fontina cheese

Nutmeg, salt and freshly
ground pepper to taste

4 ounces mozzarella cheese

4 ounces Parmesan cheese

1 teaspoon paprika

- Preheat oven to 350 degrees.
- Cook ziti *al dente* using package directions; drain.
- Mix butter and flour in saucepan. Cook over medium heat for 1 minute, stirring constantly. Whisk in milk gradually. Cook until slightly thickened, stirring constantly.
- Add crumbled Gorgonzola cheese and shredded Fontina cheese; mix well. Cook until smooth, stirring constantly. Season with nutmeg, salt and pepper.
- Stir in cooked ziti. Cut mozzarella cheese into 1/4-inch pieces. Add to ziti; mix well. Spoon into buttered 2-quart baking dish. Sprinkle with grated Parmesan cheese and paprika.
- Bake for 30 to 40 minutes or until brown and bubbly.
- Yield: 4 servings.

"PICTURE BOOK" SEA SHELL MACARONI CASSEROLE

Ingredients

16 ounces shell macaroni

1/2 cup each chopped onion
and green bell pepper

3/4 cup mayonnaise

2 (10-ounce) cans cream
of mushroom soup

1 1/2 cups shredded sharp
Cheddar cheese

1/2 cup chopped pimentos

Salt and pepper to taste

1/2 cup melted butter

1 cup crushed butter crackers

- Preheat oven to 350 degrees.
- Cook macaroni using package directions; drain.
- Combine onion, green pepper, mayonnaise, soup, cheese, pimentos, salt and pepper in bowl; mix well. Stir in macaroni.
- Spoon mixture into nonstick baking pan. Sprinkle with mixture of melted butter and crackers.
- Bake for 30 to 40 minutes or until bubbly.
- Yield: 8 servings.

Lasagna "Fantasia"

- Preheat oven to 350 degrees.
- Brown ground beef with onion and garlic in skillet, stirring until ground beef is crumbly; drain.
- Stir in tomato paste, plum tomatoes, sugar, salt and pepper. Simmer for 30 to 45 minutes or until of desired consistency, stirring occasionally. May add water or wine if necessary for desired consistency.
- Combine sour cream, cream cheese and green onions in bowl; mix well.
- Layer noodles, sour cream mixture and ground beef mixture in buttered 9x13-inch baking dish. Sprinkle with Cheddar cheese.
- Bake for 30 minutes. Cool slightly before cutting.
- Yield: 8 servings.

Ingredients

1½ pounds ground beef

1 small onion, chopped

2 cloves of garlic, minced

1 (6-ounce) can tomato paste

1 (16-ounce) can crushed plum tomatoes

1 tablespoon sugar

Salt and pepper to taste

1 cup sour cream

8 ounces cream cheese, softened

6 green onions, chopped

1 (12-ounce) package lasagna noodles, cooked, drained

1 cup shredded Cheddar cheese

"Briar Patch" Pesto Pizza

We sometimes cut the pizza into small pieces and serve as an appetizer.

- Preheat oven to 425 degrees.
- Spread crust with pesto sauce and pizza sauce. Sprinkle with assorted meats and vegetables; sprinkle with cheese.
- Bake for 10 minutes or until cheese melts.
- Yield: 6 servings.

Over the Fence: *We frequently make this pizza as a family, using leftovers. Each family member does his own thing on a section of the crust.*

Ingredients

1 frozen pizza crust

2 to 4 ounces pesto sauce

Pizza sauce

Assorted cooked meats

Assorted cooked vegetables

1 cup shredded mozzarella cheese, goat cheese or brie

LINGUINE WITH PESTO SAUCE

Sauce Ingredients

1 cup fresh basil leaves
2 large cloves of garlic, chopped
1/2 cup walnuts
6 tablespoons extra-virgin
olive oil
Salt and freshly ground
pepper to taste
1/2 cup freshly grated
Parmesan cheese
2 tablespoons freshly
grated Romano cheese

Pasta Ingredients

4 quarts water
1 1/2 tablespoons salt
1 (16-ounce) package linguine
2 tablespoons whipping cream
2 to 4 tablespoons white wine
1/4 cup freshly grated
Parmesan cheese

- Combine basil, garlic and walnuts in blender container. Process until chopped.
- Add olive oil in fine stream, processing constantly at high speed until completely blended.
- Add salt and pepper to taste, 1/2 cup Parmesan cheese and Romano cheese. Process just until combined.
- Bring 4 quarts water to a boil in saucepan. Stir in 1 1/2 tablespoons salt and linguine. Cook using package directions; drain.
- Toss linguine with mixture of whipping cream and white wine in bowl. Stir in pesto sauce, tossing to coat. Sprinkle with freshly ground pepper and 1/4 cup Parmesan cheese.
- Yield: 6 servings.

~

Over the Fence: *The first basil from the garden— and the resulting pesto—officially welcome summer. Combine equal parts pesto sauce and sour cream to serve with soups or add pesto sauce to scrambled eggs or potato salad.*

"ALLISON COTTAGE" PASTA AND CHICKEN SALAD

This is a perfect lunch entrée for a picnic or an outdoor concert at Seaside.

- Combine mayonnaise, sour cream, vinegar, dillweed, mustard, sugar, white pepper and seasoned salt in bowl; mix well.
- Combine macaroni, chicken, grapes and green onions in bowl; mix well. Stir in dressing.
- Chill, covered, for 6 hours to overnight.
- Yield: 8 servings.

Ingredients

1/2 cup each mayonnaise and sour cream
2 tablespoons cider vinegar
1/4 teaspoon dillweed
1 1/2 tablespoons Dijon mustard
1 teaspoon sugar
1/2 teaspoon white pepper
1/4 teaspoon seasoned salt
1 3/4 cups macaroni shells, cooked
2 cups chopped cooked chicken
2 cups seedless white grape halves
1/2 cup chopped green onions

"LOWE COTTAGE" ROTINI AND SPINACH SALAD

Make this salad your very own creation by adding the ingredients you prefer.

- Combine spinach, basil, garlic, cheese, olive oil, salt, pepper and wine vinegar in bowl; mix well. Add rotini; mix well.
- Chill, covered, for 2 hours or longer.
- May add one or more of the following: black olives, crumbled bacon, cherry tomatoes, chopped salami, chopped onions or pecans.
- Yield: 4 servings.

Ingredients

1 (10-ounce) package frozen spinach, cooked, drained
2 teaspoons basil
4 cloves of garlic, minced
1/2 cup grated Parmesan cheese
2/3 cup olive oil
3/4 teaspoon salt
1/2 teaspoon pepper
2 tablespoons red wine vinegar
1 (12-ounce) package rotini, cooked, drained, chilled

"VISTA DEL MAR" ANGEL HAIR PASTA

Ingredients

3 to 6 cloves of garlic, pressed

1 medium onion, chopped

1/4 cup extra-virgin olive oil

2 tablespoons fresh
chopped oregano

3/4 tablespoon fresh
chopped basil

1/4 tablespoon fresh
chopped parsley

1 bay leaf

1 (16-ounce) can tomato sauce

6 tomatoes, chopped

12 mushrooms, sliced

1/2 cup red wine

1 (16-ounce) package fresh
angel hair or rotelle pasta,
cooked, drained

1/4 cup freshly grated
Parmesan cheese

- Sauté garlic and onion in olive oil in large saucepan. Stir in oregano, basil, parsley, bay leaf and tomato sauce. Bring to a boil; reduce heat.

- Simmer for 15 to 20 minutes or until flavors of herbs are distributed through sauce. Stir in tomatoes, mushrooms and wine. Simmer, covered, for 1 hour or until of desired consistency. Discard bay leaf.

- Arrange pasta on serving platter; top with sauce. Sprinkle with Parmesan cheese.

- May substitute 1/3 cup Cabernet Sauvignon or Chianti for red wine.

- Yield: 6 servings.

Over the Fence: When cooking vegetables, cover those that grew underground, and leave uncovered those that grew above ground.

"BURNETT COTTAGE"
RED SAUCE

- Sauté garlic in olive oil in saucepan for 3 to 4 minutes or until light brown. Add onion and green pepper. Cook until tender, stirring constantly.

- Stir in red wine and mushrooms. Simmer for 5 minutes or until mushrooms are tender and wine has been absorbed, stirring frequently. Stir in tomatoes and tomato paste. Add red pepper, basil, oregano and sugar; mix well.

- Simmer for 3 hours, stirring occasionally. Season with salt and pepper.

- Serve immediately with your favorite pasta.

- May add Italian sausage to create a heartier dish or add a combination of shrimp, scallops, mussels, clams or lobster 10 to 15 minutes before serving.

- Yield: 8 servings.

Over the Fence: I grew up in a small New Jersey town where it seemed every other family was Italian and every one of my Italian buddies had a mother or grandmother who made a red sauce "to die for." When I left New Jersey in 1979, one of my friends threw me a terrific going-away party and gave me this recipe from his grandmother so that I would always be reminded of home when I prepared this dish. Enjoy it as I do and, although I know it can't be proved scientifically, I swear the sauce comes out better if you put a couple of Sinatra compact discs on while preparing it!

Ingredients

4 cloves of garlic, finely chopped

5 tablespoons olive oil

1 large yellow onion, chopped

1 small green bell pepper, chopped

3/4 cup dry red wine

1 cup sliced fresh mushrooms

1 (28-ounce) can tomatoes, drained, chopped

1 (28-ounce) can diced tomatoes

1/2 (6-ounce) can tomato paste

1/4 teaspoon red pepper, crushed

1/3 cup chopped fresh basil

1 teaspoon oregano

2 teaspoons sugar

Salt and pepper to taste

SAUSAGE AND SPAGHETTI "BELVEDERE"

Ingredients

1 pound sausage

4 slices bacon

8 ounces fresh mushrooms, sliced

1 green bell pepper, chopped

1 medium onion, chopped

1/2 (7-ounce) bottle of stuffed olives, drained, sliced

8 ounces sharp Cheddar cheese, shredded

1 cup canned tomatoes

1 (6-ounce) can tomato paste

3/4 cup water

Salt and pepper to taste

1 (8-ounce) package spaghetti, cooked, drained

Prepare the sauce one day in advance to enhance the flavors.

- Preheat oven to 350 degrees.
- Brown sausage in skillet, stirring until crumbly; drain.
- Fry bacon until crisp; crumble.
- Sauté mushrooms, green pepper, onion and olives in large nonstick skillet. Add sausage, bacon, cheese, tomatoes, tomato paste, water, salt and pepper; mix well. Simmer for 5 minutes, stirring occasionally.
- Combine sauce with spaghetti in bowl; mix well. Spoon into baking dish.
- Bake for 1 hour.
- Yield: 8 servings.

Over the Fence: *My mother served this to my fiancé and his family the day before our wedding in January of 1957. We have loved this hearty casserole ever since!*

~

Over the Fence: *Almost any meat sauce may be prepared ahead and chilled overnight. This process enables excess fat to be skimmed as well as increasing flavor.*

Spaghetti with Chicken and Sausage

- Cook spaghetti *al dente* using package directions. Drain and keep warm.

- Rinse chicken and pat dry; cut into 1/2-inch strips.

- Slice onion and cut green pepper into strips. Mince garlic. Cut sausage into 1/2-inch slices.

- Sauté onion, green pepper and garlic in olive oil in saucepan over medium-high heat until vegetables are light brown. Add chicken, sausage, undrained tomatoes, red wine, oregano, basil and sugar; mix well.

- Bring mixture to a boil; reduce heat. Simmer for 10 minutes, stirring occasionally. Stir in cream, salt and pepper. Simmer for 3 minutes or until slightly thickened.

- Arrange spaghetti on 2 plates; top with sauce.

- Yield: 2 servings.

Ingredients

1 (12-ounce) package spaghetti

8 ounces chicken breast filets

1 each onion and green bell pepper

1 clove of garlic

8 ounces sweet or hot Italian sausage links

1 tablespoon olive oil

1 (16-ounce) can diced tomatoes

1/4 cup dry red wine

1/2 teaspoon oregano, crumbled

1/4 teaspoon each crumbled basil and sugar

1/4 cup whipping cream

Salt and pepper to taste

"Coquina" Seafood Pasta

- Bring lemon and 2 quarts water to a boil in stockpot. Add shrimp and scallops. Cook for 1 minute. Remove seafood to bowl, reserving liquid.

- Pour mixture of olive oil, lemon juice, tomatoes, dillweed and pepper over seafood, tossing to coat. Let stand at room temperature for 20 minutes or store in refrigerator for up to 12 hours.

- Cook spaghetti in reserved liquid using package directions; drain. Toss with seafood mixture in bowl.

- Yield: 6 servings.

Ingredients

1 lemon, cut into halves

1 pound peeled shrimp

8 ounces bay scallops

1 cup light olive oil

1/2 cup lemon juice

3/4 cup chopped tomatoes

1/2 cup chopped fresh dillweed

1 teaspoon pepper

1 (16-ounce) package spaghetti

"PERSIMMON" JAPANESE SESAME NOODLES

Ingredients

1 pound soba (buckwheat noodles)
1 cup soy sauce
1/4 cup chicken broth
1 tablespoon sugar
3 tablespoons sesame seeds, toasted
1 pound asparagus
6 green onions, cut diagonally into 1/2-inch pieces

- Cook buckwheat noodles *al dente*; drain.
- Process soy sauce, chicken broth, sugar and 1½ tablespoons sesame seeds in blender until smooth.
- Cut asparagus into 1-inch pieces. Steam until tender-crisp.
- Toss soy sauce mixture with noodles in bowl. Mix in asparagus and green onions. Sprinkle with remaining 1½ tablespoons sesame seeds.
- Serve at room temperature.
- Linguine may be substituted for the soba.
- Yield: 10 servings.

PASTA-STUFFED ZUCCHINI

Ingredients

2 (10-inch) zucchini
2 tablespoons olive oil
1 cup small shell macaroni
4 Italian sausages, crumbled
1 onion, chopped
1 clove of garlic, minced
1 tomato, peeled, seeded, chopped
1 cup shredded Cheddar cheese
2 tablespoons chopped fresh parsley
1 teaspoon oregano
Salt and pepper to taste
1/4 cup grated Parmesan cheese

Here is a great way to utilize those overgrown zucchini!

- Preheat oven to 350 degrees.
- Split zucchini lengthwise into halves. Remove pulp carefully, leaving 1/4-inch to 1/2-inch shells. Chop pulp, reserving 2 cups. Brush inside of shells with olive oil.
- Cook macaroni *al dente* using package directions; drain.
- Cook sausage in skillet until some of fat has been rendered. Stir in reserved zucchini pulp, onion and garlic. Cook until sausage is crumbly; drain.
- Stir in macaroni and next 6 ingredients. Spoon into zucchini shells. Place in shallow baking dish. Add about 1/2 inch hot water to dish.
- Bake, covered with foil, for 30 minutes or until zucchini is tender. Remove from oven; drain.
- Preheat broiler.
- Sprinkle zucchini with Parmesan cheese. Broil until bubbly and brown.
- Yield: 4 servings.

"PLUM CRAZY" FILLED NOODLES

- Mix ground beef, salt, pepper, nutmeg, parsley, onions, spinach, oats, bread crumbs and 7 eggs in bowl; mix well.

- Combine flour, 5 eggs, salt to taste and enough water to make easy to handle dough in bowl; mix well. Knead until dough is smooth and elastic. Divide into 3 portions.

- Roll each portion into paper-thin circle on lightly floured surface; spread with ground beef mixture on 1/2 of the circle.

- Fold to enclose filling, pressing edges firmly together.

- Cut into 2-inch strips parallel to the fold. Cut strips diagonally into 2-inch pieces. Repeat with remaining dough semicircles.

- Drop noodles into boiling salted water in stockpot. Boil for 10 minutes. Remove to racks to cool. Store, covered, in refrigerator or freeze for future use.

- Yield: 25 servings.

Over the Fence: Served in homemade chicken soup, these filled noodles were often the first course at large family gatherings. The Saturday night before the party saw the whole family in the kitchen. Mom started the dough and mixed the filling, using a half eggshell to measure the water. Dad beat the dough smooth, rolled it out and helped Mom form the noodles. Mom cut the noodles by rolling a thin dinner plate across the dough. The whole family watched the pot, waiting for my mother to fish out the first batch and lay them out to cool. My father was usually the first to snitch one of those steaming noodles. My brother and I were right behind him, disregarding my mother's warnings about how we would burn our tongues.

Ingredients

3 pounds ground beef

Salt and pepper to taste

Nutmeg to taste

Fresh chopped parsley to taste

2 onions, chopped

2 to 3 packages frozen chopped spinach, thawed, drained

2 cups rolled oats

1 cup bread crumbs

7 eggs, beaten

4 cups flour

5 eggs, beaten

1/2 cup (about) water

Vegetables & Side Dishes

oral Cove • Corn Cottage • Crackerbox • Craige Cottage • Crawfo
ge • Dapper's Den • Dargusch Cottage • Daydream Believer • Days
lphin Inn • Domino • Dove Crest • Dragon's Lair • Dragonette • Drea
Duffy Cottage • Dune • Dunseth Cottage • DuPuis Cottage • East
ge • Enon • Eyer Cottage • Fantasia • Fernleigh • Flamingo • Fletch
umio • Gre age • G
Hayfo enhous
s • Hu ge • Ivy
Kenn . Hous
onard er • Lit
ttage Marisc
ge • M t's Drea
larnia a • Ols
! • Pa Crean
cture • Porte
Rena Roanok
an's C ndi Sho
Cotta ea View
Sho Seeker • Sisters Three By The Sea • Skinny Dip • Smith Cotta
tanziale Cottage • Starry Night • Stillman Cottage • Stringer Cottag

...Whose dwelling is the light of setting suns,
And the round ocean and the living air,
And the blue sky, and in the mind of man;... William Wordsworth

ms • Suntime • Taupelo • Temple Cottage • Thanksgiving • The Bea
on-the-Sea • Time Out • Toasty Sunset • Tommy T • Topisaw • Tow
ker Tower • Up On The Roof • Veranda • Villa Whimsey • Vista del M
• Windler Cottage • Windsept II • Windward • Woodlawn • Wright

Vegetables

Bacon and Green Bean Bundles, 101

Sesame Broccoli, 101

Broccoli and Rice Casserole, 102

Carrot Casserole, 102

Creole Black-Eyed Peas
and Rice, 103

Hopping John, 104

Sautéed Corn with Bacon
and Scallions, 104

Baked Onions with Balsamic
Vinaigrette, 105

Scalloped Green Peppers, 105

Golden Stuffed Baked Potatoes, 106

Potato Casserole, 106

Spinach Quiche, 107

Squash Casserole with Bacon
and Green Chilies, 107

Green Tomato Ratatouille, 108

Tomato Pudding, 108

Cheesy Vegetable Casserole, 109

Zucchini Pancakes, 109

Side Dishes

Pot Stickers, 110

Polenta with Two Cheeses, 111

Cheesy Rice, 111

Curried Rice, 112

Mixed Fruit Chutney, 112

Doctored Dills, 113

Mango Salsa, 113

"WILDER" BACON AND GREEN BEAN BUNDLES

- Preheat oven to 325 degrees.
- Drain beans and arrange into bundles of 5 beans. Wrap each bundle with ½ slice bacon. Arrange seam side down in baking dish with sides not touching.
- Sprinkle with garlic powder. Drizzle with mixture of butter and brown sugar.
- Bake for 30 minutes or until bacon is cooked through.
- Yield: 16 servings.

Over the Fence: *This is the most popular dish at our Christmas buffet for employees. Even when the menu theme is Mexican or Italian, this request has to be filled.*

Ingredients

2 (16-ounce) cans whole
Blue Lake green beans

8 slices bacon, cut into halves

Garlic powder to taste

½ cup melted butter

½ cup packed brown sugar or
granulated brown sugar

SESAME BROCCOLI

- Cook broccoli in a small amount of salted water in saucepan until tender.
- Combine sesame oil, vinegar, soy sauce and sugar in small saucepan; mix well. Bring to a boil.
- Drain broccoli. Place in warm bowl. Drizzle with oil mixture; sprinkle with sesame seeds.
- Yield: 6 servings.

Ingredients

1 pound broccoli, cut into spears

Salt to taste

1 tablespoon sesame oil

1 tablespoon vinegar

1 tablespoon soy sauce

4 teaspoons sugar

1 tablespoon toasted
sesame seeds

BROCCOLI AND RICE CASSEROLE "SHANGRI-LA"

Ingredients

1 (10-ounce) package
   frozen broccoli
1 cup hot cooked rice
6 ounces hot pepper
   cheese, shredded
1 (10-ounce) can cream of
   mushroom soup
1 cup shredded Cheddar cheese

- Preheat oven to 325 degrees.
- Cook broccoli using package directions; drain. Combine with rice, pepper cheese and soup in bowl; mix well.
- Spoon into baking dish; sprinkle with Cheddar cheese. Bake for 30 minutes.
- Yield: 4 servings.

"JUST PEACHY" CARROT CASSEROLE

Ingredients

2 cups mashed cooked carrots
1/2 cup melted margarine
1 cup sugar
3 tablespoons flour
1 teaspoon baking powder
3 eggs, beaten
1/4 teaspoon cinnamon

- Preheat oven to 400 degrees.
- Combine carrots, margarine, sugar, flour, baking powder, eggs and cinnamon in order listed in bowl, mixing well after each addition.
- Spoon into baking dish. Bake for 15 minutes. Reduce oven temperature to 350 degrees. Bake for 45 minutes longer.
- Yield: 6 servings.

CREOLE BLACK-EYED PEAS AND RICE

Great served with French bread and salad.

- Rinse and sort peas. Combine with water to cover in heavy saucepan. Soak overnight; drain.

- Add salt pork and fresh water to cover. Cook, covered, over low heat for 45 minutes.

- Add onions, green onions, parsley, green pepper, garlic, tomato sauce, Worcestershire sauce, hot sauce, oregano, thyme, salt, red pepper and black pepper.

- Simmer, covered, for 45 to 60 minutes, stirring occasionally.

- Add sausage. Simmer, uncovered, for 45 minutes. Serve over cooked rice. Garnish with green onion fans.

- May substitute grilled venison sausage for smoked sausage.

- Yield: 10 servings.

Over the Fence: *This is what we eat at Briar Patch on New Year's Day during all those ball games.*

~

Over the Fence: *Black-eyed peas are a must for good luck on New Year's Day, even if you only use the canned variety. If freshly opened canned vegetables are allowed to stand for 15 minutes before heating, oxygen lost in the canning process will be regained, making a big difference in the flavor.*

Ingredients

1 (16-ounce) package dried black-eyed peas

8 ounces salt pork

3 cups chopped onions

1 bunch green onions, chopped

1 cup chopped fresh parsley

1 cup chopped green bell pepper

2 cloves of garlic, crushed

1 (8-ounce) can tomato sauce

1 tablespoon Worcestershire sauce

3 dashes of hot sauce

1/4 teaspoon dried whole oregano

1/4 teaspoon dried whole thyme

1 teaspoon salt

1 teaspoon red pepper

1 teaspoon black pepper

2 pounds smoked sausage, cut into 1-inch pieces

8 cups cooked rice

"MELROSE" HOPPING JOHN

Ingredients

6 slices bacon, cut into quarters

1 cup thinly sliced celery

2/3 cup chopped onion

6 cups water

1 (16-ounce) package frozen
black-eyed peas

4 ounces cooked ham, cut
into 1/4-inch cubes

5 beef bouillon cubes

1/4 teaspoon crushed red pepper

1 bay leaf

1 cup uncooked rice

- Cook bacon in heavy saucepan until crisp; remove bacon, reserving drippings. Sauté celery and onion in reserved drippings in saucepan until tender.

- Add water, peas, bacon, ham, bouillon, red pepper and bay leaf. Bring to a boil; reduce heat. Simmer, covered, for 40 to 45 minutes or until peas are tender.

- Stir in rice. Simmer, covered, over medium heat for 35 minutes or until rice is tender and most of the liquid is absorbed, stirring occasionally. Discard bay leaf.

- Yield: 6 servings.

Over the Fence: *I got this recipe at a cooking school and if I hadn't tasted the dish that night, I would never have tried it, because I don't even like black-eyed peas. Now it is a favorite at Melrose Cottage on New Year's Day; we leave the bay leaf in on that day to bring extra good luck to the one who finds it.*

SAUTÉED CORN WITH BACON AND SCALLIONS

Ingredients

1 tablespoon olive oil

1 1/2 cups cooked fresh
corn kernels

2 or 3 scallions, finely chopped

2 or 3 slices bacon,
crisp-fried, crumbled

Dried hot red pepper
flakes to taste

- Heat olive oil in nonstick skillet over medium-high heat until hot but not smoking. Add corn and scallions.

- Cook for 1 minute, stirring constantly. Stir in bacon and pepper flakes. Cook for 15 seconds longer.

- May substitute one 12-ounce can drained whole kernel corn for fresh corn.

- Yield: 2 servings.

BAKED ONIONS WITH BALSAMIC VINAIGRETTE

These onions are magnificent! They are especially good with pork or meats marinated and cooked with pungent herbs.

- Preheat oven to 350 degrees.
- Cut off ends of onions. Cut a deep X in top of each onion, cutting halfway through. Place each on 6x6-inch foil square.
- Drizzle each onion with 1 teaspoon olive oil. Pull up corners of foil to enclose onions and seal.
- Place foil packets sealed side up on baking sheet. Bake for 40 minutes or until very tender.
- Combine mustard, vinegar, salt and pepper in small bowl; mix well. Whisk in 3 tablespoons olive oil gradually.
- Arrange unwrapped onions on serving plate. Spoon vinaigrette over onions; adjust seasonings.
- Yield: 6 servings.

Ingredients

6 medium Vidalia or
Walla Walla onions
2 tablespoons olive oil
1 1/2 teaspoons Dijon mustard
2 tablespoons balsamic vinegar
1/2 teaspoon salt
1/4 teaspoon freshly
ground pepper
3 tablespoons olive oil

"MOORE FUN" SCALLOPED GREEN PEPPERS

A light and unusual accompaniment!

- Preheat oven to 350 degrees.
- Process green peppers in blender or food processor until finely chopped. Simmer, covered, in saucepan over low heat for 10 minutes. Add milk, cheeses and bread crumbs; mix gently.
- Spoon into greased baking dish. Bake for 30 to 40 minutes or until bubbly and set.
- Yield: 6 servings.

Ingredients

2 cups coarsely chopped green
bell peppers
1 cup milk
1 cup shredded Swiss cheese
1 cup shredded Cheddar cheese
1 cup seasoned bread crumbs

GOLDEN STUFFED BAKED POTATOES

Ingredients

4 potatoes
1 cup grated carrot
1/4 cup chopped fresh parsley
1/4 cup minced chives
1/2 to 2 teaspoons horseradish
2/3 cup plain yogurt
1/4 to 1/2 cup melted butter
Salt and pepper to taste
1/4 cup grated Parmesan cheese
Paprika to taste

- Preheat oven to 350 degrees. Bake potatoes until tender.
- Cut potatoes into halves and scoop pulp into mixer bowl, reserving shells. Add carrot, parsley, chives, horseradish, yogurt, butter, salt and pepper; beat until smooth.
- Spoon mixture into potato shells; top with cheese and paprika. Place on baking sheet. Bake for 15 minutes or until filling is heated through and cheese melts.
- Yield: 8 servings.

Over the Fence: Wrap these individually and store them in the refrigerator or freezer to have handy. Thaw frozen potatoes in the microwave and bake potatoes for 20 to 25 minutes.

"THIS IS THE LIFE" KLEIN POTATO CASSEROLE

Ingredients

1 (32-ounce) package frozen hashed brown potatoes, thawed
1/2 cup melted margarine
1 (10-ounce) can cream of chicken soup
8 ounces light Cheddar cheese, shredded
1 cup sour cream
1 onion, grated
Pepper to taste
2 cups crushed cornflakes
1/4 cup melted margarine

- Preheat oven to 350 degrees.
- Combine hashed brown potatoes, 1/2 cup margarine, soup, cheese, sour cream, onion and pepper in bowl; mix well.
- Spoon mixture into greased 9x13-inch baking dish. Top with mixture of cornflakes and 1/4 cup margarine. Bake for 1 hour.
- Yield: 12 servings.

"PERSIMMON" SPINACH QUICHE

Cut into smaller pieces to serve as an appetizer.

- Preheat oven to 425 degrees.
- Combine spinach, eggs, ricotta cheese, Swiss cheese, Parmesan cheese and garlic salt in bowl; mix well.
- Spoon into pie shell. Bake for 15 minutes. Reduce oven temperature to 325 degrees. Bake for 35 minutes longer.
- Yield: 6 servings.

Ingredients

1 (10-ounce) package frozen chopped spinach, thawed, drained

3 eggs

2 pounds ricotta cheese

1 cup shredded Swiss cheese

1/2 cup grated Parmesan cheese

1/2 teaspoon garlic salt

1 unbaked (9-inch) pie shell

SQUASH CASSEROLE WITH BACON AND GREEN CHILIES

- Preheat oven to 350 degrees.
- Combine squash with a small amount of water in glass dish. Microwave on High until tender; drain.
- Combine with butter, onion flakes, eggs, bread crumbs, bacon, green chilies, cheese, sugar, salt and pepper in bowl; mix well.
- Spoon into baking dish. Bake for 20 minutes.
- Yield: 10 servings.

Ingredients

5 pounds yellow squash, chopped

2 tablespoons butter

1 tablespoon onion flakes

4 eggs, slightly beaten

1/2 cup bread crumbs

6 slices bacon, crisp-fried, crumbled

1 (4-ounce) can chopped green chilies

1 cup shredded Cheddar cheese

1 teaspoon sugar

1 teaspoon salt

1 teaspoon pepper

GREEN TOMATO RATATOUILLE

Ingredients

1 pound green tomatoes,
coarsely chopped

1 large green bell pepper,
coarsely chopped

1 pound onions,
coarsely chopped

3 large cloves of garlic, minced

6 tablespoons olive oil

1³/4 pounds ripe tomatoes,
coarsely chopped

1 pound zucchini, sliced

¹/2 teaspoon dried basil

1 teaspoon salt

¹/8 teaspoon crushed red pepper

1 teaspoon black pepper

This is a good way to use green tomatoes from the garden.

- Sauté green tomatoes, green pepper, onions and garlic in olive oil in large skillet for 7 to 8 minutes or until vegetables are wilted.

- Add ripe tomatoes and zucchini. Cook until vegetables are tender and juicy. Stir in basil, salt, red pepper and black pepper.

- Increase heat slightly. Cook until liquid has evaporated and mixture is thickened to desired consistency, stirring frequently.

- Serve slightly warm or at room temperature with Parmesan cheese.

- May reheat in double boiler.

- Yield: 6 servings.

"CURPHEY COTTAGE" TOMATO PUDDING

Ingredients

2 cups 2-inch day-old
bread cubes

1 (20-ounce) can tomato purée

1 cup packed brown sugar

¹/4 teaspoon cinnamon

¹/2 cup melted butter

- Preheat oven to 350 degrees. Spread bread cubes in buttered 2-quart baking dish.

- Combine tomato purée, brown sugar and cinnamon in saucepan. Bring to a boil; reduce heat. Simmer for 15 minutes. Pour tomato mixture over bread cubes; drizzle with butter. Bake for 30 minutes.

- Yield: 8 servings.

Over the Fence: I got this recipe from the old Tally-Ho Restaurant and Tea Room in Toledo, where it was a specialty. We think it is wonderful with poultry and meat.

"SANDPIPER" CHEESY VEGETABLE CASSEROLE

- Preheat oven to 350 degrees.
- Combine vegetables, soup, sour cream, pepper and half the cheese and onions in bowl; mix well.
- Spoon into 1-quart baking dish. Bake, covered, for 30 minutes.
- Top with remaining cheese and onions. Bake, uncovered, for 5 minutes longer.
- Yield: 6 servings.

Ingredients

1 (16-ounce) package frozen mixed broccoli, carrots and cauliflower

1 (10-ounce) can cream of mushroom soup

1/3 cup sour cream

1/4 teaspoon pepper

1 cup shredded Swiss cheese

1 (3-ounce) can French-fried onions

"MAIDEN'S CHAMBER" ZUCCHINI PANCAKES

- Grate or grind zucchini; drain well. Combine with eggs, flour, parsley, garlic powder, salt and pepper in bowl; mix well.
- Heat oil in large skillet over medium heat. Drop zucchini mixture by heaping tablespoonfuls into oil. Fry until golden brown on both sides; drain. Serve hot.
- Yield: 8 servings.

Over the Fence: These are interesting served as a side dish or great as finger food hors d'oeuvres. Add a few caraway seeds and try with your favorite sour cream dip. Please—no maple syrup!

Ingredients

6 to 8 medium zucchini

4 eggs

1/2 cup flour

1/4 cup chopped parsley

1/4 teaspoon garlic powder

1 teaspoon salt

1/8 teaspoon pepper

2 or 3 tablespoons vegetable oil

POT STICKERS

Ingredients

11 ounces ground pork

1 cup minced cabbage

2 green onions, minced

1 egg

1 tablespoon reduced-sodium
soy sauce

1/2 teaspoon grated orange rind

1/2 teaspoon salt

1/2 teaspoon hot chili oil

40 won ton skins

1/2 cup peanut oil

1 cup water

- Combine pork, cabbage, green onions, egg, soy sauce, orange rind, salt and chili oil in large bowl; mix well.

- Cut won ton skins into largest circles possible. Place 1 won ton skin at a time on waxed paper dusted with cornstarch.

- Spoon 1 rounded teaspoonful filling in narrow band across center of skin; moisten edges. Bring opposite sides up to enclose filling, forming semicircle.

- Pinch corners and center of arc together. Pleat edges by making 3 or 4 pleats on each side toward center to form a flat-bottomed crescent with pleated top.

- Tap lightly on bottom if necessary to make dumpling stand upright. Place on waxed paper dusted with cornstarch; cover with towel.

- Repeat with remaining won tons and filling.

- Heat 1/4 cup peanut oil in each of 2 heavy 12-inch skillets over low heat. Arrange pot stickers in close rows in skillets. Increase heat to medium-high.

- Cook for 2 minutes or until bottoms are deep golden brown. Add 1/2 cup water to each skillet. Steam, covered, for 3 minutes or until won ton skins are translucent. Cook, uncovered, until bottoms are very crisp and brown.

- Loosen pot stickers with spatula and remove to serving dish. Serve immediately with additional hot chili oil and Chinese vinegar or wine vinegar.

- Yield: 40 dumplings.

"PEACHES 'N CREAM" POLENTA WITH TWO CHEESES

- Preheat oven to 350 degrees.
- Heat butter in large saucepan over medium heat until foam subsides. Add onion. Sauté for 5 minutes or until tender. Add chicken stock. Bring to a boil.
- Sprinkle in cornmeal gradually, stirring constantly. Cook over medium-low heat for 15 minutes or until very thick, stirring frequently. Stir in half and half, 2 teaspoons Parmesan cheese and salt; remove from heat.
- Layer cornmeal mixture, mozzarella cheese and remaining Parmesan cheese ½ at a time in buttered shallow 2-quart baking dish.
- Bake until mixture is bubbly and edges begin to brown. Let stand for 10 minutes before serving.
- Yield: 8 servings.

Ingredients

¼ cup unsalted butter

½ cup finely chopped onion

5 cups unsalted chicken stock

2 cups yellow cornmeal

1 cup half and half, heated

2 teaspoons grated Parmesan cheese

1 teaspoon salt

8 ounces mozzarella cheese, shredded

2 teaspoons grated Parmesan cheese

"BRIERMOR BY THE SEA" CHEESY RICE

- Preheat oven to 350 degrees.
- Combine rice, 1 cup cheese, soup, eggs, 2 tablespoons almonds and pimentos in bowl; mix well.
- Spoon into baking dish. Sprinkle with 2 tablespoons almonds and ½ cup cheese. Bake until heated through.
- Yield: 6 servings.

Ingredients

2 cups cooked rice

1 cup shredded hoop cheese

1 (10-ounce) can cream of mushroom soup

1 or 2 eggs

2 tablespoons chopped almonds

1 cup chopped pimentos

2 tablespoons chopped almonds

½ cup shredded hoop cheese

CURRIED RICE "McCLOY"

- Sauté rice, green pepper and onion in bacon drippings in saucepan. Add consommé, water, chili powder, curry powder and salt.
- Cover saucepan. Bring to a boil; reduce heat. Simmer for 25 minutes without removing cover.
- Yield: 6 servings.

Over the Fence: I grew up eating this rice, and I love it as much today as I did as a child.

Ingredients

1 cup uncooked rice

2 teaspoons chopped green bell pepper

1 small onion, chopped

2 teaspoons bacon drippings

1 (10-ounce) can each beef consommé and water

1/2 teaspoon chili powder

1 teaspoon each curry powder and salt

"FANTASIA" MIXED FRUIT CHUTNEY

- Cook gingerroot in water in saucepan until tender. Peel and chop fine. Chop chili peppers.
- Combine gingerroot with chili peppers, chopped fruit, raisins, currants, onions, garlic, sugar, vinegar, mustard seeds, cinnamon, allspice, cloves and salt in large saucepan.
- Simmer for 1 to 2 hours or until of desired consistency, stirring occasionally. Cool to room temperature.
- Spoon into sterilized jars, leaving 1/2 inch headspace; seal with 2-piece lids. Process in boiling water bath for 10 minutes.
- May add chopped cashews or walnuts.
- Yield: 10 cups.

Over the Fence: To Fantasia Cottage by way of Memphis. I use at least three different fruits, but the mangos give it that real Florida flavor.

Ingredients

8 ounces gingerroot

4 ounces red chili peppers

6 pounds chopped fruit, such as mangos, plums, apricots, bananas, pears and apples

1 (15-ounce) package each raisins and currants

2 onions, minced

2 ounces garlic, chopped

2 pounds sugar

1 quart cider vinegar

4 ounces mustard seeds

1/2 teaspoon each cinnamon, allspice and ground cloves

2 tablespoons salt

"PICTURE BOOK" DOCTORED DILLS

Makes wonderful Christmas presents.

- Combine sugar, vinegar and pickling spices in glass bowl; mix well.
- Cut pickles into chunks or strips. Add to vinegar mixture. Let stand, covered with foil, for 4 days.
- Stir pickles. Let stand, covered with foil, for 3 days longer, stirring several times a day.
- Pack into sterilized jars. Store in refrigerator.
- Yield: 2 pints (24 servings).

Ingredients

3 cups sugar

1/2 cup vinegar

1 teaspoon pickling spices

1 (1-quart) jar kosher dill pickles, drained

"NEWNUM-QUEEN" MANGO SALSA

This salsa is great with grilled fish, beef or lamb.

- Combine mangos, pepper, lime juice, mint, gingerroot, cayenne pepper and salt in bowl; mix well.
- Chill, covered, for 1 hour to blend flavors.
- Yield: 6 servings.

Ingredients

3 large mangos, peeled, cubed

1 jalapeño pepper, seeded, finely minced

1/4 cup fresh lime juice

1 1/2 tablespoons finely chopped fresh mint

1 teaspoon finely grated fresh gingerroot

Cayenne pepper and salt to taste

Beef & Veal
Pork & Lamb

*...And 'tis my faith that every flower
Enjoys the air it breathes....*
William Wordsworth

• About Time • Acadia • Adagio • Alcorn Cottage • Allegro • Allis
hley • As You Like It • At Last • Auberge • Avondale • Bagby-Jam
terside • Bit-O-Heaven • Bloomsbury • Blue Belle • Blue Moon • B
the Sea • Brigadoon • B's Nest • Burnett Cottage • Callan Cottag
arriage House • Casa del Mar • Casablanca • Charleston • Chatha
oral Cove • ... age • Crawfo
age • Dapper ... liever • Days
lphin Inn • D ... onette • Drea
Duffy Cotta ... ottage • Eas
age • Enon • ... mingo • Fletch
rumious Ba ... o • Getaway
o • Green Co ... t Cottage • G
Hayford Co ... s Greenhous
ls • Hurrah! ... Cottage • Iv
Kennedy C ... er • La. Hous
onardo da ... Dipper • Li
ottage • Ma ... tage • Maris
age • Mellow ... Night's Drea
Narnia • Nat ... irvana • Ols
d! • Park Pla ... hes 'n Crear
icture Book ... Crazy • Port
Renaissan ... y's • Roanok
an's Castle ... e • Sandi Sho
Cottage • Scott Cottage • Scruggs Cottage • Sea for Two • Sea Vie
Shell Seeker • Sisters Three By The Sea • Skinny Dip • Smith Cotta

Beef & Veal

Brisket, 117

Tenderloin with Creamy Horseradish Spread, 117

London Grill, 118

Rapid Roast, 118

Bohemian Pot Roast, 119

Rolladen and Rotkohl, 120

Grilled Flank Steak, 121

Grayton Steaks, 121

London Broil Steak, 122

Beef and Noodles, 122

Grilled Venison with Green Peppercorn Sauce, 123

Lemon Veal Piccata, 124

Pork & Lamb

Grilled Pork Tenderloin, 124

Spinach Meat Loaf with Tomato Olive Sauce, 125

Sunday Night Skillet Supper, 126

Stuffed Artichokes, 126

Grilled Butterflied Lamb with Mustard Vinaigrette, 127

"BRIAR PATCH" BRISKET

- Slice briskets into 1½- to 2-inch slices. Sprinkle heavily with pepper.
- Preheat oven to 250 degrees.
- Place briskets in heavy baking pan. Pour beer over meat.
- Bake, covered, for 4 to 6 hours or until tender. Grill for 1 hour over hot coals, basting frequently with barbecue sauce.
- May substitute venison for beef. Soak in ice water in stockpot for 2 hours, changing water 1 or 2 times; drain and pat dry.
- Yield: 50 servings.

Ingredients

2 (8-pound) beef briskets
Pepper to taste
2 (12-ounce) bottles of beer
1 (18-ounce) bottle of
barbecue sauce

TENDERLOIN WITH CREAMY HORSERADISH SPREAD

- Combine horseradish, onion dip, Worcestershire sauce and cream cheese in bowl; mix well.
- Serve horseradish spread with tenderloin.
- Yield: 8 servings.

Ingredients

1 (5-ounce) jar horseradish
1 cup French onion dip
1 teaspoon Worcestershire sauce
3 ounces cream cheese, softened
2 pounds sliced cooked beef
tenderloin

Over the Fence: For foolproof standing rib roast, let the roast stand at room temperature for 1 hour. Sprinkle with salt and pepper; place fat side up in a shallow roasting pan. Roast at 375 degrees for 1 hour; turn off the oven. Do not open door. Let the roast stand in the closed oven for 3 hours or longer. Set the oven temperature to 375 degrees. Roast for 30 to 40 minutes longer. Cut into thin slices.

LONDON GRILL

This is the first recipe I found as a newlywed in 1967.
It has remained a family favorite. Serve hot or cold.

Ingredients

1 tablespoon olive oil
2 teaspoons chopped
fresh parsley
1 clove of garlic, crushed
1 teaspoon salt
1 teaspoon lemon juice
1/8 teaspoon pepper
1 (1½- to 2-pound) flank steak

- Preheat grill.
- Combine olive oil, parsley, garlic, salt, lemon juice and pepper in small bowl. Brush both sides of flank steak with mixture. Place in shallow dish.
- Marinate, covered, in refrigerator for 30 minutes to several hours.
- Grill over hot coals for 7 minutes per side or until done to taste. Cut into thin slices cross grain.
- Yield: 6 servings.

RAPID ROAST

Ingredients

1 (3-pound) eye-of-round roast
Freshly ground pepper to taste
Garlic salt to taste

- Preheat oven to 500 degrees.
- Sprinkle roast heavily with pepper and garlic salt. Place on rack in shallow roasting pan.
- Cook for 4 minutes per pound for rare, for 5 minutes per pound for medium and for 6 minutes per pound for well done. Turn off oven. Let stand in closed oven for 2 hours.
- Yield: 6 servings.

Over the Fence: *This is a God-sent recipe. I slice it very thin for parties, take it to the beach for sandwiches or give it to new moms home from the hospital for easy meals.*

"DuPuis Cottage" Bohemian Pot Roast

Spicy and great for fall or winter evenings.

- Coat chuck roast with mixture of flour, salt and pepper. Brown in bacon drippings in heavy saucepan; drain.

- Add onions, pickling spice and enough water to cover roast; mix well. Bring to a boil; reduce heat.

- Cook, covered, over low heat for 1½ to 2 hours or until roast is tender. Remove roast to warm platter; cover.

- Cook noodles using package directions. Drain and keep warm.

- Pour pan drippings through sieve into saucepan, mashing onions against side of sieve. Discard onions.

- Stir in mixture of cornstarch, cold water and Kitchen Bouquet. Cook until thickened, stirring constantly. Serve with roast and hot noodles.

- Yield: 6 servings.

Over the Fence: *This is a traditional Bohemian-style pot roast. (Mark's mother was Bohemian, and this is her recipe.)*

Pot Roast Ingredients

1 (2- to 3-pound) chuck roast, 2 to 3 inches thick
¼ cup flour
Salt and pepper to taste
2 tablespoons bacon drippings
2 to 3 onions, chopped
1 tablespoon pickling spice
1 (12-ounce) package wide egg noodles

Gravy Ingredients

1 tablespoon cornstarch
½ cup (or less) cold water
½ teaspoon Kitchen Bouquet

"Tupelo Honey" Rolladen and Rotkohl

Rolladen Ingredients

4 sirloin tip breakfast steaks, 1/8-inch thick

Salt and pepper to taste

4 teaspoons Grey Poupon mustard

4 slices bacon

1 medium onion, cut into quarters

12 dill pickle slices

3 tablespoons oil

1 1/2 cups water

1 teaspoon (heaping) cornstarch

1 tablespoon cold water

Rotkohl Ingredients

1 (2-pound) head red cabbage, coarsely shredded

2 tablespoons melted margarine

1/2 cup water

2 bay leaves

8 whole cloves

5 juniper berries

1 teaspoon sugar

1 teaspoon salt

1 Granny Smith apple, peeled, sliced

2 tablespoons lemon juice

Salt to taste

- Preheat oven to 325 degrees.

- Rinse steaks with cold water; pat dry. Season lightly with salt and pepper.

- Spread 1 teaspoon mustard on each steak. Lay 1 slice bacon lengthwise over mustard. Top each with onion quarter and 3 pickle slices. Fold sides slightly over filling; roll from top to enclose filling. Secure with wooden picks.

- Brown rolladens on all sides in hot oil in skillet. Place in baking dish. Combine 1 cup water with pan drippings in skillet; mix well. Pour over rolladens.

- Bake, covered, for 1 hour. Remove rolladens to warm platter. Add 1/2 cup water to pan drippings. Bring to a boil. Stir in mixture of cornstarch and 1 tablespoon cold water. Cook until thickened, stirring constantly. Pour over rolladens.

- Combine cabbage, margarine, 1/2 cup water, bay leaves, cloves, juniper berries, sugar and salt in large saucepan; mix well. Arrange apple slices over mixture.

- Cook, covered, over medium-low heat for 20 minutes; keep moist. Stir in lemon juice. Cook for 10 minutes. Discard bay leaves, juniper berries and cloves. Season with salt.

- Yield: 4 servings.

Over the Fence: My mom and dad, Cathy and Henry Steinbeck, immigrated to Canada and then to the United States from West Germany. They are both wonderful cooks. When guests come to their home in Jackson, Mississippi, they are often treated to this very traditional German dinner, served with mashed potatoes and applesauce.

"TIDE'S INN" GRILLED FLANK STEAK

- Place steaks in shallow dish. Pour mixture of green onions, oil, soy sauce, ginger, garlic powder, honey and vinegar over steaks. Marinate, covered, in refrigerator for 8 hours, turning occasionally. Drain, discarding marinade.

- Preheat grill.

- Grill steaks over hot coals for 5 minutes per side or until done to taste. Slice into 1-inch strips. Serve with a vegetable casserole and tossed green salad.

- Yield: 6 servings.

Ingredients

2 (1-pound) flank steaks
5 green onions, chopped
3/4 cup vegetable oil
1/2 cup soy sauce
1 1/2 teaspoons ginger
1 1/2 teaspoons garlic powder
3 tablespoons honey
2 tablespoons vinegar

GRAYTON STEAKS "NIRVANA"

This recipe originated at the Grayton Corner Cafe. It is truly great eating and fun to prepare.

- Sauté green pepper, onion, celery and garlic in butter in skillet over medium heat for 5 to 10 minutes or until vegetables are tender. Stir in mushrooms halfway through cycle. Stir in oysters with liquid during last minute of cooking. Remove from heat.

- Stir in bread crumbs with enough water to thicken. Cool. Stir in egg, oregano, salt, black pepper and cayenne pepper.

- Preheat grill.

- Grill steaks over hot coals until done to taste; butterfly. Lay split steaks on baking sheet. Spread with vegetable mixture; sprinkle with cheese.

- Broil until light brown.

- Yield: 4 servings.

Ingredients

1 green bell pepper, chopped
1 small yellow onion, chopped
1 stalk celery, chopped
2 cloves of garlic, finely chopped
1 tablespoon butter
1 cup chopped mushrooms
1 cup chopped oysters with liquid
1 cup bread crumbs
1 egg, beaten
1 1/2 teaspoons oregano
Salt and black pepper to taste
Cayenne pepper to taste
4 (8-ounce) filet mignon steaks, 1 inch thick
1/4 cup grated Parmesan cheese

"MAIDEN'S CHAMBER" LONDON BROIL STEAK

Ingredients

1 clove of garlic, sliced

1 cup vegetable oil

½ cup wine vinegar

2 teaspoons
Worcestershire sauce

Several drops of Tabasco sauce

2 teaspoons dry mustard

1 teaspoon salt

Cayenne pepper to taste

¼ teaspoon black pepper

1 (1½-pound) Londen broil steak

- Combine garlic, oil, vinegar, Worcestershire sauce, Tabasco sauce, dry mustard, salt, cayenne pepper and black pepper in bowl or blender container; mix or process until smooth.

- Pour marinade over steak in shallow dish. Marinate, covered, in refrigerator for 3 hours to overnight. Drain, reserving marinade.

- Grill steak for 45 minutes or until done to taste, basting occasionally with reserved marinade. Cut steak diagonally into thin slices.

- Yield: 6 servings.

BEEF AND NOODLES

Ingredients

2 pounds ground chuck

1 onion, chopped

1 (8-ounce) package thin noodles, cooked, drained

1 cup light sour cream

1 (10-ounce) can reduced-fat cream of mushroom soup

1 (10-ounce) can reduced-fat cream of chicken soup

1 (16-ounce) can whole kernel corn, drained

1 cup light shredded Cheddar cheese

Children love this recipe!

- Preheat oven to 350 degrees.

- Brown ground chuck with onion in skillet, stirring until ground chuck is crumbly; drain.

- Combine ground chuck mixture with noodles, sour cream, soups, corn and cheese in bowl; mix well. Spoon into nonstick baking pan.

- Bake for 30 to 45 minutes or until bubbly.

- Yield: 6 servings.

"BRIAR PATCH" GRILLED VENISON WITH GREEN PEPPERCORN SAUCE

- Bring peppercorns, butter and brandy to a boil in saucepan, stirring frequently. Remove from heat.
- Soak venison steak in ice water in dish for 2 hours, changing water 1 to 2 times; drain and pat dry.
- Brush both sides of steak with mixture of olive oil, parsley, garlic, salt, lemon juice and pepper.
- Place in shallow dish. Marinate, covered, in refrigerator for several hours.
- Preheat grill.
- Grill over hot coals for 7 minutes per side or until done to taste.
- Slice; serve with peppercorn sauce.
- Yield: 6 servings.

Over the Fence: I didn't even know my husband was a hunter of deer and wild turkey until four years ago when he got a third partner and a bit of free time. Now I know a lot about venison and wild turkey—more than I ever wanted!! But it's great and good for you.

Sauce Ingredients

1 to 2 tablespoons green peppercorns, crushed
2 tablespoons butter
2 tablespoons brandy

Venison Ingredients

1 (1½- to 2-pound) venison or beef steak
1 tablespoon olive oil
2 teaspoons chopped fresh parsley
1 clove of garlic, crushed
1 teaspoon salt
1 teaspoon lemon juice
⅛ teaspoon pepper

"DOBSON" LEMON VEAL PICCATA

Ingredients

8 (2-ounce) veal cutlets
2/3 cup flour
1 teaspoon salt
1/2 teaspoon pepper
1/4 teaspoon garlic powder
1/3 cup butter
1/3 cup lemon juice
1 tablespoon chopped
fresh parsley

- Dredge veal in mixture of flour, salt, pepper and garlic powder.
- Cook veal in butter in skillet for 1 minute on each side. Remove cutlets to paper towel to drain.
- Add lemon juice to pan drippings; mix well. Cook until heated through, stirring constantly.
- Return veal to skillet; sprinkle with parsley. Cook just until heated through.
- Arrange veal cutlets on plates; drizzle with pan drippings.
- Yield: 4 servings.

"PERSIMMON" GRILLED PORK TENDERLOIN

Ingredients

1 (1 1/2-pound) pork
tenderloin, trimmed
3/4 cup vegetable oil
1/4 cup dry white wine
3 cloves of garlic, crushed
3/4 cup white wine
1 tablespoon finely
chopped shallot
1 cup whipping cream
3 tablespoons Dijon mustard
Salt and white pepper to taste

- Place pork in shallow dish. Pour mixture of oil, 1/4 cup white wine and garlic over pork. Marinate, covered, in refrigerator overnight. Drain, discarding marinade.
- Preheat grill. Grill over hot coals for 25 minutes or until cooked through and tender, turning occasionally.
- Transfer pork to cutting board. Let stand while making mustard sauce.
- Bring 3/4 cup white wine and shallot to a boil in saucepan. Cook until reduced to 2 tablespoons, stirring constantly.
- Stir in cream. Bring to a boil; reduce heat. Simmer for 2 minutes, stirring constantly.
- Strain mixture into bowl. Stir in Dijon mustard, salt and white pepper. Serve with sliced pork tenderloin.
- Yield: 6 servings.

SPINACH MEAT LOAF WITH TOMATO OLIVE SAUCE

- Sauté 1 medium onion, 3 cloves of garlic, ½ teaspoon basil, ½ teaspoon oregano, ½ teaspoon thyme and ½ teaspoon red pepper in 3 tablespoons olive oil in saucepan over low heat for 20 minutes. Add tomatoes and ½ teaspoon salt; break up tomatoes with spoon. Simmer for 45 to 50 minutes or until reduced to 3 cups, stirring occasionally.

- Process in food processor until smooth. Combine with parsley and olives in saucepan; set aside.

- Sauté 1 large onion, 4 cloves of garlic, 1 teaspoon basil, 1 teaspoon oregano, 1 teaspoon thyme and 1 teaspoon red pepper in 3 tablespoons hot olive oil in large skillet over low heat for 20 minutes or until onion is very tender.

- Squeeze spinach dry; chop finely. Add to skillet. Cook for 3 minutes. Cool to room temperature.

- Preheat oven to 350 degrees.

- Combine sausage, ground beef, spinach mixture, bread crumbs, eggs, cheese and 1½ teaspoons salt in large bowl; mix well. Shape into rounded loaf; place in large shallow baking dish.

- Bake for 1½ hours or until cooked through. Let stand for 10 minutes before serving.

- Reheat sauce. Spoon into serving bowl. Serve with meat loaf.

- Yield: 10 servings.

Sauce Ingredients

1 medium onion, chopped

3 cloves of garlic, minced

½ teaspoon each basil, oregano, thyme and crushed hot red pepper

3 tablespoons olive oil

1 (15-ounce) can peeled Italian tomatoes

½ teaspoon salt

½ cup finely chopped flat-leaf parsley

12 brine-cured black olives, chopped

Meat Loaf Ingredients

1 large onion, finely chopped

4 cloves of garlic, minced

1 teaspoon each basil, oregano, thyme and crushed hot red pepper

3 tablespoons olive oil

2 (10-ounce) packages frozen spinach, thawed, drained

1 pound Italian-style sweet sausage, removed from casings and crumbled

2 pounds lean ground beef

¾ cup fine dry bread crumbs

3 eggs, beaten

½ cup grated Parmesan cheese

1½ teaspoons salt

SUNDAY NIGHT SKILLET SUPPER

Ingredients

1 (16-ounce) package frozen
hashed brown potatoes

1/3 cup chopped onion

1/3 cup chopped green bell pepper

Salt and pepper to taste

1/4 cup margarine

4 eggs, beaten

1 (12-ounce) package
bulk sausage, cooked,
crumbled, drained

1/2 cup shredded Cheddar cheese

- Cook vegetables with seasonings in margarine in covered skillet over low heat for 20 minutes.

- Add eggs and sausage. Cook, covered, for 15 minutes or until set.

- Sprinkle with cheese. Cook until cheese melts. Cut into wedges.

- Yield: 6 servings.

"SEAQUEL" STUFFED ARTICHOKES

Ingredients

8 ounces sausage, crumbled

Parsley flakes to taste

Salt and black pepper to taste

Parmesan cheese to taste

Red pepper flakes to taste

1/2 cup bread crumbs

2 eggs, beaten

1/4 to 1/2 cup milk

6 large artichokes

Olive oil to taste

1 clove of garlic, finely minced

2 chicken bouillon cubes

- Brown sausage in skillet, stirring until crumbly; drain. Remove from heat.

- Add parsley flakes, salt, black pepper, cheese, red pepper flakes, bread crumbs and eggs; mix well. Stir in milk.

- Cut off artichoke stem with scissors; trim top leaves by one-fourth. Snap off tough bottom row of leaves.

- Turn artichoke upside down, pressing hard to force leaves apart. Reverse; remove choke. Season inside with salt. Repeat with remaining artichokes.

- Stuff inside of artichokes and between layers of leaves with sausage mixture. Drizzle with olive oil.

- Place in stockpot. Combine garlic, bouillon cubes and salt with enough water to cover artichokes half way.

- Bring to a boil; reduce heat. Simmer, covered, for 40 minutes or until artichokes are tender.

- Yield: 6 servings.

GRILLED BUTTERFLIED LAMB WITH MUSTARD VINAIGRETTE

The marinade and vinaigrette turn lamb into something special.

- Trim excess fat from lamb.
- Rub surface of lamb with 3 cloves of garlic, rosemary, 1/4 cup Dijon mustard and pepper. Place in plastic food storage bag.
- Pour mixture of juice of 1 lemon, sherry, soy sauce, and 1/4 cup olive oil over lamb. Expel air from bag; seal tightly.
- Marinate, at room temperature, for 1 to 3 hours, turning occasionally. Drain, discarding marinade.
- Preheat grill.
- Grill over hot coals until done to taste. Remove lamb to warm platter; cover. Let stand for several minutes before carving.
- Whisk 2 tablespoons Dijon mustard, onion, 1 clove of garlic, juice of 2 lemons and salt together in bowl. Add 3/4 cup olive oil gradually, whisking until creamy. Stir in mint.
- Serve with grilled lamb.
- Yield: 6 servings.

Lamb Ingredients

1 (6- to 7-pound) leg of lamb, boned, butterflied
3 cloves of garlic, crushed
2 teaspoons rosemary, crumbled
1/4 cup Dijon mustard
Freshly ground pepper to taste

Marinade Ingredients

Juice of 1 lemon
2 tablespoons dry sherry
2 tablespoons soy sauce
1/4 cup olive oil

Vinaigrette Ingredients

2 tablespoons Dijon mustard
1 to 2 tablespoons finely chopped onion
1 clove of garlic, finely chopped
Juice of 2 small lemons
Salt to taste
3/4 cup olive oil
2 to 3 tablespoons finely chopped fresh mint

Poultry Main Dishes

Somewhere In Time • Southern Comfort • Southern Splendor • Spinn
undance • Sundaze • Sunnyside Up • Sunrise • Sunrise Wishes • Sur
use • The Conservatory • This Is the Life • Tide's Inn • Tiger Paw
eeze • Toye • Treetops • Trio • Tropical Holiday • Tupelo Honey • Tu
Wakeham Cottage • Waterside • Wayback • Weber Cottage • Wilder
e Beach • Zebulon • Zeidman Cottage • Zum Details • A Summe
ttage • American • Anderson Andersen Cottage • April 10
ttage • Beach Walk • Bella Vista • Belvedere • Benedictus • Beside
te • Boswell Cottage • Briar Patch • Brickwalk • Bridgeport • Brie
llaway Cottage • Cape May • Carey Cottage • Caribbean • Carpe D
elSea • Clark Cottage • Colony • Colors • Compass Rose • Coqu
ttage • Creole • C'Scape • Cubbie Hole • Curphey Cottage • Dahlgr
stle • Delor Cottage • DeoGratis • Desire • DoLittle House • Dollhou
tcher • Dream Chaser • Dream On • Dreamsicle • Dreamweaver
ttage • Eclipse • Ecstasea • Eden • Elegance • Enchantment • Engli
ttage • Floridays • For Keeps • Forsythe Cottage • Frascogna Cott
ant's Roost • GoodnightMoon • Gorlin Cottage • Grayton One • Gra
nor • Gulfview • Gull Cottage • Haardt Cottage • Hampton • Harvest
dges Cottage • Home Alone • Honalee • Hoover Cottage • House
smine • Jasper • Jennifer's Castle • Josephine's • Jubilee • Kaleido
st Edition • Latitude • LeBlanc Cottage • Leeward • Lehman Cotta

ndpine Lodge • Lonesome Dove • Lost Goggles • Lowe Cottage •
rtha Green • McChesney Cottage • McCollister Cottage • McLaughl
Mirador • Mis B'Haven • Modica Cottage • Moore Fun • Nancy's F
ttage • On the Veranda • Ondine • Orth Cottage • Outer Banks • O

tanziale Cottage • Starry Night • Stillman Cottage • Stringer Cottage
ms • Suntime • Taupelo • Temple Cottage • Thanksgiving • The Bea
on-the-Sea • Time Out • Toasty Sunset • Tommy T • Topisaw • Tow
ker Tower • Up On The Roof • Veranda • Villa Whimsey • Vista del M
• ndler Cottage • Windsept II • Windward • Woodlawn •   ight
• Abd   • Alliso
nley •   by-Jam
tersid   on • Blu
the S   Cottage
rriag   hatham
ral C   Crawfo
ge • D   • Days
phin   • Drea
Duffy   • Eas
ge •   Fletch
umio   taway
• Gre   age • G
Hayfo   nhous
s • H   ge • Iv
Ken edy Cottage • Key West • Kitchens Cottage • Krier • La Hous
onardo da Bicci • Lewis Cottage • Limehouse • Little Dipper • Lit

...Like many a voice of one delight,
The winds, the birds, the ocean floods,
The City's voice itself is soft like Solitude's. Percy Bysshe Shelley

ottage • Magnolia • Maiden's Chamber • Marietta's Cottage • Marisc
ge • Mellow Yellow • Melrose • Memories • Midsummer Night's Dre
arnia • Natchez House • Next Wave • Nightshade • Nirvana • Ols
! • Park Place • Parvey Cottage • Peach Delight • Peaches 'n Crea

Poultry Main Dishes

Broiled Marinated Chicken, 131

Chicken Stack, 132

Marinated Chicken Breasts, 132

Chinese Smoked Chicken, 133

Chicken Caper, 133

Chicken Maciel, 134

Braised Chili Chicken, 134

Company Chicken, 135

Coq au Vin, 135

Crazy Chicken, 136

Grilled Lemon and Tarragon Chicken, 136

King Ranch Casserole, 137

Hawaiian Chicken, 137

Keystone Chicken, 138

Lemon Chicken, 138

Lightly Lemon Chicken, 139

Chicken Pie, 139

Miss Pat's Quick Chicken Pie, 140

Chicken Tetrazzini, 140

Chicken Pontalba, 141

BROILED MARINATED CHICKEN

- Toast garlic cloves in cast-iron skillet over medium heat for 15 to 20 minutes or until spotted dark brown on outside and soft inside, turning frequently.

- Peel and chop garlic. Mash with ½ teaspoon salt in small bowl. Add pepper, oregano, cumin and cloves; mix well. Stir in lime juice gradually.

- Rinse chicken and pat dry. Spread with garlic paste. Marinate, tightly covered, in refrigerator for 12 to 24 hours.

- Preheat broiler. Broil green peppers or roast over gas flame until evenly charred. Place in paper bag; steam for 5 minutes. Peel peppers under gently running warm water. Cut into ½-inch strips, discarding seeds.

- Score cut sides of vegetables deeply at ½ inch intervals. Arrange in single layer on foil-lined broiler pan. Brush with 2 teaspoons oil.

- Broil 4 inches from heat source for 5 to 7 minutes or until slightly blackened on top and tender. Cover with foil; set aside.

- Let chicken stand until room temperature. Drain, reserving marinade. Place chicken in foil-lined broiler pan. Broil for 3 minutes or until speckled dark brown; turn. Broil for 1 to 2 minutes or until tender. Add drippings to reserved marinade. Wrap chicken in foil; set aside.

- Sauté chopped onion in 1 teaspoon oil in small heavy nonstick skillet over medium heat for 3 minutes or until golden brown. Stir in flour. Cook for 1 minute.

- Whisk in reserved marinade, chicken broth and wine. Bring to a boil, whisking constantly. Simmer for 5 minutes or until reduced to 1 cup, stirring frequently; remove from heat. Stir in parsley and salt to taste.

- Slice chicken cross grain. Arrange each fan-style in center of each of 4 plates. Arrange vegetables on plates. Drizzle with sauce. Serve warm or at room temperature.

- Yield: 4 servings.

Marinade Ingredients

5 large unpeeled cloves of garlic
½ teaspoon salt
1 teaspoon freshly ground pepper
½ teaspoon oregano
½ teaspoon ground cumin
⅛ teaspoon ground cloves
2 tablespoons fresh lime juice

Chicken Ingredients

4 (4-ounce) chicken breast filets
2 (6-ounce) green bell peppers
4 (6-ounce) zucchini, cut into halves lengthwise
4 (4-ounce) eggplant, cut into halves lengthwise
4 (3-ounce) plum tomatoes, cut into halves lengthwise
4 (2-ounce) onions, cut into halves crosswise
2 teaspoons vegetable oil
½ cup finely chopped onion
1 teaspoon vegetable oil
2 teaspoons flour
1 cup chicken broth
¼ cup dry white wine
¼ cup chopped fresh parsley
Salt to taste

"APRIL 16TH" CHICKEN STACK

Ingredients

4 chicken breast filets

1 (10-ounce) can chopped tomatoes with green chilies

1 1/3 cups shredded mild Cheddar cheese

1 1/3 cups shredded white American cheese

10 flour tortillas

1/2 cup chopped jalapeño peppers

1/2 cup sliced green onions

1/2 cup sliced black olives

2 tablespoons melted butter

- Preheat oven to 325 degrees.

- Rinse chicken and pat dry; arrange in baking dish. Top with tomatoes and green chilies. Bake for 1 hour. Chop chicken and return to tomato mixture.

- Increase oven temperature to 350 degrees. Mix cheeses in bowl. Spray 2 pie plates with nonstick cooking spray.

- Layer 1 tortilla, 2 tablespoons chicken mixture, 1 tablespoon jalapeño peppers, 1 tablespoon green onions, 1 tablespoon olives and 1/3 cup cheese mixture in each prepared plate. Repeat layers to make 4 layers in each plate. Top with tortillas; brush with butter.

- Bake for 20 to 25 minutes or until heated through. Cut into wedges. Serve with sour cream, salsa and guacamole.

- Yield: 4 servings.

"BRIAR PATCH" MARINATED CHICKEN BREASTS

Ingredients

3 medium cloves of garlic, crushed

1/2 cup packed brown sugar

3 tablespoons creamy Dijon mustard

1/4 cup cider vinegar

Juice of 1 lime

Juice of 1/2 large lemon

6 tablespoons olive oil

1 teaspoon salt

Pepper to taste

6 small whole chicken breasts, boned

- Combine garlic, brown sugar, mustard, vinegar, lime juice, lemon juice, olive oil, salt and pepper in bowl; mix well.

- Rinse chicken and pat dry. Add to marinade. Marinate in refrigerator for several hours.

- Preheat grill. Drain chicken, reserving marinade.

- Grill chicken until cooked through, brushing with reserved marinade.

- May also use marinade for wild turkey breasts.

- Yield: 8 servings.

Over the Fence: *We serve this fabulous grilled marinated chicken cold for tailgate parties.*

CHINESE SMOKED CHICKEN

- Combine chopped green onion, soy sauce, hoisin sauce, wine, brown sugar, liquid smoke, ginger and salt in oven cooking bag.

- Rinse chicken and pat dry. Tie wings. Add to marinade; seal oven cooking bag. Turn to coat chicken well. Marinate in refrigerator for several hours to overnight.

- Preheat oven to 350 degrees. Cut slits in top of oven cooking bag; place in baking dish.

- Bake chicken for 1½ hours or until brown and tender. Cool slightly. Place chicken on serving plate; cut into serving pieces. Spoon cooking juices over chicken. Garnish with slivered green onions. Serve with rice.

- Yield: 4 servings.

Ingredients

1 green onion, chopped
6 tablespoons soy sauce
2 tablespoons hoisin sauce
2 tablespoons dry white wine
1 teaspoon brown sugar
1 teaspoon liquid smoke
1 teaspoon finely minced ginger
1 teaspoon salt
1 (3- to 4-pound) chicken
Slivered green onions

THE "PETERSON COTTAGE" CHICKEN CAPER

- Rinse chicken and pat dry. Coat with mixture of flour, salt and pepper.

- Brown chicken in butter in skillet. Simmer, covered, for 40 minutes. Add garlic, olives, capers, capers liquid, water and parsley.

- Cook for 3 to 5 minutes or until heated through. Serve with buttered and parslied new potatoes.

- May substitute ¼ cup dry white wine for capers liquid.

- Yield: 4 servings.

Over the Fence: *This recipe has been a mystery for years.*

Ingredients

1 (2½-pound) chicken
¼ cup flour
1 teaspoon salt
¼ teaspoon pepper
3 tablespoons butter
2 large cloves of garlic, minced
¾ cup sliced pimento-stuffed olives
3 tablespoons capers
1½ tablespoons capers liquid
1 tablespoon water
½ cup minced parsley

CHICKEN MACIEL

- Sauté chicken with curry powder in butter in skillet.
- Bring half and half just to a simmer in saucepan. Stir in mixture of wine and cornstarch with fork. Cook until thickened, stirring constantly.
- Stir in chicken, rice, salt and pepper. Cook until heated through.
- Yield: 6 servings.

Ingredients

2 pounds chicken, cooked, chopped, chilled

1 teaspoon curry powder

6 tablespoons butter

2 cups half and half

1/4 cup sherry

1 teaspoon (heaping) cornstarch

1 cup rice, cooked

Salt and pepper to taste

"NEWNUM-QUEEN" BRAISED CHILI CHICKEN

- Cut chicken into small pieces. Rinse and pat dry. Brown with sliced onion, garlic and salt in 1/2 cup oil and 2 tablespoons butter in skillet until garlic is brown; remove garlic. Sauté chicken until cooked through. Add wine.
- Sauté finely chopped onion and rosemary in 1/2 cup heated oil in small saucepan until onion is tender. Add tomatoes, salt and chili pepper. Simmer for 20 minutes.
- Preheat oven to 400 degrees.
- Combine sauce, chicken and 1 tablespoon butter in baking dish; mix gently. Bake for 20 minutes.
- Yield: 4 servings.

Over the Fence: I serve this dish from the Marches region of Italy in the winter. It is "warm" in flavor and is good served with pasta or steamed fennel sprinkled with Parmesan cheese.

Ingredients

1 (2¼-pound) chicken

1 medium onion, sliced

2 cloves of garlic, minced

Salt to taste

1/2 cup vegetable oil

2 tablespoons butter

1/2 cup dry white wine

1 onion, finely chopped

1 sprig of rosemary, chopped

1/2 cup vegetable oil

14 ounces ripe tomatoes, peeled, chopped, seeded

1 piece of red chili pepper, finely chopped

1 tablespoon butter

"HAVFORD" COMPANY CHICKEN

Even children love this easy chicken dish!

- Preheat oven to 350 degrees.
- Place chicken in rectangular baking dish. Spread with mixture of sour cream and soup.
- Prepare stuffing mix using package directions. Sprinkle over casserole.
- Bake for 30 to 45 minutes or until golden brown and bubbly.
- Yield: 8 servings.

Ingredients

3 chicken breasts, cooked, chopped

2 cups sour cream

1 (10-ounce) can cream of mushroom soup

1 (7-ounce) package stuffing mix

"DUPUIS COTTAGE" COQ AU VIN

- Rinse chicken and pat dry; sprinkle with salt and pepper.
- Brown on all sides in butter in heavy saucepan. Add green onions, mushrooms, wine, tomatoes and chicken bouillon dissolved in water.
- Simmer over medium heat for 35 to 40 minutes or until cooked through. Garnish with fresh parsley and chives.
- Yield: 4 servings.

Ingredients

1 chicken, cut up

Salt and pepper to taste

1/2 cup butter

3 or 4 green onions, sliced

1 pound mushrooms, sliced

1/2 cup dry white wine

1 (16-ounce) can stewed tomatoes

2 to 3 chicken bouillon cubes

1/2 cup hot water

Fresh parsley

Chopped chives

"PEACHES 'N CREAM" CRAZY CHICKEN

Ingredients

1 chicken, cut up

1 (16-ounce) can whole cranberry sauce

1 (8-ounce) bottle of French salad dressing

1 envelope onion soup mix

1 (11-ounce) can mandarin oranges, drained

Quick to prepare as well as very good.

- Preheat oven to 300 to 325 degrees. Rinse chicken and pat dry; place in baking dish.
- Combine cranberry sauce, salad dressing, soup mix and oranges in bowl; mix well. Spoon over chicken.
- Bake, covered, for 2 hours. Serve with sauce over rice.
- Yield: 4 servings.

GRILLED LEMON AND TARRAGON CHICKEN "MCCLOY"

Ingredients

1 chicken, cut into quarters

2 tablespoons Dijon mustard

Pepper to taste

1/2 cup melted butter

2 teaspoons lemon juice

1 teaspoon tarragon

1/2 teaspoon garlic salt

- Rinse chicken and pat dry. Spread with mustard; sprinkle with pepper. Marinate, covered, in refrigerator for 3 to 4 hours.
- Preheat grill. Combine butter, lemon juice, tarragon and garlic salt in bowl; mix well.
- Grill chicken until tender, basting frequently with lemon-tarragon mixture.
- Yield: 4 servings.

"TIDE'S INN"
KING RANCH CASSEROLE

- Preheat oven to 350 degrees.
- Cut tortillas into quarters. Dip into chicken broth; arrange in greased rectangular baking dish.
- Combine chicken, onion, green pepper, cheese, soups and tomatoes with green chilies in bowl; mix well. Spoon into prepared baking dish.
- Bake for 30 to 45 minutes or until bubbly. Serve with tossed salad and French bread.
- Yield: 8 servings.

Over the Fence: The King Ranch, which spreads over much of south Texas, has always been known for this recipe. It is a favorite in the Lone Star State and at our house.

Ingredients

1 (12-count) package tortillas

1 cup chicken broth

3 cups chopped cooked chicken

1 yellow onion, chopped

1 green bell pepper, chopped

2 cups shredded Cheddar cheese

1 (10-ounce) can each cream of chicken and cream of mushroom soup

1 (10-ounce) can tomatoes with green chilies

"GULF MANOR"
HAWAIIAN CHICKEN

- Preheat grill; let coals burn to low heat. Rinse chicken and pat dry; rub with oil.
- Combine brown sugar, vinegar, mustard, pineapple, salt and pepper in bowl; mix well.
- Grill chicken on 1 side for 15 minutes. Turn chicken and brush with pineapple mixture. Grill for 15 minutes. Turn chicken and brush remaining side with pineapple sauce. Grill for 10 minutes longer or until chicken is cooked through.
- Place chicken on serving plate; serve with fresh pineapple.
- Yield: 8 servings.

Ingredients

4 pounds cut-up chicken

1 tablespoon vegetable oil

2 cups packed light brown sugar

2 tablespoons light vinegar

2 tablespoons Dijon mustard

1 (16-ounce) can crushed pineapple, drained

1 teaspoon salt

1/2 teaspoon pepper

"MOORE FUN" KEYSTONE CHICKEN

Ingredients

4 whole medium chicken
breasts, cut into halves
1 medium onion, chopped
2 tablespoons butter
1 (15-ounce) can tomato sauce
2/3 cup beer
1/2 teaspoon each oregano, basil
and white pepper
1/4 cup grated Parmesan cheese

- Preheat oven to 350 degrees. Rinse chicken and pat dry; arrange in 8x12-inch baking dish.
- Sauté onion in butter in saucepan until tender. Stir in tomato sauce, beer, oregano, basil and pepper. Simmer over medium heat for 10 minutes.
- Pour sauce over chicken. Bake for 50 to 55 minutes or until chicken is tender. Sprinkle with cheese.
- May substitute chicken thighs or legs for chicken breasts or crushed canned tomatoes for tomato sauce.
- Yield: 8 servings.

"DOBSON COTTAGE" LEMON CHICKEN

Ingredients

6 chicken breast filets
1/2 cup butter
Salt and pepper to taste
2 tablespoons cooking sherry
2 tablespoons lemon juice
2 tablespoons grated lemon rind
1 cup whipping cream
1/4 cup grated Parmesan cheese

- Preheat oven to 350 degrees.
- Rinse chicken and pat dry. Sauté in butter in skillet until light brown. Sprinkle with salt and pepper. Remove chicken to baking dish.
- Stir wine, lemon juice and lemon rind into drippings in skillet. Cook over low heat for 3 to 4 minutes, stirring constantly. Stir in cream gradually.
- Pour sauce over chicken; sprinkle with cheese. Bake for 20 to 30 minutes or until golden brown.
- Yield: 6 servings.

"ADAGIO" LIGHTLY LEMON CHICKEN

*A light, quick and easy dish good served with
long grain and wild rice and a vegetable.*

- Cut chicken breasts into halves; pound until thin. Rinse chicken and pat dry. Dip into egg substitute; coat with mixture of bread crumbs and parsley.
- Sauté garlic in margarine in skillet over medium-high heat for 1 minute. Add chicken. Cook until brown on both sides. Top with lemon slices from 1/2 lemon.
- Add mixture of chicken broth and lemon juice from 1/2 lemon. Bring to a boil; reduce heat. Simmer for 10 minutes or until chicken is tender.
- Yield: 4 servings.

Ingredients

2 whole chicken breasts
1/4 cup egg substitute
3/4 cup fine dry bread crumbs
1 tablespoon chopped parsley
1 clove of garlic, crushed
3 tablespoons margarine
1 lemon
1/4 cup reduced-sodium
chicken broth

"ROBINS" CHICKEN PIE

- Preheat oven to 400 degrees.
- Sauté onion in margarine in skillet until tender but not brown. Stir in flour and salt. Add broth gradually. Cook until thickened, stirring constantly.
- Add chicken, mixed vegetables, mushrooms and carrots; mix well. Spoon into 2-quart baking dish. Top with pastry.
- Bake for 30 minutes or until pastry is golden brown.
- Yield: 6 servings.

Ingredients

1/2 cup chopped onion
1/3 cup margarine
1/3 cup flour
1 1/2 teaspoons salt
3 cups chicken broth
4 cups coarsely chopped
cooked chicken
1 (10-ounce) package frozen
mixed vegetables
1 (8-ounce) can
mushrooms, drained
8 ounces carrots, sliced, cooked
1 All Ready pie pastry

MISS PAT'S QUICK CHICKEN PIE

Ingredients

1 chicken, cooked, chopped

1 (10-ounce) can cream of
chicken soup

3 cups chicken broth

1 1/2 cups self-rising flour

1 cup buttermilk

1/4 cup melted margarine

- Preheat oven to 350 degrees.
- Spread chicken in 9x13-inch baking dish. Add mixture of soup and chicken broth.
- Combine flour, buttermilk and margarine in bowl; mix well. Spoon over chicken.
- Bake for 45 minutes or until crust is golden brown.
- May add peas and mushrooms if desired.
- Yield: 8 servings.

"FANTASIA" CHICKEN TETRAZZINI

Ingredients

4 pounds chicken breasts

8 ounces uncooked spaghetti

6 stalks celery, chopped

2 large onions, chopped

1 green or red bell pepper,
chopped into 1/4-inch pieces

3 tablespoons margarine

8 ounces fresh mushrooms, sliced

1 tablespoon
Worcestershire sauce

Black or red pepper to taste

1 (10-ounce) can cream of
mushroom soup

2 cups shredded Cheddar cheese

1/4 cup chopped pecans

1 cup bread crumbs

1/2 cup grated Parmesan cheese

- Rinse chicken well. Cook in water to cover in saucepan until tender. Drain, reserving broth. Chop chicken, discarding skin and bones.
- Set aside 2 cups (or more) chicken broth. Cook spaghetti *al dente* in reserved broth in large saucepan; drain.
- Sauté celery, onions and bell pepper in margarine in saucepan until tender. Add mushrooms. Sauté lightly. Add 2 cups reserved broth, Worcestershire sauce and pepper.
- Stir in soup and Cheddar cheese. Add chicken and spaghetti; mix gently. Adjust seasoning. Spoon into 2 baking dishes; add additional broth if needed for desired consistency. Top with pecans and mixture of bread crumbs and Parmesan cheese.
- Preheat oven to 350 degrees. Bake casseroles for 1 hour.
- May add 1 small bottle of sliced stuffed olives to sauce.
- Yield: 16 servings.

Chicken Pontalba

- Whisk egg yolks and lemon juice in double boiler until thick and smooth. Place over hot water. Add cooled melted butter 2 tablespoons at a time, lifting pan occasionally to cool bottom. Whisk in vinegar. Cook until thickened, whisking constantly. Season with salt and pepper. Keep warm.

- Brown potatoes in 2 tablespoons 375-degree oil in skillet; drain on paper towel. Add onion, green onions and garlic to drippings in skillet. Stir in mushrooms, ham and potatoes. Sauté for 5 minutes.

- Stir in wine and parsley; remove from heat. Season with salt and pepper. Keep mixture warm.

- Rinse chicken and pat dry. Coat with mixture of flour, salt and pepper. Sauté in 1/4 cup oil in skillet until cooked through.

- Place potato mixture on serving plate. Arrange chicken over potatoes.

- Spoon sauce over chicken. Sprinkle with mixture of bread crumbs and 2 tablespoons butter.

- Yield: 8 servings.

Sauce Ingredients

6 egg yolks
Juice of 1 1/2 lemons
2 cups minus 2 tablespoons
butter, melted, cooled
3/4 tablespoon tarragon vinegar
Salt and pepper to taste

Potato Ingredients

2 cups chopped potatoes
2 tablespoons vegetable oil
1 1/2 cups thinly sliced
white onion
3/4 cup chopped green onions
3 cloves of garlic, minced
1 cup sliced fresh mushrooms
1 1/2 cups chopped cooked ham
3/4 cup Sauterne
3 tablespoons minced parsley
Salt and pepper to taste

Chicken Ingredients

8 large boneless chicken
breast halves
1 cup flour
Salt and pepper to taste
1/4 cup oil
1/2 to 3/4 cup bread crumbs
2 tablespoons melted butter

Fish & Shellfish

ican Perch • Periwinkle • Persimmon • Persuasion • Peterson Cott
ttage • Postcard • Precious • Propinquity • Puglin • Rainbow • Ren
bin's Nest • Roger's Lighthouse • Romance • Rooftops • Rose Cotta
andia • Sandpail • Sandpiper • Savannah Rose • Savannah Sands •
alink • Seaquel • Seaspell • Seastar • Seawynds • Serendipity • Shan
omewhere In Time • Southern Comfort • Southern Splendor • Spinn
ndance • Sundaze • Sunny Side Up • Sunset • These Wishes • Suna
use • The Conservatory • This Is the Life • Tide's Inn • Tiger Paw •
eze • Toye • Treetops • Trio • Tropical Holiday • Tupelo Honey • Tup
akeham Cottage • Waterside • Wayback • Weber Cottage • Wilder
Beach • Zebulon • Zeidman Cottage • Zurn Cottage • A Summer
ttage • American Dream • Anderson Cottage • Anniston • April 16
ttage • Beach Walk • Bella Vista • Belvedere • Benedictus • Beside
e • Boswell Cottage • Briar Patch • Brickwalk • Bridgeport • Brier
away Cottage • Cape May • Carey Cottage • Caribbean • Carpe Di
elSea • Clark Cottage • Colony • Colors • Compass Rose • Coqu
ttage • Creole • C'Scape • Cubbie Hole • Curphey Cottage • Dahlgre
stle • Delor Cottage • DeoGratis • Desire • DoLittle House • Dollhou
cher • Dream Chaser • Dream On • Dreamsicle • Dreamweaver •
ttage • Eclipse • Ecstasea • Eden • Elegance • Enchantment • Englis
ttage • Floridays • For Keeps • Forsythe Cottage • Frascogna Cotta
nt's Roost • GoodnightMoon • Gorlin Cottage • Grayton One • Gray
nor • Gulfview • Gull Cottage • Haardt Cottage • Hampton • Harvest
dges Cottage • Home Alone • Honalee • Hoover Cottage • House
mine • Jasper • Jennifer's Castle • Josephine's • Jubilee • Kaleidos

ture Book • Pitter Patter • Pleasure Principal • Plum Crazy • Porte
Renaissance • Rendezvous • Rhett's Revenge • Ricky's • Roanoke
an's Castle • Sabella Cottage • Salad Days • Sandcastle • Sandi Sho
Cottage • Scott Cottage • Scruggs Cottage • Sea for Two • Sea View
Sho Seeker • Sisters Three By The Sea • Skinny Dip • Smith Cotta
Stanzi Cottage
ams The Bea
on-the Tow
ker To a del M
Win Wright
Abo Allis
nley y-Jam
tersid on • Bl
the S Cottage
arriage hatham
ral C Crawfo
ge • D • Days
lphin e • Drea
Duffy East
age Enon • Eyer Cottage • Fantasia • Fernleigh • Flamingo Fletch
umious Bandersnatch • Gadsden • Gatewalk • Gazebo • Getaway

...I am a part of all that I have met;
Yet all experience is an arch wherethrough
Gleams that untraveled world whose margin fades.... Alfred, Lord Tennyson

Green Cottage • Green Gables • Greenpeace • Guest Cottage • G
Hayford Cottage • Heavenly Days • Helvie Cottage • His Greenhous
s • Hurrah! • Idlewild South • Irvine Cottage • Isaacs Cottage • Iv
Kennedy Cottage • Key West • Kitchens Cottage • Krier • La. Hous

Fish

Grilled Fish, 145

Corney Grouper, 145

Smoked King Mackerel, 146

Grilled Salmon Fillet, 146

Grilled Red Snapper with Garlic and Lime, 147

Grilled Tuna, 147

Shellfish

Seafood Lasagna, 148

Crab Claws, 149

Best Scalloped Oysters, 149

Oysters Rockefeller, 150

Cold Bay Scallops, 150

Barbecued Shrimp, 151

Curried Barbecued Shrimp, 151

Cold Boiled Shrimp with Herb
Mayonnaise, 152

Louisiana Heads On Shrimp, 152

DeJean's Shrimp Remoulade, 153

Shrimp Scampi, 153

Swiss Fondue with Shrimp, 154

Shrimp with Artichoke Hearts and Feta, 154

Shrimp with Roasted Red Pepper Sauce, 155

"MAGNOLIA COTTAGE" GRILLED FISH

- Place fish steaks in shallow dish.
- Combine olive oil, wine vinegar, lemon juice, sherry, soy sauce, ginger, garlic, peppercorns and oregano in bowl; mix well. Pour over fish steaks.
- Marinate in refrigerator for 6 hours, turning 2 to 3 times.
- Drain, discarding marinade.
- Grill over hot coals until fish flakes easily, turning occasionally.
- Yield: 6 servings.

Ingredients

6 (6-ounce) dolphin, mackerel, salmon or tuna steaks

1/3 cup olive oil

3 tablespoons wine vinegar

Juice of 1 lemon or lime

1/3 cup dry sherry

2 tablespoons soy sauce

2 tablespoons grated fresh ginger

2 cloves of garlic, minced

Peppercorns to taste

Oregano to taste

"APRIL 16TH" CORNEY GROUPER

- Sprinkle grouper fillets with salt. Dip in mixture of eggs and water; roll in cornflakes.
- Fry in hot peanut oil in deep-fryer over medium-high heat for 1 to 2 minutes or until golden brown; drain.
- Serve with seafood or tartar sauce.
- Yield: 6 servings.

Ingredients

2 pounds (1 1/2-inch) grouper fillets

Salt to taste

2 eggs, beaten

2 tablespoons water

1 (12-ounce) package cornflakes, crushed

Peanut oil for deep frying

"DUNSETH COTTAGE"
SMOKED KING MACKEREL

Ingredients

16 ounces king mackerel fillets
2 tablespoons olive oil
Salt and pepper to taste
Garlic salt to taste
1 lime, sliced
4 green onions, chopped
1/2 cup lemon juice
1/4 cup butter
1/4 cup Durkee Famous Sauce

- Preheat grill to medium-high.
- Rub both sides of fillets with olive oil; sprinkle with salt, pepper and garlic salt.
- Arrange fillets on heavy-duty foil. Top with lime slices and green onions.
- Place on grill. Pierce foil around fillets with fork. Grill, covered, over hot coals for 15 minutes; do not peek.
- Combine lemon juice, butter and Durkee Famous Sauce in saucepan; mix well. Cook until heated through. Spoon over fillets.
- Yield: 3 servings.

"FLORIDAYS"
GRILLED SALMON FILLET

Ingredients

1 (8-ounce) salmon fillet
Salt and pepper to taste
1 tablespoon melted margarine
2 tablespoons dry white wine
Dillweed to taste
1/2 lemon, sliced

- Preheat grill to medium.
- Rinse fillet with cold water; pat dry.
- Rub both sides of fillet with salt and pepper; brush with margarine. Place on heavy-duty foil. Pour white wine over fish; sprinkle with dillweed. Fold foil to enclose fillet; seal ends.
- Grill over hot coals for 15 minutes. Top salmon with lemon slices.
- Yield: 1 serving.

GRILLED RED SNAPPER WITH GARLIC AND LIME

- Arrange fillets in single layer in shallow dish.

- Whisk lime juice and olive oil in bowl until blended. Stir in parsley, onion, garlic and jalapeño pepper. Pour olive oil mixture over fillets, tossing to coat.

- Let stand at room temperature for 1 hour, turning occasionally. Drain, reserving marinade.

- Preheat grill to high for 4 to 6 minutes; reduce temperature to medium.

- Grill fillets over hot coals until red snapper flakes easily.

- Heat reserved marinade in saucepan. Serve with red snapper.

- Yield: 4 servings.

Ingredients

16 ounces red snapper fillets

1/4 cup fresh lime juice

1/4 cup extra-virgin olive oil

1 tablespoon chopped fresh parsley

1 small onion, finely chopped

6 cloves of garlic, minced

1 large jalapeño pepper, finely chopped

"SEASTAR" GRILLED TUNA

- Combine orange juice, soy sauce, sugar, garlic, honey, onion flakes, cilantro, ginger, salt and pepper in bowl; mix well. Let stand for 1 hour.

- Arrange tuna steaks in shallow dish. Pour orange juice mixture over tuna, tossing to coat. Let stand, covered, for 20 minutes. Drain, discarding marinade.

- Preheat grill.

- Place tuna steaks in wire fish basket. Grill over hot coals for 4 minutes per side or until tuna flakes easily.

- Serve with lemon slices, sliced fresh ginger and Chinese horseradish.

- Yield: 6 servings.

Ingredients

1 cup orange juice

2 tablespoons soy sauce

2 tablespoons sugar

4 cloves of garlic, finely minced

3 tablespoons honey

1 tablespoon onion flakes

2 tablespoons chopped fresh cilantro

2 tablespoons finely minced fresh ginger

Salt and freshly ground pepper to taste

6 (6-ounce) tuna steaks

"TOASTY SUNSET" SEAFOOD LASAGNA

Sauce Ingredients

1 large yellow onion, chopped

4 cloves of garlic, minced

3 tablespoons olive oil

5 cups chopped canned Italian
plum tomatoes in purée

1/2 cup dry white wine

1/2 cup chopped fresh basil

2 teaspoons fennel seeds

Salt and freshly ground pepper

1 cup whipping cream

2 tablespoons Pernod

1 pound medium shrimp, peeled

1 pound scallops, poached

3 dozen mussels, steamed

24 littleneck clams, steamed

Filling Ingredients

3 cups ricotta cheese

8 ounces cream cheese, softened

2 eggs, beaten

1 (10-ounce) package frozen
chopped spinach, cooked, drained

1 pound cooked crab meat

1 red bell pepper, chopped

1 bunch green onions, sliced

1/2 cup chopped fresh basil

Salt and freshly ground pepper

1 1/4 pounds lasagna noodles

1 1/2 pounds mozzarella cheese,
thinly sliced

- Preheat oven to 350 degrees.

- Sauté onion and garlic in olive oil in large saucepan for 5 minutes. Stir in tomatoes. Cook for 5 minutes.

- Add white wine, basil, fennel seeds and salt and pepper to taste; mix well. Simmer over medium heat for 45 minutes, stirring occasionally. Stir in whipping cream and Pernod.

- Poach shrimp slightly. Add shrimp, scallops, mussels and clams to cream mixture; mix well. Simmer for 5 minutes, stirring occasionally. Remove from heat.

- Beat ricotta cheese, cream cheese and eggs in bowl until smooth. Stir in spinach, shredded crab meat, bell pepper, green onions, basil and salt and pepper to taste.

- Cook lasagna noodles *al dente* using package directions.

- Spread a small amount of seafood sauce without any shellfish over bottom of buttered baking pan. Layer 1/3 of the noodles, 1/2 of the filling, 1/2 of the remaining seafood sauce and 1/3 of the mozzarella cheese over prepared layer.

- Arrange 1/2 of the remaining noodles over layers. Spread with remaining filling and 1/2 of the remaining mozzarella cheese.

- Arrange remaining noodles over top. Spread with remaining seafood sauce and remaining mozzarella cheese.

- Bake for 50 minutes or until bubbly and brown. Let stand for 10 minutes before cutting.

- Yield: 10 servings.

"ABOUT TIME" CRAB CLAWS

- Combine Worcestershire sauce, pepper, cheese, salt, parsley, green onions, garlic, lemon juice, oregano, basil, olive oil, wine vinegar and salad dressing mix in bowl; mix well.
- Pour marinade into plastic food storage bag. Add crab claws gently; seal bag.
- Marinate in refrigerator for 8 to 24 hours, turning occasionally.
- Yield: 8 servings.

~

Over the Fence: "Blue Belle" Soft-shell Crabs make a wonderful sandwich filling. Dredge 2 soft-shell crabs in mixture of 1/2 cup flour, 1 teaspoon garlic powder, 1/4 teaspoon black pepper and cayenne pepper to taste. Sauté in 2 tablespoons margarine. Sprinkle with 2 tablespoons minced parsley and the juice of a lemon.

Ingredients

1 tablespoon Worcestershire sauce
1 tablespoon freshly
ground pepper
1/2 cup grated Parmesan cheese
1/2 teaspoon salt
1/4 cup chopped fresh parsley
1/4 cup finely chopped
green onions
3 cloves of garlic, finely chopped
1 tablespoon lemon juice
1/2 teaspoon oregano
1 teaspoon basil
1 cup olive oil
1/2 cup wine vinegar
1 envelope Italian salad
dressing mix
1 pound fresh crab claws

"IRVINE COTTAGE" BEST SCALLOPED OYSTERS

- Preheat oven to 375 degrees.
- Layer crackers, oysters, butter, salt and pepper alternately in buttered 3- or 4-quart round baking dish until ingredients are 1 inch from top, ending with crackers.
- Fill the baking dish with milk.
- Bake for 45 to 60 minutes or until oysters begin to curl.
- Yield: 6 servings.

Ingredients

Crushed saltine crackers
1 quart oysters, drained
Butter, chopped
Salt and pepper to taste
Milk

"PEACHES 'N CREAM" OYSTERS ROCKEFELLER

Ingredients

2 bunches shallots, chopped

1 large stalk celery, chopped

1 cup melted butter

1 teaspoon Tabasco sauce

1/2 (7-ounce) tube anchovy paste

8 teaspoons Herbsaint

2 (10-ounce) packages frozen chopped spinach, thawed

2 large cloves of garlic

1 cup butter

Salt to taste

2 pints medium oysters, cooked

- Process shallots and celery with 1 cup melted butter in blender or food processor. Spoon into large saucepan. Stir in Tabasco sauce, anchovy paste and Herbsaint.

- Cook, covered, over medium heat for 15 minutes, stirring occasionally.

- Purée well drained spinach and garlic with 1 cup butter in blender or food processor. Stir into celery mixture. Cook for 15 minutes, stirring occasionally. Season with salt.

- Stir in oysters. Cook just until heated through. Transfer to chafing dish. Serve with toast points.

- May steep 1/2 teaspoon anise seeds in 1/2 cup boiling water for 3 minutes for Herbsaint.

- Yield: 10 servings.

"C'SCAPE" COLD BAY SCALLOPS

Ingredients

1 cup each sour cream and mayonnaise

2 tablespoons chopped dillweed

1 tablespoon fresh lemon juice

1 teaspoon salt

1/4 teaspoon each crushed garlic and ground pepper

1 cup each water and white wine

1 bay leaf

1 large lemon, sliced

6 peppercorns

1 pound bay scallops

This is a delicious cool lunch for a warm summer day at Seaside. Great served with hot homemade French bread.

- Combine sour cream, mayonnaise, dillweed, lemon juice, salt, garlic and pepper in bowl; mix well. Chill, covered, in refrigerator.

- Bring water, white wine, bay leaf, sliced lemon and peppercorns to a boil in saucepan; reduce heat. Simmer for 5 minutes.

- Stir in scallops. Cook for 2 to 3 minutes or until scallops are tender. Drain; rinse in cold water. Chill, covered, in refrigerator.

- Arrange chilled scallops on lettuce-lined platter. Top with chilled sauce.

- Yield: 6 servings.

"DREAMWEAVER" BARBECUED SHRIMP

- Preheat oven to 400 degrees.
- Arrange shrimp in single layer in large baking dish. Sprinkle with parsley flakes, garlic powder, Italian seasoning, pepper, soy sauce and Worcestershire sauce.
- Drizzle shrimp with melted margarine.
- Bake for 12 minutes or until shrimp turn pink.
- Yield: 3 servings.

Ingredients

2 pounds unpeeled jumbo shrimp
Parsley flakes to taste
Garlic powder to taste
Italian seasoning to taste
Pepper to taste
Soy sauce to taste
Worcestershire sauce to taste
1 cup melted margarine

CURRIED BARBECUED SHRIMP

- Preheat oven to 375 degrees.
- Pour olive oil, butter, lemon juice, Tabasco sauce and Worcestershire sauce in order listed into large cast-iron skillet. Add paprika and curry powder.
- Simmer for 5 minutes, stirring frequently. Remove from heat.
- Add shrimp, stirring to mix. Sprinkle with salt, cayenne pepper and garlic powder.
- Bake for 35 minutes. Serve from skillet with hot French bread, dipping shrimp and bread in pan drippings.
- Yield: 6 servings.

Ingredients

2 tablespoons olive oil
1/4 cup melted butter
Juice of 2 lemons
2 large dashes of Tabasco sauce
2 tablespoons Worcestershire sauce
1 teaspoon (heaping) paprika
2 teaspoons curry powder
1 1/2 pounds large unpeeled shrimp
Salt to taste
Cayenne pepper to taste
Garlic powder to taste

COLD BOILED SHRIMP WITH HERB MAYONNAISE

Ingredients

2 cups mayonnaise

1/3 cup finely minced parsley

4 cloves of garlic, minced

1/3 cup minced spinach leaves

1/3 cup minced fresh basil

1/2 cup sour cream

1/4 cup fresh lemon juice

2 tablespoons grated onion

Worcestershire sauce to taste

Salt and freshly ground pepper to taste

3 pounds cooked peeled shrimp, chilled

- Combine mayonnaise, parsley, garlic, spinach, basil, sour cream, lemon juice, onion, Worcestershire sauce, salt and pepper in blender or food processor container. Process until smooth. Chill, covered, in refrigerator.

- Serve herb mayonnaise with shrimp.

- May also serve the herb mayonnaise with crab, fresh vegetables or cooked chicken breast.

- Yield: 10 servings.

LOUISIANA HEADS ON SHRIMP

Ingredients

2 pounds large shrimp, heads on

1/2 teaspoon cayenne pepper

1/2 teaspoon black pepper

1 teaspoon garlic powder

1/2 cup butter

1/4 cup Worcestershire sauce

Juice of 1 lemon

1/8 teaspoon Tabasco sauce

1 lemon, sliced

1 teaspoon salt

1 loaf French bread

A favorite meal on a summer night after a day on the beach.

- Rinse shrimp; drain. Arrange in shallow microwave-safe dish. Sprinkle with cayenne pepper, black pepper and garlic powder, stirring to coat.

- Combine next 4 ingredients in microwave-safe dish. Microwave on High for 2 minutes or until butter melts, stirring once. Pour over shrimp.

- Stir in lemon slices. Microwave on High for 10 to 12 minutes or until shrimp turn pink, stirring twice. Season with salt.

- Let stand at room temperature for 4 minutes.

- Dip French bread in pan drippings.

- Yield: 6 servings.

DeJean's Shrimp Remoulade

- Combine vinegar, mustard, horseradish, salt, cayenne pepper, paprika, catsup and garlic in large bowl; mix well. Whisk in oil. Stir in shallots and celery.
- Add shrimp to marinade. Marinate, covered, in refrigerator for several hours to overnight, tossing occasionally; drain.
- Yield: 6 servings.

Over the Fence: My father fixed this delicious treat for get-togethers of family and friends. At About Time Cottage it always brings back special memories of good times for me.

Ingredients

1/4 cup vinegar

1 1/2 tablespoons mustard

2 teaspoons horseradish

1/2 teaspoon salt

1/2 teaspoon cayenne pepper

1 1/2 teaspoons paprika

1 tablespoon catsup

1/2 clove of garlic, minced

1/2 cup vegetable oil

1/4 cup minced shallots with tops

1/4 cup chopped celery

2 pounds cooked peeled shrimp

"Wilder" Shrimp Scampi

Great dish for entertaining! It can be assembled in the morning, refrigerated and baked when your guests arrive.

- Preheat oven to 450 degrees.
- Arrange shrimp in shallow baking pan. Pour mixture of butter, olive oil, parsley flakes, basil, oregano, garlic powder, salt and lemon juice over shrimp.
- Bake for 5 minutes. Turn oven to broil. Broil shrimp for 5 minutes or until brown. Serve over rice.
- Yield: 4 servings.

Ingredients

2 pounds large shrimp, peeled, deveined

2 cups melted butter

1 cup olive oil

2 tablespoons parsley flakes

1 teaspoon basil

1 teaspoon oregano

3/4 teaspoon garlic powder

3/4 teaspoon salt

3 tablespoons lemon juice

"Fantasia" Swiss Fondue with Shrimp

Ingredients

2 cups whipping cream
1 cup shredded Swiss cheese
3 tablespoons flour
1/4 teaspoon cayenne pepper
1 teaspoon dillweed
1 teaspoon salt
1 pound cooked peeled shrimp
2 loaves French bread, sliced

- Combine cream, cheese, flour, cayenne pepper, dillweed and salt in saucepan; mix well. Cook until cheese melts, stirring constantly.
- Spoon into fondue pot. Dip shrimp in cheese mixture. Serve over French bread.
- Yield: 6 servings.

"For Keeps" Shrimp with Artichoke Hearts and Feta

Ingredients

3 cloves of garlic, minced
3 tablespoons olive oil
1 1/2 pounds jumbo shrimp, peeled, deveined
1 (16-ounce) can chopped tomatoes
3 tablespoons chopped fresh parsley
2 (9-ounce) cans artichoke hearts, drained
1 tablespoon chopped fresh parsley
1 (12-ounce) package fettucini, cooked, drained
2 ounces feta cheese, crumbled

- Sauté garlic in olive oil in large skillet. Add shrimp. Cook until shrimp turn pink, stirring frequently. Remove shrimp to warm platter.
- Stir undrained tomatoes and 3 tablespoons parsley into pan drippings. Cook for 5 minutes or until slightly thickened, stirring frequently. Add artichoke hearts, shrimp and 1 tablespoon parsley; mix well. Cook just until heated through.
- Arrange fettucini on serving platter; top with shrimp mixture. Sprinkle with feta cheese.
- Yield: 4 servings.

"KRIER COTTAGE" SHRIMP WITH ROASTED RED PEPPER SAUCE

- Preheat broiler. Place bell peppers on top oven rack; place pan of water on lower rack.
- Broil until peppers are blackened, turning to broil evenly. Place in paper bag; let stand to steam.
- Slice off stem of entire head of garlic. Poach garlic in water in saucepan for 30 to 45 minutes or until tender.
- Peel and seed peppers. Place in food processor container. Squeeze garlic cloves from skins into container. Add anchovies and lemon juice; process until smooth. Add oil gradually, processing constantly until mixture has consistency of thin mayonnaise. Season with salt, cayenne pepper and additional lemon juice if needed.
- Bring water, wine, lemon juice, bay leaf and peppercorns to a boil in saucepan. Boil for 5 to 10 minutes. Add shrimp; cover.
- Bring to a simmer; remove from heat. Let stand for 3 to 5 minutes or until cooked through.
- Drain shrimp and place on serving plate. Serve with the roasted red pepper sauce.
- Yield: 10 servings.

Over the Fence: *We subscribe to the theory that only wimps buy shrimp that have been headed. The heads add flavor and can provide evidence that the shrimp are fresh.*

Sauce Ingredients

3 red bell peppers
1 entire head garlic
3 anchovies
Juice of 1/2 lemon
2/3 cup olive oil
Salt and cayenne pepper to taste

Shrimp Ingredients

3 cups water
1 cup dry white wine
Juice of 1 lemon
1 bay leaf
2 tablespoons peppercorns
5 pounds heads-on shrimp

...st Edition • Latitude • LeBlanc Cottage • Leeward • Lehman Cotta...
...ndpine Lodge • Lonesome Dove • Lost Goggles • Lowe Cottage • L...
...rtha Green • McChesney Cottage • McCollister Cottage • McLaughli...
...Mirador • Mis B'Haven • Modica Cottage • Moore Fun • Nancy's F...
...ttage • On the Veranda • Ondine • Orth Cottage • Outer Banks • Ov...
...lican Perch • Periwinkle • Persimmon • Persuasion • Peterson Cott...
...ttage • Postcard • Precipulation • Rainbow • Ren...
...bin's Nest • Roger's Lighthouse • Romance • Rooftops • Rose Cotta...
...andia • Sandpail • Sandpiper • Savannah Rose • Savannah Sands • ...
...alink • Seaquel • Seaspell • Seastar • Seawynds • Serendipity • Shar...
...omewhere In Time • Southern Comfort • Southern Splendor • Spinn...
...ndance • Sundaze • Sunnyside Up • Sunrise • Sunrise Wishes • Sun...
...use • The Conservatory • This Is the Life • Tide's Inn • Tiger Paw •...
...eeze • Toye • Treetops • Trio • Tropical Holiday • Tupelo Honey • Tup...
...Wakeham Cottage • Waterside • Wayback • Weber Cottage • Wilder...
...Beach • Zebulon • Zeidman Cottage • Zurn Cottage • A Summe...
...ttage • American Dream • Anderson Cottage • Anniston • April 16...
...ttage • Beach Walk • Bella Vista • Belvedere • Benedictus • Beside...
...te • Boswell Cottage • Briar Patch • Brickwalk • Bridgeport • Brier...
...laway Cottage • Cape May • Carey Cottage • Caribbean • Carpe D...
...elSea • Clark Cottage • Colony • Colors • Compass Rose • Coqu...
...ttage • Creole • C'Scape • Cubbie Hole • Curphey Cottage • Dahlgre...
...stle • Delor Cottage • DeoGratis • Desire • DoLittle House • Dollhou...
...tcher • Dream Chaser • Dream On • Dreamsicle • Dreamweaver •...
...ttage • Eclipse • Ecstasea • Eden • Elegance • Enchantment • Engli...

Just Desserts

eonardo da Bicci • Lewis Cottage • Limehouse • Little Dipper • Lit
ottage • Magnolia • Maiden's Chamber • Marietta's Cottage • Mariso
ge • Mellow Yellow • Melrose • Memories • Midsummer Night's Drea
Narnia • Natchez House • Next Wave • Nightshade • Nirvana • Ols
l! • rk Place • Parvey Cottage • Peach Delight • Peaches 'n Crea
icture Porte
Rena Roanok
an's C ndi Sho
Cotta ea Vie
Shell Cotta
tanzi Cottag
ams • e Bea
-on-th w • Tow
ker To a del M
• Win Wright
• Abo • Allis
hley by-Jam
tersid on • Bl
the S Cottag
arriage House • Casa del Mar • Casablanca • Charleston • C athar
oral Cove • Corn Cottage • Crackerbox • Craige Cottage • Crawf

...What little town by river or sea shore,..?
John Keats

ge • Dapper's Den • Dargusch Cottage • Daydream Believer • Days
lphin Inn • Domino • Dove Crest • Dragon's Lair • Dragonette • Drea
Duffy Cottage • Dune • Dunseth Cottage • DuPuis Cottage • East
ge • Enon • Eyer Cottage • Fantasia • Fernleigh • Flamingo • Fletch

Just Desserts

French Apple Dessert, 159

Deep-Dish Blueberry Cobbler, 159

Brazilian Mousse, 160

Death by Chocolate, 160

Chocolate Mousse, 161

Chocolate Icebox Torte, 161

Chocolate Icebox Cake, 162

Bundt Kugel, 162

Lemon Ice Cream Trifle, 163

Lemon Mousse with Blueberries, 163

Homemade Peach Ice Cream, 164

Russian Creme with Strawberry Sauce, 164

Buttermilk Strawberry Sherbet, 165

Sauce for Fresh Fruit, 165

Amaretto Cheesecake, 166

Cheesecake, 166

Praline Cheesecake, 167

Cheesecake with Raspberries, 167

Cakes

Apple Pecan Cake, 168

Mexican Chocolate Cake, 168

Fresh Coconut Cake, 169

Hazelnut Cake, 169

Chocolate Chip Pound Cake, 170

Five-Flavor Pound Cake, 170

Fabulous Lemon Pound Cake, 171

Cookies

Kathryn Hepburn's Brownies, 171

Almond Chocolate Squares, 172

Clipper Chocolate Chip Squares, 173

Filled Cookies, 173

Macadamia Nut Tea Cookies, 174

Pecan Sandies, 174

Salted Nut Bars, 175

Carolina Spice Cookies, 175

Pies

Black Bottom Pie, 176

Chocolate Chess Pie, 176

Brownie Pie, 177

Chocolate Pecan Pie, 177

Coconut Caramel Pies, 178

Kahlua Pie, 178

Cookie Crust Lemon Pie, 179

Margarita Pie, 179

Melba Pie, 180

Praline Peach Pie, 180

White Peach Pie, 181

Southern Pecan Pie, 181

FRENCH APPLE DESSERT

- Preheat oven to 350 degrees.
- Combine 1 cup baking mix, brown sugar and pecans in bowl. Cut in 3 tablespoons margarine until crumbly; set aside.
- Spread apples in greased 9x13-inch baking dish. Combine eggs, sugar, 3/4 cup baking mix, 2 tablespoons margarine, milk, cinnamon and nutmeg in mixer bowl or blender container; beat or process until smooth.
- Spoon over apples. Sprinkle with crumb mixture. Bake for 55 minutes or until knife inserted in center comes out clean.
- Yield: 12 servings.

Ingredients

1 cup baking mix

1/3 cup packed brown sugar

1/2 cup chopped pecans

3 tablespoons margarine

6 cups thinly sliced peeled tart apples

2 eggs

1 cup sugar

3/4 cup baking mix

2 tablespoons margarine, softened

3/4 cup milk

1 1/4 teaspoons cinnamon

1/4 teaspoon nutmeg

"DuPuis Cottage" Deep-dish Blueberry Cobbler

It is a great summer dessert and is just as good with peaches.

- Preheat oven to 350 degrees.
- Melt butter in 2-quart baking dish in oven.
- Mix sugar and flour in mixer bowl. Add milk, vanilla and cinnamon; mix well. Pour into butter in baking dish. Spoon blueberries over top; do not stir.
- Bake for 40 minutes or until crust is golden brown.
- Yield: 8 servings.

Ingredients

1/2 cup butter

1 cup sugar

3/4 cup self-rising flour

3/4 cup milk

1/2 teaspoon vanilla extract

1 teaspoon cinnamon

3 to 4 cups blueberries

BRAZILIAN MOUSSE

A traditional holiday dessert.

- Combine unopened cans of condensed milk with water to cover in large saucepan. Bring to a boil; reduce heat. Simmer for 2 to 2½ hours, adding water as needed to keep cans covered.
- Remove cans from saucepan. Let stand until cool. Open cans and spoon caramelized condensed milk into bowl; beat until smooth.
- Reserve a small amount of whipped cream for garnish. Fold remaining whipped cream gently into condensed milk. Fold in pecans. Chill until serving time. Stir before serving. Garnish servings with the reserved whipped cream.
- Yield: 12 servings.

Over the Fence: The family story about this recipe is that a cousin allowed the water to boil away while cooking the condensed milk and the cans exploded all over the kitchen. It took longer to clean up the mess than to prepare the entire turkey dinner.

Ingredients

2 (14-ounce) cans sweetened condensed milk

4 cups whipping cream, whipped

1 cup chopped pecans

DEATH BY CHOCOLATE

- Preheat oven to 350 degrees.
- Prepare and bake cake mix using package directions for 9x13-inch cake pan; do not overbake.
- Pierce holes in warm cake. Drizzle with Kahlua. Cool on wire rack. Let stand overnight. Crumble cake.
- Prepare chocolate mousse using package directions, substituting 1% milk for whole milk.
- Layer cake crumbs, mousse, whipped topping and candy ½ at a time in trifle bowl. Chill for 6 to 12 hours.
- Yield: 16 servings.

Ingredients

1 (2-layer) package devil's food cake mix

¼ cup (or more) Kahlua

3 packages instant chocolate mousse mix

12 ounces whipped topping

6 (1.5-ounce) Heath bars, frozen, crushed

"MIS B' HAVEN" CHOCOLATE MOUSSE

- Beat egg yolks and confectioners' sugar in mixer bowl until thick and lemon-colored. Melt chocolate chips with water in double boiler, stirring to mix well. Fold into egg yolk mixture.

- Beat egg whites in mixer bowl until stiff peaks form. Fold into chocolate mixture.

- Whip cream in mixer bowl until soft peaks form. Fold into chocolate mixture with vanilla.

- Spoon into 1 large bowl or individual bowls. Chill for 6 hours or longer. Garnish with additional whipped cream.

- Yield: 8 servings.

Ingredients

4 egg yolks
3/4 cup confectioners' sugar
1 1/2 cups chocolate chips
1/4 cup water
4 egg whites
1 cup whipping cream
1 teaspoon vanilla extract
Whipped cream

"DOBSON COTTAGE" CHOCOLATE ICEBOX TORTE

- Whip cream in mixer bowl until soft peaks form. Beat in sugar. Beat egg whites in mixer bowl until stiff peaks form.

- Soften gelatin in cold water in bowl. Add to egg whites; beat until smooth. Fold in whipped cream and cherries.

- Spread 3/4 of the cookie crumbs in torte pan. Spoon whipped cream mixture into prepared torte pan; top with remaining cookie crumbs. Chill for 3 to 4 hours.

- Yield: 8 servings.

Ingredients

1 pint whipping cream
2 tablespoons sugar
6 egg whites
1 envelope unflavored gelatin
1/2 cup cold water
1 cup finely chopped maraschino cherries, drained
1 (8-ounce) package chocolate wafers, finely crushed

"TUPELO STREET" CHOCOLATE ICEBOX CAKE

A divine birthday "cake" for chocolate lovers.

Ingredients

1 cup unsalted butter, softened

1 1/4 cups confectioners' sugar

6 egg yolks

1/2 (1-ounce) square unsweetened baking chocolate

1 (4-ounce) bar German's sweet chocolate

6 egg whites, stiffly beaten

2 (3-ounce) packages ladyfingers

- Cream butter and confectioners' sugar in mixer bowl until light and fluffy. Beat in egg yolks 1 at a time. Beat for 5 minutes longer.
- Melt chocolate in double boiler. Add to egg yolk mixture; mix well. Fold in stiffly beaten egg whites.
- Line springform pan with ladyfingers. Spoon filling into prepared springform pan. Chill overnight.
- Place dessert on serving plate; remove side of pan. Serve with whipped cream if desired.
- Yield: 12 servings.

"THIS IS THE LIFE" KLEIN BUNDT KUGEL

Ingredients

1/4 cup margarine

1/2 cup pecan halves

1 (16-ounce) package wide noodles, cooked

1/4 cup margarine, softened

1/2 cup sugar

1/2 cup packed dark brown sugar

3 eggs, beaten

3/4 cup raisins

1 tablespoon (heaping) cinnamon

1/2 teaspoon salt

1/2 cup chopped pecans

- Preheat oven to 350 degrees.
- Melt 1/4 cup margarine in bundt pan, tilting to coat well. Arrange pecan halves in pattern in margarine in bundt pan.
- Combine noodles, 1/4 cup margarine, sugar, brown sugar, eggs, raisins, cinnamon and salt in bowl; mix well. Fold in chopped pecans.
- Spoon into prepared bundt pan. Bake for 1 hour. Invert onto serving plate.
- May use egg substitute instead of eggs.
- Yield: 8 servings.

"Peaches 'n Cream" Lemon Ice Cream Trifle

- Melt butter in double boiler. Stir in lemon rind, lemon juice, sugar and salt. Blend in eggs. Cook over boiling water until thickened, stirring constantly. Cool to room temperature.
- Layer cake slices, ice cream and lemon sauce 1/3 at a time in trifle bowl; swirl top with spatula.
- Freeze for several hours or until firm.
- Yield: 8 servings.

Ingredients

1/3 cup butter

2 teaspoons grated lemon rind

1/3 cup lemon juice

1 cup sugar

1 1/4 teaspoons salt

3 eggs, beaten

1 (11-ounce) pound cake, cut into 1/2-inch slices

3 pints vanilla ice cream, softened

Lemon Mousse with Blueberries

- Beat egg yolks with 3/4 cup sugar in double boiler. Cook over hot water until frothy and lemon-colored, stirring constantly. Stir in lemon juice. Cook for 8 minutes or until thickened, stirring constantly.
- Cool to room temperature. Chill in refrigerator.
- Beat egg whites in mixer bowl until stiff peaks form. Beat whipping cream in mixer bowl until soft peaks form. Stir in lemon rind. Fold egg whites and whipped cream into cooled mousse. Chill in refrigerator.
- Sprinkle blueberries with 1/4 cup sugar in glass bowl. Chill until serving time. Serve the lemon mousse over blueberries.
- Yield: 6 servings.

Ingredients

5 egg yolks

3/4 cup sugar

Juice of 2 lemons

5 egg whites

1 cup whipping cream

2 teaspoons grated lemon rind

2 pints blueberries

1/4 cup sugar

"CAREY COTTAGE"
HOMEMADE PEACH ICE CREAM

Ingredients

2 envelopes unflavored gelatin
3 cups milk
2 cups sugar
1/4 teaspoon salt
6 eggs
1 1/2 cups half and half
1 (4-ounce) package vanilla
instant pudding mix
5 teaspoons vanilla extract
4 cups (or more) crushed very
ripe peaches

- Soften gelatin in 1/2 cup milk in small bowl. Scald 1 1/2 cups milk in saucepan. Add gelatin mixture, stirring until dissolved. Add remaining 1 cup milk, sugar and salt.
- Beat eggs at high speed in mixer bowl for 5 minutes. Add half and half, pudding mix, vanilla and gelatin mixture; beat until smooth. Stir in peaches.
- Spoon into 1-gallon ice cream freezer container. Freeze using manufacturer's directions. Pack well and ripen for 2 hours before serving.
- Yield: 12 servings.

"SUNDAZE" RUSSIAN CREME WITH
STRAWBERRY SAUCE

Ingredients

3 (10-ounce) packages
frozen sliced strawberries
in syrup, thawed
1/2 cup sugar
4 1/2 teaspoons lemon juice
1 envelope unflavored gelatin
1/2 cup cold water
1/2 cup sugar
1 cup half and half
1 cup sour cream
1 teaspoon vanilla extract

- Combine strawberries with 1/2 cup sugar and lemon juice in blender container; process until smooth.
- Spoon into nonaluminum saucepan. Cook over low heat for 10 minutes or until thickened, stirring occasionally.
- Cool to room temperature. Chill until serving time.
- Soften gelatin in cold water in small bowl. Blend 1/2 cup sugar into half and half in small saucepan. Heat until lukewarm, whisking constantly. Add gelatin, stirring until dissolved. Chill until mixture begins to thicken.
- Beat sour cream and vanilla in mixer bowl until smooth. Add gelatin mixture gradually, beating constantly. Beat for 1 minute longer.
- Spoon into 2/3-cup molds sprayed with nonstick cooking spray. Chill until firm. Unmold onto dessert plates. Top with the strawberry sauce.
- Yield: 5 servings.

BUTTERMILK STRAWBERRY SHERBET

This is a wonderful light dessert.

- Combine buttermilk, honey, lemon juice, lemon rind and vanilla in food processor or blender container; process until smooth.
- Process strawberries in food processor or blender until coarsely puréed. Fold into buttermilk mixture.
- Spoon into 9x13-inch dish. Freeze, covered, until firm.
- Spoon frozen mixture into large bowl; stir with wooden spoon until softened. Stir in egg whites.
- Spoon into 9x13-inch dish. Freeze until firm. Spoon into serving glasses. Garnish with sliced strawberries.
- Yield: 6 servings.

Ingredients

3 cups buttermilk
6 tablespoons honey
Juice and grated rind of 1/2 lemon
2 teaspoons vanilla extract
4 cups unsweetened fresh or
frozen strawberries
4 egg whites, stiffly beaten
Sliced strawberries

"PICTURE BOOK" SAUCE FOR FRESH FRUIT

Layer with blueberries, strawberries, peaches and bananas in a compote for a light summer dessert.

- Combine milk, orange juice and pudding mix in mixer bowl; beat at low speed for 1 minute.
- Add whipped topping; beat for 1 minute.
- May substitute orange liqueur for orange juice.
- Yield: 6 servings.

Ingredients

1 3/4 cups milk
1 tablespoon orange juice
1 (4-ounce) package vanilla
instant pudding mix
1 cup whipped topping

"PERSIMMON" AMARETTO CHEESECAKE

Ingredients

1 recipe for favorite
graham cracker pie shell
16 ounces each ricotta cheese
and sour cream
16 ounces cream cheese, softened
1 1/2 cups sugar
1/2 cup butter, softened
3 eggs
3 tablespoons each flour
and cornstarch
1 1/2 teaspoons lemon juice
1 1/2 teaspoons Amaretto

- Preheat oven to 300 degrees.
- Press graham cracker pie shell mixture into springform pan.
- Combine ricotta cheese, sour cream, cream cheese, sugar, butter, eggs, flour, cornstarch, lemon juice and Amaretto in mixer bowl; mix well.
- Spoon into prepared springform pan. Bake for 1 1/2 hours or until set. Cool on wire rack. Chill until serving time. Place on serving plate; remove side of pan.
- May substitute vanilla extract for Amaretto.
- Yield: 12 servings.

"FANTASIA" CHEESECAKE

Ingredients

1/2 cup butter, softened
1/4 cup packed brown sugar
1 cup sifted cake flour
1/2 cup chopped pecans
16 ounces cream cheese, softened
4 egg yolks
2 tablespoons flour
1/2 teaspoon salt
1/2 cup sugar
2/3 cup evaporated milk
1 teaspoon vanilla extract
4 egg whites
1/4 cup sugar

- Preheat oven to 400 degrees.
- Combine first 4 ingredients in bowl; mix well. Spoon into baking pan. Bake for 15 minutes; stir mixture with fork. Press mixture into springform pan. Reduce oven temperature to 325 degrees.
- Beat cream cheese in mixer bowl until smooth. Beat in egg yolks. Add 2 tablespoons flour, salt and 1/2 cup sugar; mix well. Blend in evaporated milk and vanilla.
- Beat egg whites in mixer bowl until soft peaks form. Add 1/4 cup sugar. Beat until stiff peaks form. Fold into cream cheese mixture.
- Spoon into crust. Bake for 55 minutes. Cool to room temperature. Chill until serving time. Place on serving plate; remove side of pan.
- Yield: 12 servings.

"DREAMWEAVER" PRALINE CHEESECAKE

- Preheat oven to 350 degrees.
- Mix graham cracker crumbs and ¼ cup butter in bowl. Press into bottom of 9-inch springform pan.
- Blend cream cheese and 1¼ cups brown sugar in large mixer bowl until smooth. Beat in eggs 1 at a time. Stir in vanilla and salt. Add chopped pecans and flour; mix well.
- Spoon into prepared pan. Bake for 50 to 55 minutes or until set. Cool. Chill, covered, overnight.
- Combine ¼ cup butter and remaining ½ cup brown sugar in small saucepan. Cook over low heat for 5 minutes or until smooth, stirring occasionally. Spoon over cheesecake. Place cheesecake on serving plate; remove side of pan. Arrange pecan halves around edge.
- Yield: 12 servings.

Ingredients

1 cup graham cracker crumbs
¼ cup melted butter
24 ounces cream cheese, softened
1¾ cups packed light brown sugar
3 eggs
1½ teaspoons vanilla extract
Salt to taste
1 cup chopped pecans plus 12 (or more) pecan halves
2 tablespoons flour
¼ cup butter

"DREAM CHASER" CHEESECAKE WITH RASPBERRIES

A favorite because it's easy with no crust and fail-proof!

- Preheat oven to 350 degrees.
- Beat cream cheese and ⅔ cup sugar in bowl until light and fluffy. Beat in eggs 1 at a time. Stir in almond extract.
- Pour into lightly buttered 10-inch pie plate. Bake for 25 minutes. Let stand until cool.
- Combine sour cream, 6 tablespoons sugar and vanilla in bowl; mix well. Pour over baked layer.
- Bake for 10 minutes longer. Let stand until cool.
- Chill in refrigerator. Top with raspberries.
- Yield: 12 servings.

Ingredients

16 ounces cream cheese, softened
⅔ cup sugar
3 eggs
1 teaspoon almond extract
2 cups sour cream
6 tablespoons sugar
1 teaspoon vanilla extract
1 pint fresh raspberries

APPLE PECAN CAKE

Best served hot out of the oven.

- Preheat oven to 350 degrees.
- Sprinkle sugar over apples in bowl; let stand for 20 minutes.
- Add oil and egg; mix well. Sift in flour, baking soda, cinnamon, allspice and salt; mix well. Stir in pecans.
- Spoon into loaf pan. Bake for 1 hour. Serve warm.
- Yield: 8 servings.

Ingredients

1 cup sugar
2 cups chopped peeled apples
1/2 cup vegetable oil
1 egg
1 1/2 cups flour
1 teaspoon baking soda
1/2 teaspoon cinnamon
1/4 teaspoon allspice
1/4 teaspoon salt
1 cup chopped pecans

MEXICAN CHOCOLATE CAKE

- Preheat oven to 350 degrees.
- Grate 3/4 cup chocolate chips and walnuts in blender.
- Beat eggs in large mixer bowl. Add sugar, brown sugar and butter; mix well. Fold in chocolate and walnut mixture. Add 2 1/2 teaspoons cinnamon, buttermilk and vanilla; mix well.
- Fold in flour, baking powder, baking soda and salt. Spoon into greased 10-inch tube pan.
- Bake for 45 to 60 minutes or until cake tests done. Cool in pan for 5 minutes. Invert onto serving plate to cool completely.
- Melt 1 cup chocolate chips in double boiler over hot water. Stir in sour cream and 1/4 teaspoon cinnamon.
- Split cake horizontally into 3 layers. Spread frosting between layers and over top and side of cake.
- Yield: 16 servings.

Ingredients

3/4 cup semisweet chocolate chips
1/2 cup walnuts
3 eggs
1/2 cup sugar
1/2 cup packed light brown sugar
2 tablespoons butter, softened
2 1/2 teaspoons cinnamon
1 cup buttermilk
1 teaspoon vanilla extract
2 cups sifted flour
1 1/2 teaspoons baking powder
1/2 teaspoon baking soda
1/4 teaspoon salt
1 cup semisweet chocolate chips
1 cup sour cream
1/4 teaspoon cinnamon

"MAIDEN'S CHAMBER" FRESH COCONUT CAKE

Use absolutely fresh coconut! Grating the coconut is a chore—but worth it!

- Preheat oven to 350 degrees.
- Spray 10-inch tube pan with nonstick cooking spray; grease and flour pan.
- Cream butter, margarine and sugar in mixer bowl until light and fluffy. Beat in eggs 1 at a time.
- Sift flour, baking powder and salt together. Add to batter alternately with milk and ½ teaspoon each flavoring, mixing well after each addition. Fold in 1 cup coconut.
- Spoon into prepared pan. Bake for 1¼ to 1½ hours or until cake tests done. Cool in pan for 20 minutes. Remove to serving plate to cool completely.
- Combine confectioners' sugar, half and half and 1 teaspoon coconut extract in bowl. Add enough evaporated milk to make of spreading consistency. Spread over cooled cake. Sprinkle with ½ cup remaining coconut.
- Yield: 16 servings.

Ingredients

1 cup each butter and margarine, softened

3 cups sugar

6 eggs

3 cups flour

1 teaspoon baking powder

½ teaspoon salt

1 cup milk

½ teaspoon each coconut and almond extract

1½ cups grated fresh coconut

1 cup confectioners' sugar, sifted

2 tablespoons half and half

1 teaspoon coconut extract

2 tablespoons evaporated milk

HAZELNUT CAKE

- Preheat oven to 375 degrees.
- Beat eggs and sugar in mixer bowl until smooth. Add 8 ounces ground hazelnuts and baking powder.
- Spoon into greased and floured 9-inch cake pan. Bake for 45 minutes. Remove to wire rack to cool; split layers.
- Whip cream in mixer bowl until soft peaks form. Fold in 4 ounces chopped hazelnuts. Spread between layers and over top of cake. Garnish with chocolate chips.
- Yield: 12 servings.

Ingredients

4 eggs

1 cup sugar

8 ounces hazelnuts, ground

1 teaspoon baking powder

2 cups whipping cream

4 ounces hazelnuts, chopped, toasted

Chocolate chips

CHOCOLATE CHIP POUND CAKE

A good groom's cake.

- Preheat oven to 325 degrees.
- Combine cream cheese, butter and sugar in food processor container; pulse 3 times. Process for 30 seconds or until smooth, scraping bowl as necessary.
- Add eggs, processing constantly for 40 seconds. Add sour cream and vanilla; process for 10 seconds. Add flour, baking powder, salt and chocolate chips; pulse 8 to 10 times or just until moistened. Fold in any remaining flour with spatula.
- Spoon batter into greased and floured 10-cup tube pan. Tap pan on counter twice. Bake in center of oven for 1 hour or until cake tests done. Cool cake in pan for 10 minutes; remove to wire rack to cool completely. Garnish with confectioners' sugar.
- Yield: 16 servings.

Ingredients

8 ounces cream cheese or light cream cheese, softened

1 cup unsalted butter, cut into 8 pieces, softened

1½ cups sugar

4 eggs

2 tablespoons sour cream

2 teaspoons vanilla extract

2¼ cups flour

2 teaspoons baking powder

¼ teaspoon salt

1 cup semisweet chocolate chips

Confectioners' sugar

"POSTCARD" FIVE-FLAVOR POUND CAKE

- Preheat oven to 325 degrees.
- Cream butter, shortening and sugar in mixer bowl until light and fluffy. Beat in eggs.
- Sift flour with baking powder. Add to batter alternately with milk, mixing well after each addition. Stir in flavorings.
- Spoon into greased and floured 10-inch tube pan. Bake for 1½ hours. Cool in pan for several minutes. Remove to wire rack to cool completely.
- Yield: 16 servings.

Ingredients

1 cup butter, softened

½ cup shortening

3 cups sugar

5 eggs, slightly beaten

3 cups flour

½ teaspoon baking powder

1 cup milk

1 teaspoon each vanilla, butternut, coconut, lemon and rum flavorings

FABULOUS LEMON POUND CAKE

- Cream butter and sugar in mixer bowl until light and fluffy. Beat in eggs.
- Add flour 1 cup at a time, mixing well after each addition. Add salt, flavorings and cream; mix well.
- Spoon into greased and floured 10-cup tube or bundt pan. Place in cold oven; set oven temperature at 325 degrees. Bake for 1 hour and 10 minutes or until cake tests done. Invert onto wire rack to cool.
- Yield: 16 servings.

Ingredients

1 cup butter, softened
3 cups sugar, sifted
6 eggs
3 cups flour, sifted twice
Salt to taste
1 teaspoon each vanilla and lemon extract
1 cup whipping cream

KATHRYN HEPBURN'S BROWNIES

- Preheat oven to 325 degrees.
- Melt 1/2 cup butter in heavy saucepan; remove from heat. Stir in 1/2 cup baking cocoa, oil and sugar. Add eggs and 1/2 teaspoon vanilla; stir to mix well. Stir in flour, salt and pecans.
- Spoon into greased 8x8-inch baking pan. Bake for 30 minutes. Cool on wire rack.
- Cream 1/4 cup butter in mixer bowl until light. Add 1/2 cup baking cocoa, 1 teaspoon vanilla, salt, confectioners' sugar and milk. Blend until smooth.
- Spread over brownies. Cut into squares.
- Yield: 16 servings.

Over the Fence: *This recipe was published in an interview with Kathryn Hepburn years ago. The secret is in the small amount of flour.*

Ingredients

1/2 cup butter
1/2 cup baking cocoa
2 tablespoons vegetable oil
1 cup sugar
2 eggs
1/2 teaspoon vanilla extract
1/4 cup flour
1/4 teaspoon salt
1 cup chopped pecans
1/4 cup butter, softened
1/2 cup baking cocoa
1 teaspoon vanilla extract
Salt to taste
2 cups confectioners' sugar
3 tablespoons milk

"ABOUT TIME"
ALMOND CHOCOLATE SQUARES

Ingredients

1/2 cup butter, softened

1/2 cup packed light brown sugar

1 1/2 cups flour

1/4 teaspoon salt

1 teaspoon vanilla extract

3/4 cup seedless raspberry jam

3 eggs

8 ounces almond paste

1/2 cup sugar

*1 cup blanched almonds,
toasted, ground*

1 teaspoon almond extract

*1 (1-ounce) square
unsweetened chocolate*

2 tablespoons butter, softened

1 1/2 cups confectioners' sugar

2 tablespoons light cream

1 tablespoon coffee liqueur

- Preheat oven to 350 degrees.

- Combine 1/2 cup butter, brown sugar, flour, salt and vanilla in mixer bowl; mix until smooth. Pat into 9x13-inch baking pan. Bake for 15 minutes or until golden brown. Spread with jam.

- Combine eggs, almond paste, sugar, almonds and almond extract in mixer bowl; mix well. Spread over baked layer. Bake for 20 minutes longer or until golden brown. Cool on wire rack.

- Melt chocolate in small saucepan over low heat or in microwave. Add 2 tablespoons butter, confectioners' sugar, cream and liqueur; mix well. Spread over baked layer. Cut into squares.

- May omit liqueur if preferred.

- Yield: 36 servings.

Over the Fence: For Easy Beach Combing Brownies, spread half a package of refrigerator brownie dough in 9-inch square baking pan. Top with 4 sheets caramel for caramel apples and remaining dough. Bake using package directions.

Clipper Chocolate Chip Squares

- Preheat oven to 325 degrees.
- Combine butter, sugar, brown sugar, vanilla and liqueurs in mixer bowl; beat until light and fluffy. Beat in eggs.
- Mix flour, baking soda and salt together. Stir into batter. Stir in chocolate chips, walnuts, pecans and macadamia nuts.
- Drop from ice cream scoop onto ungreased cookie sheet. Bake for 16 minutes or until golden brown. Remove to wire rack to cool. Cut into squares.
- Yield: 36 servings.

Ingredients

1 cup unsalted butter, softened
3/4 cup sugar
3/4 cup packed light brown sugar
1 tablespoon vanilla extract
1 tablespoon hazelnut liqueur
1 tablespoon coffee liqueur
2 eggs
2 1/2 cups flour
1 teaspoon baking soda
1/2 teaspoon salt
4 cups milk chocolate chips
1 cup chopped walnuts
1/2 cup chopped pecans
1/2 cup chopped macadamia nuts

"C'Scape" Filled Cookies

- Preheat oven to 350 degrees.
- Combine margarine and cake mix in bowl; mix well. Add 1 egg. Spread in greased 11x13-inch baking pan.
- Mix cream cheese, 2 eggs and confectioners' sugar in bowl. Spread over cake mix layer. Sprinkle with pecans.
- Bake for 50 to 60 minutes or until golden brown. Cool on wire rack. Cut into squares. Sprinkle with remaining 2 tablespoons confectioners' sugar.
- Yield: 24 servings.

Over the Fence: When I served them at a P.T.A. board meeting, everyone wanted the recipe, including the principal.

Ingredients

1/2 cup margarine, softened
1 (2-layer) package
butter cake mix
1 egg
8 ounces cream cheese, softened
2 eggs
1 (16-ounce) package
confectioners' sugar minus 2
tablespoons for sprinkling
1 cup chopped pecans

"SHANGRI-LA" MACADAMIA NUT TEA COOKIES

Ingredients

1 cup butter, softened
1/2 cup sifted confectioners' sugar
1 teaspoon vanilla extract
2 1/2 cups sifted flour
1/4 teaspoon salt
1 cup finely chopped
macadamia nuts
1 cup confectioners' sugar

- Preheat oven to 400 degrees.
- Cream butter, 1/2 cup confectioners' sugar and vanilla in mixer bowl until light and fluffy. Sift in flour and salt; stir to mix well. Stir in macadamia nuts.
- Shape into 1-inch balls; place on ungreased cookie sheet. Bake for 10 to 12 minutes or until set but not brown.
- Roll warm cookies in 1 cup confectioners' sugar. Cool on wire rack. Roll in remaining confectioners' sugar again.
- Yield: 36 servings.

"McLAUGHLIN COTTAGE" PECAN SANDIES

Ingredients

1/2 cup shortening
1/2 cup vegetable oil
1 cup sugar
2 eggs
3 cups flour
1/2 teaspoon baking powder
1/2 teaspoon baking soda
1/2 teaspoon salt
1 cup finely chopped pecans
1/4 cup sugar

- Preheat oven to 350 degrees.
- Combine shortening, oil and 1 cup sugar in mixer bowl; beat until light. Beat in eggs.
- Add flour, baking powder, baking soda and salt; mix well. Stir in pecans.
- Shape into balls; place on cookie sheet. Press with bottom of glass dipped in 1/4 cup sugar. Bake until golden brown. Remove to wire rack to cool.
- Yield: 48 servings.

"FLAMINGO" SALTED NUT BARS

- Preheat oven to 350 degrees.
- Combine flour, brown sugar, salt and 1 cup butter in medium bowl; mix well. Press into ungreased 10x15-inch baking pan.
- Bake for 10 to 12 minutes. Sprinkle with mixed nuts.
- Bring corn syrup, 2 tablespoons butter, water and butterscotch chips to a boil in small saucepan. Boil for 2 minutes, stirring constantly. Pour over nuts.
- Bake for 10 to 12 minutes longer or until golden brown. Cool on wire rack. Cut into bars.
- Yield: 42 servings.

Ingredients

3 cups sifted flour
1 1/2 cups packed brown sugar
1 teaspoon salt
1 cup butter, softened
2 cups salted mixed nuts
1/2 cup corn syrup
2 tablespoons butter
1 tablespoon water
1 cup butterscotch chips

"DoLITTLE" CAROLINA SPICE COOKIES

- Cream shortening and 1 cup sugar in mixer bowl until light and fluffy. Add molasses and egg; mix well.
- Mix dry ingredients together. Add to creamed mixture; mix well.
- Chill for 2 hours or longer.
- Preheat oven to 350 degrees.
- Roll dough into small walnut-sized balls; roll in remaining 1 cup sugar.
- Place 2 inches apart on ungreased cookie sheet. Bake for 8 to 10 minutes or until brown.
- Remove to wire rack to cool.
- Yield: 24 servings.

Over the Fence: *Although not a particularly "fancy" cookie, I think it's very tasty, especially around the holidays—great with your favorite hot cider!*

Ingredients

3/4 cup shortening
2 cups sugar
1/4 cup molasses
1 egg, beaten
2 cups flour
2 teaspoons baking soda
1 teaspoon ground cloves
1 teaspoon ginger
1 teaspoon cinnamon
1/4 teaspoon salt

"GATEWALK" BLACK BOTTOM PIE

Ingredients

1 1/4 cups gingersnap crumbs
1/4 cup margarine
1 envelope unflavored gelatin
1 3/4 cups milk
4 egg yolks
1/2 cup sugar
1/2 teaspoon salt
4 teaspoons cornstarch
2 (1-ounce) squares
unsweetened chocolate
1 teaspoon vanilla extract
3 tablespoons rum
4 egg whites
1/2 cup sugar

- Preheat oven to 350 degrees.
- Mix cookie crumbs and margarine in bowl. Press into deep-dish pie plate. Bake for 8 minutes. Cool.
- Soften gelatin in 1/4 cup milk in small bowl. Scald remaining 1 1/2 cups milk. Beat egg yolks in double boiler. Add 1/2 cup sugar, salt and cornstarch; mix well. Stir in scalded milk gradually.
- Cook over simmering water for 4 minutes or until custard coats spoon, stirring constantly; remove from heat.
- Reserve 1/2 cup custard. Add melted chocolate to reserved custard. Stir in vanilla. Spread over cooled crust. Chill.
- Add gelatin to remaining custard, stirring to dissolve well. Chill until partially set. Add rum; mix well.
- Beat egg whites until soft peaks form. Add 1/2 cup sugar gradually, beating constantly until stiff peaks form. Fold into custard. Spoon over chocolate in crust. Chill until firm.
- Yield: 8 servings.

"C'SCAPE" CHOCOLATE CHESS PIE

Ingredients

1 1/2 cups sugar
3 tablespoons (heaping)
baking cocoa
2 eggs, beaten
1 (5-ounce) can evaporated milk
1/4 cup melted margarine
1 teaspoon vanilla extract
1 unbaked (9-inch) pie shell

- Preheat oven to 350 degrees.
- Mix sugar and baking cocoa in bowl. Add eggs, evaporated milk, margarine and vanilla; mix well.
- Spoon into pie shell. Bake for 30 to 40 minutes or until firm in center.
- Yield: 6 servings.

Over the Fence: *This easy pie brings back childhood memories because it is like those our grandmother prepared as a special treat.*

"Briar Patch" Brownie Pie

*An easy, fabulous dessert, but better
not make it on a humid day.*

- Preheat oven to 350 degrees.
- Beat egg whites with salt, cream of tartar and 1/2 cup sugar in mixer bowl until stiff peaks form. Fold in 1/4 cup baking cocoa, 1/2 cup sugar, vanilla and pecans.
- Spoon into buttered pie plate. Bake for 35 minutes. Cool to room temperature.
- Beat whipped topping with 3 tablespoons baking cocoa in mixer bowl. Spread over pie. Chill for 2 hours or longer. Garnish with finely ground pecans sprinkled in circle.
- Yield: 8 servings.

Ingredients

4 egg whites

1/8 teaspoon salt

1/8 teaspoon cream of tartar

1/2 cup sugar

1/4 cup baking cocoa

1/2 cup sugar

1 teaspoon vanilla extract

1 cup chopped pecans

12 ounces light whipped topping

3 tablespoons baking cocoa

Finely ground pecans

"Easter Cottage" Chocolate Pecan Pie

- Preheat oven to 375 degrees.
- Combine pecans and bourbon in bowl; set aside.
- Combine eggs, sugar, corn syrup, butter and vanilla in bowl; mix well. Stir in chocolate chips and pecan mixture. Pour into pie shell.
- Bake for 55 to 60 minutes or until set.
- Yield: 8 servings.

Over the Fence: We first tasted this pie in a restaurant near Pleasant Hill, Kentucky. I searched until I found a recipe that was very similar—a favorite of all!

Ingredients

1/2 cup chopped pecans

2 tablespoons plus
1 teaspoon bourbon

5 eggs, beaten

1 cup sugar

3/4 cup light corn syrup

1/4 cup butter, melted

1 teaspoon vanilla extract

1/2 cup semisweet chocolate chips

1 unbaked (9-inch) pie shell

"DREAMWEAVER" COCONUT CARAMEL PIES

Ingredients

1 (7-ounce) package coconut

1 cup chopped pecans

6 tablespoons melted margarine

8 ounces cream cheese, softened

1 cup sweetened condensed milk

16 ounces whipped topping

1 (12-ounce) jar caramel ice cream topping

2 baked (9-inch) deep-dish pie shells

- Toast coconut and pecans lightly in margarine in skillet; set aside.
- Combine cream cheese and condensed milk in mixer bowl; mix until smooth. Fold in whipped topping.
- Layer cream cheese mixture, caramel topping and coconut mixture 1/2 at a time in each pie shell.
- Freeze pies until firm. Serve frozen.
- Yield: 12 servings.

"LAST EDITION" KAHLUA PIE

A wonderful pie for hot summer days at Seaside.

Ingredients

20 graham crackers, crushed

3 tablespoons brown sugar

1/3 cup butter, softened

1 cup whipping cream

1/2 cup sifted confectioners' sugar

1/4 cup Kahlua

4 egg yolks

- Mix graham cracker crumbs, brown sugar and butter in bowl. Reserve 2 tablespoons mixture; press remaining mixture into 9-inch pie plate. Chill in refrigerator.
- Whip cream in mixer bowl until soft peaks form. Fold in confectioners' sugar and liqueur. Beat egg yolks in mixer bowl until thick and lemon-colored. Fold into whipped cream mixture.
- Spoon into pie shell; top with reserved crumb mixture. Freeze until firm. Serve frozen.
- Yield: 8 servings.

"SOUTHERN SPLENDOR" COOKIE CRUST LEMON PIE

- Preheat oven to 325 degrees.
- Mix vanilla wafer crumbs with 2 to 3 tablespoons butter in bowl. Press over bottom of buttered pie plate; arrange whole wafers around edge.
- Combine condensed milk, egg yolks, lemon juice and lemon rind in bowl; mix well. Spoon into prepared pie plate.
- Beat egg whites in mixer bowl until soft peaks form. Add sugar gradually, beating constantly until stiff peaks form. Spread over pie, sealing to edge. Bake for 10 to 15 minutes or until golden brown.
- Yield: 8 servings.

Ingredients

1 cup vanilla wafer crumbs
2 to 3 tablespoons butter, softened
16 whole vanilla wafers
1 (14-ounce) can sweetened condensed milk
3 egg yolks
1/2 cup fresh lemon juice
1 tablespoon grated lemon rind
3 egg whites
5 to 6 tablespoons sugar

MARGARITA PIE

- Combine pretzel crumbs, butter and 3 tablespoons sugar in bowl; mix well. Press into 9-inch pie plate. Chill in refrigerator. Sprinkle gelatin over lemon juice in small bowl; let stand until softened.
- Beat egg yolks in double boiler. Stir in 1/2 cup sugar, salt and lemon rind. Cook over boiling water until thickened, stirring constantly. Stir in gelatin until dissolved.
- Combine with Tequila and Triple Sec in bowl; mix well. Chill in refrigerator.
- Beat egg whites in mixer bowl until foamy. Add 1/2 cup sugar gradually, beating constantly until stiff peaks form. Fold into chilled mixture.
- Spoon into prepared pie plate. Chill until serving time.
- Yield: 8 servings.

Ingredients

3/4 cup finely crushed pretzels
1/3 cup butter
3 tablespoons sugar
1 envelope unflavored gelatin
1/2 cup lemon juice
4 egg yolks
1/2 cup sugar
1/4 teaspoon salt
1 teaspoon grated lemon rind
1/3 cup Tequila
3 tablespoons Triple Sec
4 egg whites
1/2 cup sugar

"BAGBY-JAMES" MELBA PIE

Ingredients

7 ounces flaked coconut

1/2 cup chopped almonds

1/4 cup (or more) melted butter

1 quart peach ice
cream, softened

1 pint vanilla ice cream, softened

2 (10-ounce) packages frozen
raspberries, thawed

1 cup sugar

2 tablespoons cornstarch

1 cup sliced fresh peaches

- Preheat oven to 325 degrees.
- Combine coconut, almonds and butter in bowl; mix well. Press firmly into buttered 9-inch pie plate. Bake until light brown. Cool to room temperature. Chill in freezer.
- Spoon peach ice cream into prepared plate. Freeze, tightly wrapped, until firm. Spread vanilla ice cream over peach ice cream. Freeze, tightly wrapped, until firm.
- Drain raspberries, reserving syrup. Combine reserved syrup with sugar and cornstarch in saucepan. Cook until thickened, stirring constantly. Fold in raspberries. Cool to room temperature.
- Arrange peach slices on top of ice cream. Drizzle with raspberry sauce.
- Yield: 6 servings.

"SANDPIPER" PRALINE PEACH PIE

Ingredients

6 or 7 large peaches,
peeled, sliced

3/4 cup sugar

3 tablespoons quick-cooking
tapioca

1 unbaked (9-inch) pie shell

1/2 cup flour

1/4 cup packed brown sugar

1/4 cup butter

1/2 cup chopped pecans

- Preheat oven to 450 degrees.
- Toss peaches with sugar and tapioca in bowl. Spoon into pie shell.
- Combine flour, brown sugar, butter and pecans in bowl; mix well. Sprinkle over pie.
- Bake pie for 10 minutes. Reduce oven temperature to 350 degrees. Bake for 20 minutes longer.
- Yield: 8 servings.

"ENGLISH COTTAGE" WHITE PEACH PIE

- Preheat oven to 425 degrees.
- Pour boiling water over shortening in bowl; stir until smooth. Sift in flour, baking powder and salt; mix to form dough. Divide into 2 portions. Roll each portion on floured surface.
- Toss peaches with lemon juice in bowl. Mix sugar, flour and cinnamon together. Add to peaches; mix lightly.
- Fit 1 portion pastry into 9-inch pie plate. Spoon peach mixture into prepared plate; dot with margarine. Top with remaining pastry; seal edges and cut vents. Cover edge with 2-inch to 3-inch strip of foil.
- Bake pie for 20 to 30 minutes. Remove foil. Bake until crust is golden brown and filling is bubbly.
- Yield: 8 servings.

Ingredients

1/3 cup boiling water

2/3 cup shortening

2 cups flour

1/2 teaspoon baking powder

1/2 teaspoon salt

6 cups sliced fresh white peaches

1 teaspoon fresh lemon juice

3/4 cup sugar

1/4 cup flour

1/4 teaspoon cinnamon

2 tablespoons margarine

"NARNIA" SOUTHERN PECAN PIE

- Preheat oven to 400 degrees.
- Beat eggs slightly in medium mixer bowl. Stir in corn syrup, sugar, butter, vanilla and salt. Stir in pecans.
- Spoon into pie shell; arrange pecans flat side down.
- Bake for 15 minutes. Reduce oven temperature to 350 degrees. Bake for 25 to 30 minutes longer or until puffed and light brown.
- Yield: 8 servings.

Over the Fence: *This recipe came from my mother, who made her own pastry. I find that the All Ready pie pastries from the refrigerator section in the market work very well; with some fancy forkwork and crimping on the edge, the crust will look like you knocked yourself out.*

Ingredients

3 eggs

1 cup light corn syrup

1 cup (scant) sugar

2 tablespoons melted butter

2 teaspoons vanilla extract

1/8 teaspoon salt

1 cup pecan halves

1 unbaked (9-inch) pie shell

ttage • Floridays • For Keeps • Forsythe Cottage • Frascogna Cott
ant's Roost • GoodnightMoon • Gorlin Cottage • Grayton One • Gray
nor • Gulfview • Gull Cottage • Haardt Cottage • Hampton • Harvest
dges Cottage • Home Alone • Honalee • Hoover Cottage • House
smine • Jasper • Jennifer's Castle • Josephine's • Jubilee • Kaleido
st Edition • Latitude • LeBlanc Cottage • Leeward • Lehman Cotta
ndpine Lodge • Loblolly Pine • Lost Cottage • Lucky's Cottage • L
rtha Green • McChesney Cottage • McCollister Cottage • McLaughli
Mirador • Mis B'Haven • Moon Shadow • Morning Fun • Nancy's F
ttage • On the Veranda • Ondine • Orth Cottage • Outer Banks • Ov
lican Perch • Periwinkle • Persimmon • Persuasion • Peterson Cott
ttage • Postcard • Precious • Propinquity • Puglin • Rainbow • Re
bin's Nest • Roger's Lighthouse • Romance • Rooftops • Rose Cotta
andia • Sandpail • Sandpiper • Savannah Rose • Savannah Sands •
alink • Seaquel • Seaspell • Seastar • Seawynds • Serendipity • Shar
omewhere In Time • Southern Comfort • Southern Splendor • Spinn
ndance • Sundaze • Sunnyside Up • Sunrise • Sunrise Wishes • Sun
use • The Conservatory • This Is the Life • Tide's Inn • Tiger Paw
eeze • Toye • Treetops • Trio • Tropical Holiday • Tupelo Honey • Tup
Wakeham Cottage • Waterside • Wayback • Weber Cottage • Wilder
e Beach • Zebulon • Zeidman Cottage • Zurn Cottage • A Summe

Rainy Days & Sunburns

(or any reason to stay indoors...)

ttage • American Dream • Anderson Cottage • Anniston • April 16
ttage • Beach Walk • Bella Vista • Belvedere • Benedictus • Beside
te • Boswell Cottage • Briar Patch • Brickwalk • Bridgeport • Brier
llaway Cottage • Cape May • Carey Cottage • Caribbean • Carpe D

...Here bout the beach I wandered, nourishing a youth sublime
With the fairy tales of science, and the long result of time;...
Alfred, Lord Tennyson

Rainy Days & Sunburns

Ice Cream Sandwiches, 185

Dirt Cake, 185

Fruit Pizza, 186

Beary Good Snack Mix, 187

Clown Face Sundae, 187

Whoopie Pies, 188

Ooey Gooey Cake, 189

Cupcake Cones, 189

Peanut Butter Fudge, 190

Peanut Butter Honeybees, 190

Sweet Spiced Nuts, 191

Quick Graham Cracker Delights, 191

"Oh Henry" Bars, 192

Peanut Butter Cup Cookies, 192

Snickerdoodles, 193

Dottie L's Cookies, 193

Stained Glass Cookies, 194

Sinkhole Cheese Pie, 194

Chocolate Bar Pie, 195

Daddy's Favorite Peanut Butter Pies, 195

Perspective

Long ago when we were smaller,
Grownups then were much, much taller,
Men were stronger, braver, bolder,
Old was ever so much older!

Skies were wider and much bluer,
Grass was greener, clouds were fewer,
Nights were darker, stars were brighter,
Snows far deeper and much whiter.

Food was yummier, odors headier,
Fun was easier, laughter readier,
Life much simpler, all in all,
In those days when we were small.

—Helen Lowrie Marshall

"DREAMWEAVER" ICE CREAM SANDWICHES

- Line 8x8-inch dish with ½ of the graham crackers.
- Combine egg yolks, sugar, flour, milk and salt in double boiler; mix well.
- Cook over boiling water until slightly thickened, stirring constantly. Cool.
- Stir in vanilla. Fold in egg whites and whipped cream. Spoon into prepared dish. Top with remaining graham crackers. Freeze until set.
- Yield: 9 servings.

Ingredients

12 to 15 whole graham crackers
2 egg yolks, slightly beaten
¾ cup sugar
2 tablespoons flour
½ cup milk
Salt to taste
1 teaspoon vanilla extract
2 egg whites, stiffly beaten
2 cups whipping cream, whipped

"WILDER" DIRT CAKE

I know I look strange, but dig right in.
The flowers are fake, but the dirt is cake.
I don't need water or Tender Loving Care.
Just eat my dirt til my pot is bare.

- Line 8-inch flowerpot or sand pail with foil.
- Cream margarine, confectioners' sugar and cream cheese in mixer bowl until smooth.
- Prepare pudding mix using package directions using 3½ cups milk. Fold in whipped topping. Add to cream cheese mixture; mix well.
- Layer ½ of the cookie crumbs and the pudding mixture in prepared flowerpot. Sprinkle with remaining cookie crumbs. Decorate with artificial flowers, gummy worms and a gardening trowel or sand shovel.
- Yield: 8 servings.

Ingredients

¼ cup margarine, softened
1 cup confectioners' sugar
8 ounces cream cheese, softened
2 (4-ounce) packages vanilla instant pudding mix
3½ cups milk
12 ounces whipped topping
40 ounces Oreo cookies, crushed

"Picture Book" Fruit Pizza

Ingredients

1/2 cup margarine, softened

3/4 cup sugar

2 cups flour

1 teaspoon vanilla extract

1 cup chopped pecans

8 ounces cream cheese, softened

3 cups confectioners' sugar

12 ounces whipped topping

1 cup sliced strawberries

1 cup chopped peaches

1 cup blueberries

1 cup purple and green
grape halves

1/4 cup cornstarch

2 cups orange juice

11/2 cups sugar

Salt to taste

- Preheat oven to 350 degrees.

- Cream margarine and 3/4 cup sugar in mixer bowl until light and fluffy. Add flour and vanilla; mix well. Pat into round baking pan. Sprinkle with pecans.

- Bake for 10 minutes. Cool for 10 minutes.

- Beat cream cheese and confectioners' sugar in mixer bowl until smooth. Fold in whipped topping.

- Spread over baked layer.

- Arrange strawberries, peaches, blueberries and grapes over cream cheese layer.

- Combine cornstarch and orange juice in saucepan, stirring until cornstarch dissolves. Stir in 11/2 cups sugar and salt. Boil for 1 minute. Cool for 5 minutes. Pour over fruit.

- Chill until serving time.

- May also use bananas, canned cherries, canned pineapple chunks, kiwifruit or any combination of fruits.

- Yield: 12 servings.

Just for Fun

Create **Spicy Sachets** for Mom. Mix 1 cup of cinnamon, 1 cup of applesauce, 1 tablespoon of allspice and 1 tablespoon of nutmeg in a bowl and shape the mixture into a ball. Roll it 1/4 inch thick on waxed paper. Cut into desired shapes and make a hole in the top of each shape with a drinking straw. Let stand on the waxed paper for 2 or 3 days or until dry, turning the shapes occasionally. Tie a ribbon through the top hole to hang it. Use Christmas cookie cutters to make ornaments at Christmas time. You also may shape the dough into beads and make holes through them with the straw. When dry, string the beads on a string.

BEARY GOOD SNACK MIX

- Combine bears, cereal, peanuts and raisins in bowl; mix gently.
- Store in plastic food storage bag.
- Yield: 8 to 10 servings.

Ingredients

2 cups bear-shaped
graham snacks
2 cups honey-nut oat cereal
1 cup peanuts
1/2 cup raisins

CLOWN FACE SUNDAE

- Place ice cream in center of dessert dish. Press cone into ice cream to resemble hat.
- Arrange chocolate chips for eyes and mouth and maraschino cherry for nose. Press points of wafers into base of ice cream for collar.
- May use any flavor ice cream.
- Yield: 1 serving.

Ingredients

1 scoop chocolate ice cream
1 pointed ice cream cone
3 chocolate chips
1 maraschino cherry
3 or 4 ice cream wafers, cut
into triangles

Just for Fun

Tissue Paper Art is fun and easy to do. Cut designs from tissue paper, using as many colors as desired. Arrange the designs on construction paper and spray them lightly with water. Let them stand for several minutes for tissue colors to bleed onto the paper. Remove the tissue paper to reveal the colored print. You can also arrange strips of tissue paper on the construction paper and paint them carefully with a wet brush. When the strips are removed, the design will remain.

"SOMEWHERE IN TIME" WHOOPIE PIES

Ingredients

1 cup sugar

1 egg

5 tablespoons shortening

1½ teaspoons baking soda

5 tablespoons baking cocoa

2 cups flour

1 cup milk

½ cup shortening

½ cup margarine

½ cup marshmallow creme

½ cup (heaping) confectioners' sugar

1 teaspoon vanilla extract

- Preheat oven to 425 degrees.
- Beat sugar, egg and 5 tablespoons shortening in mixer bowl until smooth. Add baking soda, cocoa, flour and milk; mix well.
- Drop by teaspoonfuls onto ungreased cookie sheet.
- Bake for 7 minutes. Remove to wire rack to cool.
- Beat ½ cup shortening, margarine, marshmallow creme, confectioners' sugar and vanilla in mixer bowl until smooth. Spread mixture over ½ of the cookies; top with remaining cookies.
- Yield: 12 servings.

Over the Fence: I made this recipe for my children when they were growing up in Maine. I doubled the filling recipe because they loved the extra filling. The cookies are great warm out of the oven, but my husband prefers them cold. I wrap each sandwich cookie individually in plastic wrap and store them in the refrigerator.

Just for Fun

Preparing edible play dough is a good rainy day activity. For *Chocolate Play Dough*, mix 1 package of confectioners' sugar with one 4-ounce package of chocolate instant pudding mix. Add ½ cup peanut butter, ⅓ cup softened margarine and 4 to 5 tablespoons milk and mix until smooth. You can play with this until snack time and then eat your creations, but be sure to wash your hands before you begin and play on a clean surface.

"HAYFORD COTTAGE" OOEY GOOEY CAKE

- Preheat oven to 350 degrees.
- Combine cake mix, butter and eggs in bowl; mix well. Pat into greased 9x13-inch cake pan.
- Beat confectioners' sugar and cream cheese in mixer bowl until smooth. Spoon evenly over prepared layer.
- Bake for 35 to 40 minutes or until edges pull from sides of pan. Remove to wire rack to cool completely.
- Sprinkle with additional confectioners' sugar.
- Yield: 15 servings.

Ingredients

1 (2-layer) package yellow cake mix

1/2 cup melted butter

2 eggs, beaten

1 (16-ounce) package confectioners' sugar

8 ounces cream cheese, softened

CUPCAKE CONES

- Preheat oven to 350 degrees.
- Prepare cake mix using package directions. Spoon batter into ice cream cones. Place on baking sheet.
- Bake until your mom says the cake in the cones tests done. Remove to wire rack to cool.
- Frost with your favorite icing. Sprinkle with sugar sprinkles, chocolate chips or red hot candies.
- Yield: 12 servings.

Ingredients

1 (2-layer) package chocolate cake mix

12 flat-bottom ice cream cones

Just for Fun

Chunky Chalk is fun to use, even for little hands. Mix 2 tablespoons of powdered tempera paint and 3 tablespoons of plaster of Paris in one 5-ounce paper cup. Add 3 tablespoons of cold water and mix for 1 minute. Let it stand for 1 hour or until firm. Peel away the cup and use like chalk for drawing. Dip the chalk in water to use after the first day.

"BRIERMOR BY THE SEA"
PEANUT BUTTER FUDGE

Ingredients

1 cup melted margarine

2 cups graham cracker crumbs

1 (16-ounce) package
confectioners' sugar

1 tablespoon vanilla extract

1 (18-ounce) jar chunky
peanut butter

2 (18-ounce) Hershey
bars, melted

- Combine margarine, graham cracker crumbs, confectioners' sugar and vanilla in bowl; mix well. Stir in peanut butter.

- Spoon into 9x13-inch dish. Drizzle with melted chocolate.

- May add a small amount of milk to chocolate for desired consistency.

- Yield: 30 servings.

"TUPELO HONEY"
PEANUT BUTTER HONEYBEES

Ingredients

1/2 cup peanut butter

1 tablespoon honey

1/3 cup nonfat instant dry milk

2 tablespoons sesame seeds

2 tablespoons toasted wheat germ

2 to 3 tablespoons baking cocoa

1/2 cup sliced almonds

- Combine peanut butter and honey in bowl; mix well. Stir in milk powder, sesame seeds and wheat germ.

- Shape by teaspoonfuls into bee-shaped ovals. Place on waxed paper.

- Dip wooden pick into cocoa; press across oval to make stripes. Attach sliced almonds for wings.

- Yield: 24 servings.

Over the Fence: These are a wonderful special snack to take to school or enjoy at home. I have yet to find a child who does not love them. We sometimes make sugar cookies shaped like sunflowers with chocolate sprinkles in the center to accompany the bees. Not only are they good for you, but they are fun and easy to make.

"Narnia" Sweet Spiced Nuts

My girls and I make these for Christmas gifts for our neighbors. It is easy enough for five-year-olds to help prepare and grown-ups love the results!

- Preheat oven to 250 degrees.
- Combine sugar, cinnamon, cloves, salt, ginger and nutmeg in bowl; mix well.
- Beat egg white and cold water in mixer bowl until frothy. Stir in sugar mixture. Add pecans, tossing to coat. Spread on buttered baking sheet.
- Bake for 1 hour, stirring every 15 to 20 minutes. Cool. Store in airtight container.
- May substitute any type of nuts for pecans.
- Yield: 32 servings.

Ingredients

1 cup sugar
1½ tablespoons cinnamon
1 teaspoon ground cloves
1 teaspoon salt
1 teaspoon ginger
½ teaspoon nutmeg
1 egg white
1 tablespoon cold water
1 pound pecan halves

Quick Graham Cracker Delights

Very simple and a good "first" baking project with children.

- Preheat oven to 325 degrees.
- Combine graham cracker crumbs, condensed milk and chocolate chips in bowl; mix well. Spoon into small baking pan.
- Bake for 10 to 15 minutes or until edges are crisp. Remove to wire rack to cool before slicing.
- May add chopped nuts to mixture.
- Yield: 12 servings.

Ingredients

11 graham crackers, crushed
1 (14-ounce) can sweetened condensed milk
1 cup chocolate chips

Just for Fun

Bring the ocean inside on rainy days with an *Ocean-in-a-Bottle*.
Fill a clear plastic soda bottle ¾ full with water. Add baby oil and food coloring as desired. Add tiny shells, beads, sequins and other small decorative items. Screw or glue the top securely on the bottle and shake the bottle to enjoy the designs.

"OH HENRY" BARS

Ingredients

2/3 cup butter, softened
1 cup packed brown sugar
1/3 cup light corn syrup
4 cups rolled oats
1 tablespoon vanilla extract
1 cup semisweet chocolate chips, melted
2/3 cup chunky peanut butter

- Preheat oven to 350 degrees.
- Cream butter and brown sugar in mixer bowl until light and fluffy. Stir in corn syrup, oats and vanilla. Pat into 9x13-inch baking pan.
- Bake for 15 minutes. Remove to wire rack to cool.
- Spread baked layer with mixture of chocolate chips and peanut butter. Let stand until set. Cut into bars.
- Yield: 36 servings.

"TIDE'S INN" PEANUT BUTTER CUP COOKIES

Ingredients

1 roll refrigerator cookie dough, cut into 9 slices
36 miniature peanut butter cups

Children adore these! Great for parties and after-school treats.
- Preheat oven to 350 degrees.
- Cut each cookie slice into fourths. Place each piece in a greased miniature muffin cup.
- Bake for 8 to 10 minutes or until brown. Place peanut butter cups over baked layers. Cool. Remove from pan.
- Yield: 36 servings.

Just for Fun

Watch your own **Crystal Garden** grow. Place several small pieces of charcoal in a small shallow bowl. Mix 1/4 cup water, 1 tablespoon ammonia and 1/4 cup salt together and pour over the charcoal. Dot with several drops of colored ink. After several days, crystals will begin to form and grow on the charcoal. The ink will form colored crystals; other crystals will be white.

"DREAM CHASER" SNICKERDOODLES

Nicole prepares these for her own afternoon tea.

- Cream butter, 1¼ cups sugar, eggs, flavorings and lemon juice in mixer bowl until light and fluffy. Beat in mixture of flour, cream of tartar, baking soda and salt.
- Chill, covered, for 1 hour. Shape into 1-inch balls. Roll in mixture of 2 tablespoons sugar and cinnamon. Place on cookie sheet.
- Preheat oven to 375 degrees.
- Bake for 10 minutes. Remove to wire rack to cool.
- Do not substitute margarine for butter in this recipe.
- Yield: 36 servings.

Ingredients

1 cup butter, softened
1¼ cups sugar
2 eggs
½ teaspoon vanilla extract
½ teaspoon almond extract
1 teaspoon lemon juice
2¾ cups flour
2 teaspoons cream of tartar
1 teaspoon baking soda
½ teaspoon salt
2 tablespoons sugar
1 teaspoon cinnamon

DOTTIE L'S COOKIES

- Preheat oven to 350 degrees.
- Cream brown sugar and butter in mixer bowl until light and fluffy. Add eggs, flour, baking powder, baking soda, vanilla and salt; mix well.
- Drop by teaspoonfuls onto ungreased cookie sheet.
- Bake for 5 to 7 minutes or until brown. Remove to wire rack to cool.
- Yield: 30 servings.

Over the Fence: Dottie was a good friend of my mother, and we children grew up enjoying these cookies. Now our children and grandchildren enjoy them at Curphey Cottage.

Ingredients

1 (16-ounce) package
dark brown sugar
1 cup butter, softened
2 eggs
2¼ cups flour
1 teaspoon baking powder
1 teaspoon baking soda
2 teaspoons vanilla extract
Salt to taste

"FANTASIA" STAINED GLASS COOKIES

These make great gifts for Christmas.

Ingredients

1 (16-ounce) package hard
candies in assorted colors
1/3 cup shortening
1/3 cup sugar
2/3 cup honey
1 egg
1 teaspoon lemon extract
3 cups flour
1 teaspoon baking soda
1 teaspoon salt

- Preheat oven to 300 degrees. Line cookie sheet with foil; grease foil.
- Place candy of each color in separate containers; crush.
- Cream next 5 ingredients in mixer bowl until light and fluffy. Beat in sifted mixture of flour, baking soda and salt. May knead in additional flour to make stiffer dough. Roll dough into 1/8-inch strips on lightly floured surface.
- Shape into assorted Christmas shapes on prepared cookie sheet. Spoon crushed candy into areas between strips of dough.
- Bake for 10 minutes. Cool on cookie sheet. Remove carefully from foil.
- Yield: 30 servings.

"BAGBY-JAMES" SINKHOLE CHEESE PIE

After baking, the crust will "sink" forming a shell for the filling.

Ingredients

16 ounces cream cheese, softened
3 eggs
1 cup sugar
1 teaspoon almond extract
2 cups sour cream
2/3 cup sugar
1 teaspoon vanilla extract

- Preheat oven to 325 degrees.
- Beat cream cheese in mixer bowl until smooth. Beat in eggs 1 at a time. Add 1 cup sugar and almond extract.
- Beat for 5 minutes, scraping bowl occasionally. Spread in 10-inch pie plate.
- Bake for 45 minutes. Cool on wire rack for 20 minutes.
- Beat sour cream, 2/3 cup sugar and vanilla in mixer bowl until blended. Spread evenly over baked layer.
- Bake for 20 to 30 minutes longer or until set. Chill in refrigerator. Store in refrigerator for up to 2 weeks.
- Yield: 8 servings.

"CURPHEY COTTAGE" CHOCOLATE BAR PIE

- Combine candy bars, marshmallows and milk in double boiler. Cook over boiling water until blended, stirring frequently. Cool.
- Fold whipped cream into chocolate mixture. Spoon into pie shell.
- Chill until serving time.
- Yield: 6 servings.

Ingredients

4 (2-ounce) chocolate
candy bars
16 marshmallows
1/2 cup milk
1 cup whipping cream, whipped
1 (9-inch) graham cracker
pie shell

DADDY'S FAVORITE PEANUT BUTTER PIES

- Beat confectioners' sugar, milk, peanut butter and cream cheese in mixer bowl until smooth. Fold in whipped topping.
- Spoon into pie shells. Freeze.
- Yield: 18 servings.

Ingredients

4 cups confectioners' sugar
1 cup milk
1 cup creamy peanut butter
8 ounces cream cheese, softened
16 ounces whipped topping
3 (9-inch) graham cracker
pie shells

Just for Fun

Make your own **Soap Bubbles**. Mix 1 cup of water with 2 tablespoons
of liquid detergent, 1 tablespoon of glycerine and 1/2 teaspoon of sugar in a
small plastic jar. Twist the end of a pipe cleaner to form a loop. Dip the
loop into the soap mixture and blow through the loop. An empty spool also
works well—blow gently or wave spool to float bubbles through the air.

elSea • Clark Cottage • Colony • Colors • Compass Rose • Coqu
ttage • Creole • C'Scape • Cubbie Hole • Curphey Cottage • Dahlgr
stle • Delor Cottage • DeoGratis • Desire • DoLittle House • Dollhou
tcher • Dream Chaser • Dream On • Dreamsicle • Dreamweaver
ttage • Eclipse • Ecstasea • Eden • Elegance • Enchantment • Engli
ttage • Floridays • For Keeps • Fortune Cottage • Frascogna Cott
nt's Roost • Goodnight • Gotham • Gotham One • Gray
nor • Gulfview • Gull Cottage • Haardt Cottage • Hampton • Harvest
dges Cottage • Home Alone • Honalee • Hoover Cottage • House
smine • Jasper • Jennifer's Castle • Josephine's • Jubilee • Kaleido
st Edition • Latitude • LeBlanc Cottage • Leeward • Lehman Cotta
ndpine Lodge • Lonesome Dove • Lost Goggles • Lowe Cottage • L
rtha Green • McChesney Cottage • McCollister Cottage • McLaughl
lirador • Mis B'Haven • Modica Cottage • Moore Fun • Nancy's Fa
ttage • On the Veranda • Ondine • Orth Cottage • Outer Banks • Ov
lican Perch • Periwinkle • Persimmon • Persuasion • Peterson Cott
ttage • Postcard • Precious • Propinquity • Puglin • Rainbow • Re
bin's Nest • Roger's Lighthouse • Romance • Rooftops • Rose Cotta
andia • Sandpail • Sandpiper • Savannah Rose • Savannah Sands
alink • Seaquel • Seaspell • Seastar • Seawynds • Serendipity • Shar
omewhere In Time • Southern Comfort • Southern Splendor • Spinn

Seaside Restaurant Sampler

...All things that love the sun are out of doors;
The sky rejoices in the morning's birth;...
William Wordsworth

ndance • Sundaze • Sunnyside Up • Sunrise • Sunrise Wishes • Sun
use • The Conservatory • This Is the Life • Tide's Inn • Tiger Paw
eeze • Toye • Treetops • Trio • Tropical Holiday • Tupelo Honey • Tup
akeham Cottage • Waterside • Wayback • Weber Cottage • Wilder

oral Cove • Corn Cottage • Crackerbox • Craige Cottage • Crawfo
age • Dapper's Den • Dargusch Cottage • Daydream Believer • Days
lphin Inn • Domino • Dove Crest • Dragon's Lair • Dragonette • Dre
Duffy Cottage • Dune • Dunseth Cottage • DuPuis Cottage • Eas
age • Eno Eyer Cottage • Fantasia • Fernleigh • Flam go • Fletch
rumious Ba o • Getaway
o • Green Co t Cottage • G
Hayford Co s Greenhous
ls • Hurrah! Cottage • Iv
Kennedy C er • La. Hous
onardo da Dipper • Li
ottage • Mag tage • Maris
age • Mellow Night's Dre
Narnia • Nat irvana • Ols
! • Park Pla ches 'n Crea
icture Book Crazy • Porte
Renaissan y's • Roanok
an's Castle e • Sandi Sho
Cottage • S wo • Sea Vie
Shell Seeke Smith Cotta
Stanziale Co inger Cottag

ams • Suntir ng • The Bea
on-the-Sea opisaw • Tov
ker Towe Up On The Roof • Veranda • Villa Whimsey Vista del M
• Windler Cottage • Windsept II • Windward • Woodlawn • Wright

BASMATI'S

Spring Rolls

Green Salad with
Basmati Salad Dressing

Curry Shrimp

Hot Oolong Tea

ASIAN · CUISINE

Basmati's
Quincy Circle
904-231-1366

CURRY SHRIMP

- Stir-fry green onions and ginger in heated oil in wok. Add shrimp. Stir-fry until shrimp are pink.
- Add snow peas, tomato, sugar, curry powder and salt; mix well. Stir in coconut milk. Cook for 2 minutes.
- Spoon into serving dish. Serve with rice and bowls of raisins, pineapple and peanuts for topping.
- You may substitute broccoli for snow peas.
- Yield: 4 servings.

~

Over the Fence: The name Basmati is taken from an aromatic rice that originated in Northern India, but Basmati's cuisine is more influenced by Shueh-Mei's Chinese background. The philosophy behind Basmati's is to offer a contemporary blend of Asian ingredients and techniques with locally available fresh fish, seafood and produce . . . resulting in a truly unique "nouveau Asian" dining experience. Charles Bush and Shueh-Mei Pong, husband-and-wife team, opened Basmati's in May of 1990.

Ingredients

1/4 cup chopped green onions

1 tablespoon chopped fresh gingerroot

1/4 cup vegetable oil

1 pound fresh shrimp, peeled

8 ounces snow peas

1 large tomato, chopped

1 teaspoon sugar

1/4 cup curry powder

Salt to taste

2/3 cup coconut milk

4 cups cooked basmati rice

1/2 cup sherried raisins

1/2 cup chopped pineapple

1 cup peanuts

BUD & ALLEY'S

Goat Cheese and Vegetable Quesadillas with
Cilantro Crème Fraiche and
Roasted Pumpkin Seed Purée

Yellowtail Snapper with
Fire-roasted Tomato Tarragon Sauce

Arugula Salad with
Shaved Pecorino and Roasted Pine Nuts

Girgich Hills Sauvignon Blanc

RESTAURANT

Bud & Alley's
Scenic Route 30-A
904-231-5900

YELLOWTAIL SNAPPER WITH FIRE-ROASTED TOMATO TARRAGON SAUCE

- Coat the fish fillets lightly with a mixture of flour, sea salt and pepper. Heat mixture of peanut oil and 1 tablespoon butter to 375 degrees in skillet. Sauté fish in oil mixture until golden brown on both sides. Drain fish on paper towels. Remove fish to serving plate.

- Add tarragon, garlic and shallots to drippings in skillet. Cook over medium-high heat, tossing briefly.

- Add wine, stirring to deglaze skillet. Stir in 1/3 cup fish stock and roasted tomatoes. Cook until reduced by 2/3.

- Reduce heat to medium. Whisk in 1/4 cup butter gradually. Adjust seasonings. Spoon sauce over fish. Garnish with additional sprigs of fresh tarragon.

- To make stock, combine stock ingredients.

- Add 2 quarts water. Bring to a boil. Simmer for 20 minutes, skimming foam. Strain through cheesecloth.

- Yield: 4 servings.

Over the Fence: Bud & Alley's has been a warm, friendly gathering place in Seaside for close to 10 years. The popular eatery is legendary for its consistently superb regional cuisine and comfortable beach setting. The Roof-top Bar is the favorite spot to hang out with friends for Tapas, cocktails and spectacular sunsets. Rated as one of the top restaurants in Florida by Florida Trend Magazine. Award of Excellence winner, Wine Spectator Magazine. (Serving lunch and dinner daily. Reservations recommended for dinner.)

Fish Ingredients

2 (2- to 3 1/2-pound) whole yellowtail snappers, deboned, skinned

1 cup flour

1 tablespoon sea salt

1 teaspoon freshly ground pepper

1/4 cup peanut oil

1 tablespoon butter

1/4 cup coarsely chopped tarragon leaves

3 cloves of garlic, coarsely chopped

4 shallots, coarsely chopped

1/3 cup dry sauvignon blanc

1/3 cup fish stock

4 oven-roasted plum tomatoes, coarsely chopped

1/4 cup cold butter, chopped

Stock Ingredients

2 bay leaves

2 cloves of garlic, crushed

2 stalks celery, coarsely chopped

1 medium onion, chopped

Several sprigs of parsley, and tarragon stems

6 peppercorns

1 tablespoon salt

Yellowtail snapper bones

THE DOLPHIN INN

Assorted Fresh Fruit

Dolphin Inn Fruit Sauce

Dolphin Inn Sour Cream Waffles

Cajun-style French Toast

Homemade Bread

Bagels — Danish Pastries

Orange Juice — Gevalia Kaffee — Hot Tea

The Dophin Inn
107 Savannah Street
904-231-5477

DOLPHIN INN
SOUR CREAM WAFFLES

- Beat egg yolks, milk, margarine, sour cream and vanilla in mixer bowl until smooth. Add flour, baking powder, baking soda, sugar and salt; mix well.
- Beat egg whites in mixer bowl until stiff peaks form. Fold into batter.
- Spoon batter onto waffle iron. Bake using manufacturer's directions. Serve with fresh fruit and Dolphin Inn Fruit Sauce (see below).
- Yield: 6 servings.

Ingredients

3 egg yolks

3/4 cup milk

1/2 cup melted margarine

1 cup sour cream

2 teaspoons vanilla extract or
Mexican vanilla

1 1/2 cups flour

2 teaspoons baking powder

1/2 teaspoon baking soda

1 tablespoon sugar

1/2 teaspoon salt

3 egg whites

DOLPHIN INN FRUIT SAUCE

- Combine sour cream, confectioners' sugar, almond extract and Amaretto and Cognac in bowl; whisk until smooth. Use as dip or topping for fresh fruit or waffles.
- Yield: 8 servings.

Ingredients

1 cup sour cream

1 cup confectioners' sugar

1 teaspoon almond extract

1 tablespoon Amaretto
and Cognac

Over the Fence: Breakfasts at the Dolphin Inn can best be described as "laid back" in keeping with the casual relaxed and informal style of the operation of the Inn and of the owners' own personal life.

Chilled Leek Soup

Baby Lamb Chops with Couscous Timbale

*Pan-seared Tournedos with Roasted Red Pepper and
Smoked Gouda Cheese*

Mashed Potatoes

Garden Salad

Chocolate Truffle Pie

Josephine's Bed & Breakfast
101 Seaside Avenue
904-231-1939

Baby Lamb Chops with Couscous Timbale

Couscous is a traditional North African dish made with hard wheat semolina and is considered to be the North African equivalent of pasta. It was discovered by the French during the conquest of Algeria.

- Bring chicken stock to a boil in saucepan. Stir in couscous. Simmer for 5 minutes; remove from heat. Let stand, covered, for 20 minutes. Spoon into serving bowl. Chill for 1 hour.

- Stir to separate grains. Add tomato, green onion, parsley, vinegar, 3 tablespoons olive oil, salt and pepper; mix well. Place in 3-ounce ramekin.

- Steam couscous for 10 minutes or microwave for 1 minute until heated through.

- Rub lamb with additional olive oil; sprinkle with rosemary and pepper. Cut into 8 chops. Grill for 5 minutes on each side or pan broil for 3 minutes on each side. Serve with couscous.

- Yield: 8 servings.

~

Over the Fence: *Serving breakfast, lunch and dinner. Guests at Josephine's (the family name of the owner) find the ambiance of a time long forgotten, when casual elegance and personal service were the standard. Rinse the sand from your feet at the back door and slip into your favorite deck shoes for dining, or "dress to the nines." The changing menus offer wonderful variety. Dinner features an excellent menu of casual French country cuisine, and each dish is deliciously and meticulously prepared by our Belgian chef, Olivier Petit, and served by Bruce and Judy Albert, our "resident herb growers."*

Timbale Ingredients

1 cup chicken stock

1/2 cup uncooked couscous

1/4 cup finely chopped seeded tomato

1 green onion, finely chopped

2 tablespoons chopped parsley

2 tablespoons red wine vinegar

3 tablespoons extra-virgin olive oil

Salt and pepper to taste

Lamb Ingredients

1 (12-ounce) Frenched rack of baby lamb

Olive oil

1 sprig of rosemary

Pepper to taste

Modica MARKET

Seaside, Florida

Fresh Fruit Salad

*Chicken with Goat Cheese and
Roasted Red Peppers*

Rice with Almonds

Fresh Coconut Cake

Iced Tea

Modica Market
Town Center
904-231-1214

Chicken with Goat Cheese and Roasted Red Peppers

- Cut whole peppers lengthwise into halves. Reserve one half for another purpose. Place peppers cut side down on baking sheet.

- Broil until skin is blackened. Let stand, covered with foil, for 10 minutes to steam. Discard skins; cut peppers into strips. Chill, covered, in refrigerator.

- Cut cheese into 8 rounds; sprinkle rounds with almonds. Chill, covered, in refrigerator.

- Rinse chicken and pat dry. Brush with 2 tablespoons olive oil. Grill for 10 minutes or until cooked through. Remove to baking sheet.

- Top chicken with pepper strips and cheese rounds. Bake at 350 degrees for 5 minutes or just until cheese is heated through.

- Sauté onion and garlic in 1/4 cup olive oil in heavy skillet over high heat. Add wine and rosemary. Cook for 3 minutes or until reduced by 1/2.

- Whisk in butter gradually. Season with salt and pepper. Spoon over chicken.

- Yield: 4 servings.

Chicken Ingredients

2 red bell peppers

3 ounces Montrachet or other soft fresh goat cheese

Toasted sliced almonds

4 chicken breast filets

2 tablespoons olive oil

Sauce Ingredients

1 teaspoon chopped onion

1 teaspoon chopped garlic

1/4 cup olive oil

1/2 cup dry white wine

2 teaspoons chopped fresh rosemary

1/2 cup unsalted butter, sliced

Salt and pepper to taste

~

Over the Fence: Modica Market is a 1990s take on a 19th century European food hall. The variety of fresh vegetables, fruits, meats and cheese—all beautifully displayed—make it a fun place to visit, even when the pantry at home is full.

Shrimp and Tomato Bisque

Pasta Salad with Garden Vegetables

Assorted Hard Rolls

Key Lime Ice Cream Pie

Shades
Town Center
904-231-1950

SHRIMP AND TOMATO BISQUE

- Combine shrimp, salt, pepper, garlic, seafood stock, water, tomatoes, celery, red peppers and green onions in stockpot; mix well.
- Cook over low heat for 20 minutes or until shrimp are pink and vegetables are tender, stirring occasionally. Drain excess liquid.
- Stir in cream. Simmer for 15 minutes, stirring constantly. Ladle into soup bowls.
- Yield: 8 servings.

Ingredients

5 pounds small peeled
deveined shrimp

2 teaspoons salt

2 teaspoons pepper

2 teaspoons granulated garlic

8 ounces seafood stock

2 quarts water

8 large tomatoes, finely chopped

1 stalk celery, finely chopped

2 large red bell peppers,
finely chopped

2 bunches green onions,
finely chopped

2 quarts whipping cream

~

Over the Fence: Reminiscent of "your own local Cheers Bar," Shades, located in downtown Seaside, offers a dining experience that goes beyond casual. The menu features an assortment of burgers, dogs, ribs, seafood and their famous chicken sandwich. And let's not forget about the homemade crab cakes. Whether you decide to belly-up to the bar or hang-out on the deck, you'll enjoy a laid-back, but lively, eating atmosphere . . . like the sign says, —good food —cold beer! Shoes and reservations not required. Alabama natives, Billy McConnell of Birmingham and Jimmy Rogers of Tuscaloosa are both owners and operators.

The Bucket Club Sandwich with
Turkey, Ham, Bacon and Swiss on a Roll

or

Vermont Cheddar with Sliced Green Apple
on Sourdough Bread

New Potato Salad with Scallions and Parsley

Chocolate Roulade

Freshly Squeezed Strawberry Lemonade or
Raspberry Iced Tea

Silver Bucket
Highway C 30A
904-231-1190

Chocolate Roulade

- Melt chocolate in double boiler over hot water. Add coffee, stirring until smooth.

- Beat egg yolks with half the sugar in mixer bowl until thick and lemon-colored. Fold in chocolate mixture.

- Beat egg whites with remaining sugar in mixer bowl until stiff peaks form. Fold into chocolate mixture.

- Spread mixture onto baking sheet lined with buttered and floured baking parchment.

- Bake at 350 degrees for 15 to 20 minutes or until cake springs back when lightly touched. Invert onto towel to cool. Remove parchment.

- Beat whipping cream with vanilla in mixer bowl until soft peaks form. Spread on cooled cake. Top with raspberries.

- Roll cake as for jelly roll to enclose filling. Let rest. Garnish with baking cocoa or confectioners' sugar. Slice to serve. May substitute chocolate chunks for raspberries.

- Yield: 15 servings.

Ingredients

6 ounces semisweet chocolate
1/4 cup strong coffee
8 egg yolks
3/4 cup sugar
8 egg whites
1 1/2 cups whipping cream
1/2 teaspoon vanilla extract
1 cup raspberries

Over the Fence: *If you're on the beach, or strolling through the beachside shops of Seaside and you're hungry for a gourmet snack, please stop in! We're just off the beach, among the dunes at The Silver Bucket! We saw an opportunity to bring our favorite caterer, Lisa Gail Smith, from New York City to Seaside to work her magic on fellow Seasiders and guests. Opened since May 1993, we serve gourmet sandwiches, fresh-baked confections and ice cream, plus a variety of fresh fruit juices and . . . in addition we boast the Best Bottled Beer on the Beach!*

Elegant Napkin Fold

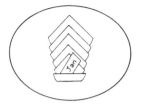

Illustration 1

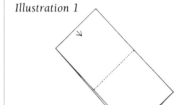

Illustration 2

Illustration 3

Fold napkin in half, bringing down right side from top. Fold in half again, bringing down left side from top (Illus. 1). Turn up lower points in succession, each one lower than the other (Illus. 2). Fold left and right corners to back. Tuck one into the other (Illus. 3). Place card may be placed in bottom fold.

THE ART OF FOOD

Presentation

- Whether you are serving your family a casual supper or entertaining at a formal dinner, think of the occasion as an expression of art; you are highlighting a scene to tantalize the eyes as well as the taste buds, and the appearance of the table and the food is very important. The table setting, even if simple, can be enhanced with an artfully folded napkin. The wine can be chosen to enhance the menu and served in the correct sparkling glass. The food on the plate can be carefully arranged and garnished to please the eye. In fact, the meal will actually taste better if it looks attractive.

- The main rule to keep in mind in food presentation, as in other art forms, is balance. We are aware that nutritional balance is important in planning meals, with a proper proportion of choices from the various levels on the food pyramid. It is also important, however, to bring a sense of proportion and harmony to cooking by balancing flavors, shapes, textures, plate arrangement and cooking techniques.

- To balance flavors, try to pair foods that complement each other, such as lamb with rosemary or mint, beef with horseradish, salmon with cucumber and dill, turkey with cranberries, duck with orange or tomato with basil. Try not to combine flavors that may overpower each other or distract from the courses to follow.

- The balance of color is one of the key ingredients in an attractive plate and to achieve it you should vary your palette to tempt your palate. You will probably want to start with your entrée and select side dishes and accompaniments in complementary colors. A dark entrée such as prime rib will need some vegetables with lighter color and appearance. A pale entrée such as broiled sole will need stronger colors to add vibrancy. Contrasting colors such as tomatoes and broccoli or julienned carrots and green beans are appealing.

- All food colors on the plate need not contrast sharply, however; several shades of the same color can be featured to achieve a monochromatic look. The dark color of broccoli can be softened with the more delicate green of cucumber slices, for example. Be sure not to overcook foods such as green beans; their faded look will make your presentation appear drab.

- Think in terms of unity when designing your plate. Try to create a focal point and arrange the remaining elements to complement the focal point. Simplicity is the golden rule in unity, without the distractions of overly complex elements. With simplicity will come elegance and a strong visual and taste appeal.

- The choice of cooking technique is important in achieving balance and will result in a more interesting and well-presented meal. Combining fried fish with fried potatoes and a fried vegetable will result in a plate without nutritional balance and bland in color and texture. A meat entrée served with two casseroles presents a too-complex array of ingredients to please the eye. Try for diversity by combining a broiled entrée with a baked or sautéed accompaniment. Balance it with something fresh or crunchy.

- Never underestimate the importance of the garnish, the table setting or the correct wine to the success of your meal. You can add elegance and excitement with careful touches such as folded napkins or small splashes of color and texture on the plate. Edible flowers, sieved egg, parsley, paprika or chopped pimento can be used to change the effect of a dish without affecting its taste appreciably. Use your own creativity with garnishes and napkin folding; follow the basic rule of balance and create your own culinary canvas.

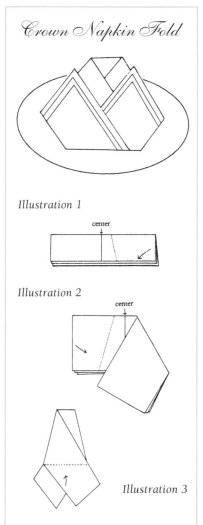

Crown Napkin Fold

Illustration 1

Illustration 2

Illustration 3

With napkin opened, fold in half, bringing top edge to bottom. Fold in half again, bringing top fold to bottom edge. Find center by folding in half; crease and open. Fold down right end along dotted line (Illus. 1). Fold down left end along dotted line (Illus. 2). Fold up along dotted line (Illus. 3).

Flower Napkin Fold

Illustration 1

Illustration 2

Illustration 3

With napkin opened, fold in half, bringing up left side from bottom. Fold in half again on dotted line, bringing up right side from bottom (Illus. 1). Turn down three points, each one higher than the last (Illus. 2). Turn right and left corners under in thirds (Illus. 3). Place flower in fold.

Garnishes

• Beautiful garnishes can elevate a commonplace meal to a special event. Beautiful does not have to mean difficult, however, and the trend is toward the natural. The leaves from celery and carrot can be added to the plate for a green touch. Clusters of fresh grapes, fresh dill or basil, edible flower petals or flowers and fans made of vegetables and fruits add the needed color and texture.

• Salads can be enhanced with the addition of capers, carrot curls, chives, julienned prosciutto, kumquats, grated citrus rind, hazelnuts, pine nuts, pistachios, croutons, dried fruits, Chinese noodles, olives, pomegranate seeds, broken tortilla chips, fresh herbs and edible flowers such as nasturtiums, violets or roses.

• Garnish soups with slivered nuts, yogurt, crumbled cheese, fennel seeds, caviar, apple or avocado slices, chopped hard-boiled eggs, croutons, lemon or orange slices or peel, mushroom slices and chives.

• At dessert time, instead of just spooning the sauce over the cake or mousse, drizzle it into a decorative pattern on the plate or top of the dessert. Make a feather pattern by piping chocolate in horizontal lines across the top of the dessert and draw a wooden pick through the lines in alternate directions at 1-inch intervals. Add a citrus twist or swan or a chocolate leaf or butterfly.

• Radishes lend themselves easily to garnishes. Cut off the stem end of a round radish for a **Radish Mum**. Make parallel cuts three quarters of the way through the radish from the stem end; make additional cuts perpendicular to the first cuts. Chill in iced water to open.

• For a **Radish Accordion**, cut a thin slice from each end of a long narrow radish. Cut crosswise into thin slices, leaving the bottom intact. Chill the radish in iced water to open.

- To make **Radish Mushrooms**, remove the root end of the radish, cutting away as little of the red skin as possible. Make a ¼-inch deep cut around the "equator" of the radish. Working from the stem end to the cut, cut away the bottom part of the radish to form a stem.

- Trim both ends of a radish for a **Radish Rosette**. Working about halfway up the sides, cut rounded petal shapes around the circumference of each radish. Cut a second scalloped row just inside the first row and remove it. Continue cutting rows of scallops, removing alternate rows. Chill in iced water to open before using.

- To make a **Beet** or **Turnip Rose**, follow the directions for the Radish Rosette, parboiling the beet or turnip for 5 to 10 minutes first or until the skins can be slipped off. Color turnip roses with beet juice or food coloring.

- Use a large firm tomato for a **Tomato Rose**. Working from the bottom, cut the peel in a continuous ½-inch strip, zigzagging the knife slightly to give a scalloped effect. Holding the peel skin side down, roll it into a spiral; hold the center in place as you roll. Add fresh herb leaves such as basil to resemble rose leaves.

- For a **Cherry Tomato Rose**, cut an X into the stem end of the tomato and peel back the skin partway down the side with a sharp knife to form 4 petals.

- Follow the instructions for the Tomato Rose to make **Lime**, **Lemon** or **Orange Roses**. **Kumquat Roses** can be made in the same manner as the Cherry Tomato Rose.

- To make **Green Onion Frills**, cut off the root end and most of the stem portion of green onions. Make narrow lengthwise cuts at both ends with a sharp knife to produce a fringe. Chill in iced water until the ends curl.

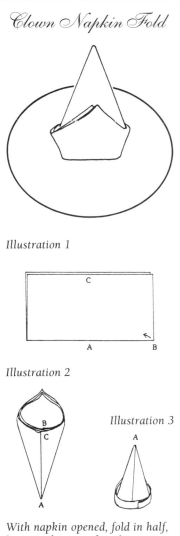

Clown Napkin Fold

Illustration 1

Illustration 2

Illustration 3

With napkin opened, fold in half, bringing bottom of napkin to top (Illus. 1). Holding point A carefully with thumb, roll B loosely over and up to center (C), without creasing. Continue rolling cone (Illus. 2). Turn napkin upside down. Turn up hem all around (Illus. 3).

Heart Napkin Fold

Illustration 1

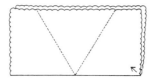

Illustration 2

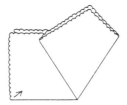

With napkin opened, fold in half, bringing bottom of napkin to top (Illus. 1). Fold into thirds along dotted lines, picking up lower right corner. Repeat with left corner (Illus. 2).

- Cut off the top and remove the skin of small onions for **Onion Mums**. Cut the onion into thin wedges, cutting from the top to within ¼ inch of the stem end. Soak the onion in iced water in the refrigerator for several hours or until some of the outer sections can be pulled back gently to form petals. Tint the soaking water with food coloring to color the mums.

- Select firm, round white mushrooms for **Fluted Mushrooms**. Rub gently with lemon juice to prevent discoloration. Press the flat tip of a knife into the center of the mushroom cap in a star design. Continue making indentations in rows around the mushroom cap. Another method is to cut 5 or 6 inverted Vs from the center to the rim of the cap.

- **Pepper Flowers** go well with a Southwestern menu. Make several lengthwise slashes through a 2-inch to 3-inch Serrano chili pepper to form a fringe; do not cut through stem end. Chill until the ends curl.

- For **Fluted Fruit Wheels**, cut thin strips of rind evenly from the stem end to the blossom end of lemons, oranges and limes. Cut the fruit into slices of desired thickness. To make **Fruit Twists**, cut from 1 side to the center and twist. For **Fruit Fans**, cut fruit into slices, cutting to but not through the bottom and fan out the slices.

- To make **Frosted Fruit**, rinse and dry grapes, cranberries or cherries. Dip into egg white beaten until frothy and then into granulated sugar. Shake off the excess sugar and let stand until dry.

- For **Citrus Swans**, cut citrus slices into halves and cut the peel from the fruit three-quarters of the way to the opposite side. Tuck the free end under to form the swan's neck.

- Select large firm strawberries with caps for *Strawberry Fans*. Cut several parallel slices from the top of each berry to just below the cap with a sharp knife. Fan the slices gently.

- For *Chocolate Leaves*, wash fresh rose, lemon, camellia, gardenia or ivy leaves and pat them dry. Melt 4 ounces of sweet or semisweet chocolate and brush on the undersides of the leaves. Place on waxed paper and chill for 15 minutes. Peel the leaves carefully from the chocolate. Spoon the melted chocolate into a decorating bag fitted with a writing tip for *Chocolate Butterflies*. Pipe the chocolate into butterfly designs on waxed paper and chill until firm. For three-dimensional butterflies, let the chocolate stand just until it begins to set. Lift the wings 1 at a time with a spatula, folding them gently toward the center to resemble wings in flight. Place them between the cups of an inverted egg carton and chill until firm.

- Spread melted chocolate in a very thin layer on the underside of a metal tray for *Chocolate Curls*. Chill for 10 minutes or until firm but still pliable. Slip the straight tip of a metal spatula under the edges of the chocolate and push to form curls. For quick curls, warm a large chocolate bar in hands and draw a vegetable peeler over the smooth side to form curls.

- *Crystallized Flower Blossoms* make beautiful garnishes. Use edible flowers such as violets, Johnny-jump-ups, rose petals, mint leaves or scented geraniums. Paint the flowers with a mixture of egg white and a few drops of water. Sprinkle evenly all over with superfine sugar and let stand on waxed paper for 12 to 36 hours to dry.

Butterfly Napkin Fold

Illustration 1

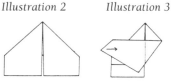

Illustration 2   Illustration 3

Illustration 4   Illustration 5

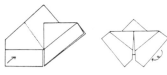

With napkin opened, fold bottom third of napkin up. Bring top edge to bottom fold, dividing napkin into thirds (Illus. 1). Bring left and right ends to meet in center (Illus. 2). Turn napkin over. Swing right flap over to left (Illus. 3). Swing same flap back to right on dotted line (Illus. 4). Repeat process with left flap (Illus. 5). Turn napkin over for finished butterfly.

Boat Napkin Fold

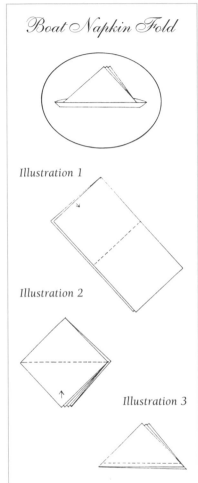

Illustration 1

Illustration 2

Illustration 3

With napkin opened, fold in half, bringing upper right side down to lower left. Fold in half again along dotted line, bringing upper edges down to lower edges (Illus. 1). Fold on dotted line, lifting top lower layer to top point. Lift remaining lower three layers toward back to top point (Illus. 2). Turn up from bottom to make a small border along dotted line all the way around (Illus. 3).

Wines

- Wines can play two very important roles in the enjoyment of a meal: first as an element in the actual preparation of the food and, second, as an accompaniment to the meal.

- The best wine to cook with is the one you will be serving at the table. If you feel that it is too expensive to cook with, use a less expensive wine in the same family for cooking. Do not sacrifice quality, however. The real secret is to cook with a good wine, as the alcohol evaporates during the cooking process, leaving only the actual flavor of the wine. A fine wine with rich body and aroma will insure a distinct and delicate flavor. Never use "cooking wines", which are heavily salted and which distort the recipe.

- When used in cooking, the wine should accent and enhance the natural flavor of the food while adding its own inviting fragrance and flavor. It should not, however, overpower the flavor of the other ingredients; when in doubt, it is better to use too little than too much. Use Madeira, sherry or Marsala very sparingly, for example, tasting carefully to avoid overpowering the dish.

- If you are adding wine at the end of the cooking process, as in soups and sauces, simmer it until the volume is reduced by half to eliminate the alcohol and concentrate the flavor.

- Flamed dishes are dramatic as well as delicious, but most wines do not have enough alcohol content to flame. Fortified wines such as Port, sherry or Madeira, with 20% alcohol, can be flamed. To flame, heat the wine gently until very hot, but not long enough to boil off the alcohol. Ignite the wine and pour it over the dish.

- The wine to serve with a meal is usually chosen to enhance the food on the menu, but there are no set rules about what wine must be served with a particular food and it is not as difficult as some people would have you think.

- Balance plays a role in selecting the wine to pair with your menu. The four basic principles to consider are sameness, contrast, equal intensity and personal preference.

- The sameness approach looks for similar characteristics in the wine and foods, to emphasize the aspects which the two have in common. A full-bodied Chardonnay with a rich "buttery" flavor goes well with a chicken dish cooked in butter and cream because they share the same impressions of flavor.

- The same chicken dish could also be paired with a crisp, lemony tasting wine such as Sauvignon Blanc to cut through the richness of the food and furnish a refreshing contrast.

- With regard to intensity, try to select a delicate wine to complement a delicate dish and an intense wine to go with a robust dish. A simple chicken dish would do well with a light white wine, but a full-flavored red wine would do more justice to a chicken dish grilled with strong flavors such as garlic and rosemary.

- Probably the most satisfying approach is that of personal preference. You are the ultimate expert when it comes to pleasing your palate and you can trust your own choice if it satisfies you.

Appetizer Wines

- Sherry, vermouth and flavored wines are considered appetizer wines.

- Appetizer wines can be served with or without food at room temperature or chilled to around 50 degrees. They are usually served in a 2½-ounce to 4-ounce glass.

- Serve appetizer wines with Baked Brie (page 13), Asparagus Roll-Ups (page 14), Sun-Dried Tomato Pâté (page 20), Artichoke Dip (page 21), Chilled Avocado Soup (page 35) or Crab Bisque (page 41).

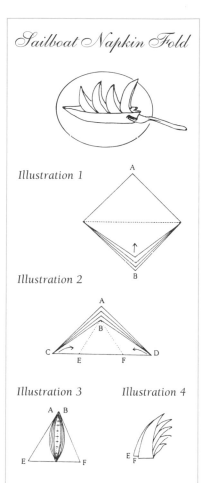

Sailboat Napkin Fold

Illustration 1

Illustration 2

Illustration 3   Illustration 4

With napkin opened, fold in half, bringing down right side from top. Fold in half again on dotted line, bringing down left side from top. Fold in half, bringing all points at B up to A (Illus. 1). Fold on dotted lines, bring AC and AD down to meet in center below. Fold up points C and D in back (Illus. 2). Place E and F together in back (Illus. 3). Pull out sails one at a time (Illus. 4). Place in tines of fork.

Candle Napkin Holder

Illustration 1

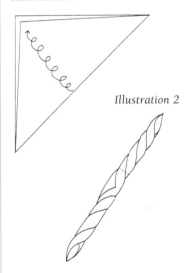

Illustration 2

With napkin opened, fold in half on the dotted line (Illus. 1). Roll up tightly from diagonal fold (Illus. 2) Fold, bringing points upward.

Red Dinner Wines

- Burgundy, Cabernet Sauvignon, Gamay, Chianti, Pinot Noir, Petite Sirah, Ruby Cabernet, Bordeaux, Beaujolais, Barbera and Zinfandel are red dinner wines.

- Red dinner wines are usually served at cool room temperature, around 65 degrees, in 6-ounce to 9-ounce glasses. They are served with hearty foods, red meats, cheese, egg dishes, pasta and highly seasoned foods.

- Try a red dinner wine with French Stew (page 47), Lasagna (page 89), Sausage and Spaghetti (page 94), Brisket (page 117), Bohemian Pot Roast (page 119), London Broil Steak (page 122) and Grilled Venison with Green Peppercorn Sauce (page 123).

Rosé Wines

- Rosés are served chilled to about 50 degrees in 6-ounce to 9-ounce glasses with ham, chicken, picnic foods, shellfish and cold beef.

- Rosé will go well with Sea Time Finger Sandwiches (page 16), California Salad (page 55), Shrimp Salad (page 60), Catch of the Day Salad (page 85), Lemon Veal Piccata (page 124), Crazy Chicken (page 136), Hawaiian Chicken (page 137), Crab Claws (page 149), Shrimp Remoulade (page 153) and Curry Shrimp (page 199).

White Dinner Wines

- Chablis, Rhine, dry Sauterne, Pinot Blanc, Bordeaux, Soave, Chardonnay, Chenin Blanc, White Riesling, French Colombard and Sauvignon Blanc are white dinner wines.

- White dinner wines are served chilled to about 50 degrees in 6-ounce to 9-ounce glasses. They complement light foods such as poultry, fish and shellfish, ham and veal.

- Serve a white dinner wine with Pecan and Chicken Salad (page 54), Pasta and Chicken Salad (page 91), Seafood Pasta (page 95), Coq au Vin (page 135), Lightly Lemon Chicken (page 139), Grilled Salmon Fillet (page 146), Best Scalloped Oysters (page 149) and Shrimp Scampi (page 153).

Dessert Wines

- Port, Tokay, Muscatel, Catawba, sweet Sauterne, Aurora and sherry are dessert wines.

- Dessert wines are served at cool room temperature, around 65 degrees, in 2½-ounce to 4-ounce glasses.

- Enjoy a dessert wine with Bundt Kugel (page 162), Russian Creme with Strawberry Sauce (page 164), Mexican Chocolate Cake (page 168), Fabulous Lemon Pound Cake (page 171), Melba Pie (page 180) and Chocolate Roulade (page 211).

Sparkling Wines

- Champagne, Sparkling White Zinfandel, Sparkling Burgundy, Sparkling Rosé, and Cold Duck are sparkling wines.

- Sparkling wines are served chilled to 45 degrees with all foods for all occasions.

- Serve a sparkling wine with Crab Grass (page 17), Bleu Cheese Dip (page 23), Cucumber Soup (page 39), Salad with Artichokes and Hearts of Palm (page 53), Mobile Bay Salad (page 57), Linguine with Pesto Sauce (page 90), Marinated Chicken Breasts (page 132), Grilled Red Snapper with Garlic and Lime (page 147), Shrimp with Artichoke Hearts and Feta (page 154), French Apple Dessert (page 159) and Cheesecake with Raspberries (page 167).

Ascot Napkin Fold

Illustration 1

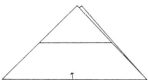

Illustration 2

Illustration 3

With napkin opened, fold in half, bringing bottom point up to top. Fold in half again, bringing bottom fold to top fold; crease and release (Illus. 1). Fold bottom up midway to crease. Bring bottom to crease made in center of triangle. Turn up fold once more (Illus. 2). Turn right point to left of top point. Turn left point to right of top point (Illus. 3).

Herbs and Spices

Allspice

- Pungent aromatic spice, whole or in powdered form. It is excellent in marinades, particularly in game marinade, or in curries.

Basil

- Can be chopped and added to cold poultry salads. If the recipe calls for tomatoes or tomato sauce, add a touch of basil to bring out a rich flavor.

Bay leaf

- The basis of many French seasonings. It is added to soups, stews, marinades and stuffings.

Celery seeds

- From wild celery rather than domestic celery. It adds pleasant flavor to bouillon or a stock base.

Chervil

- One of the traditional *fines herbes* used in French-derived cooking. (The others are tarragon, parsley and chives.) It is good in omelets or soups.

Chives

- Available fresh, dried or frozen, chives can be substituted for raw onion or shallot in any poultry recipe.

Cinnamon

- Ground from the bark of the cinnamon tree, it is important in desserts as well as savory dishes.

Coriander

- Adds an unusual flavor to soups, stews, chili dishes, curries and some desserts.

Cumin

- A staple spice in Mexican cooking. To use, rub seeds together and let them fall into the dish just before serving. Cumin also comes in powdered form.

Rosemary

Garlic

- One of the oldest herbs in the world, it must be carefully handled. For best results, press or crush the garlic clove.

Marjoram

- An aromatic herb of the mint family, it is good in soups, sauces, stuffings and stews.

Mustard

- Brings a sharp bite to sauces. Sprinkle just a touch over roast chicken for a delightful flavor treat.

Oregano

- A staple herb in Italian, Spanish and Mexican cuisines. It is very good in dishes with a tomato foundation; it adds an excellent savory taste.

Paprika

- A mild pepper that adds color to many dishes. The very best paprika is imported from Hungary.

Rosemary

- A tasty herb important in seasoning stuffing for duck, partridge, capon and other poultry.

Sage

- A perennial favorite with all kinds of poultry and stuffings. It is particularly good with goose.

Tarragon

- One of the *fines herbes*. Goes well with all poultry dishes whether hot or cold.

Thyme

- Usually used in combination with bay leaf in soups stews and sauces.

Bouquet garni

- A must in many Creole cuisine recipes. It is a bundle of herbs, spices and bay leaf tied together and added to soups, stews or sauces.

Thyme

NUTRITIONAL PROFILES

The editors have attempted to present these family recipes in a form that allows approximate nutritional profile values to be computed. Persons with dietary or health problems or whose diets require close monitoring should not rely solely on the nutritional information provided. They should consult their physicians or a registered dietitian for specific information.

Abbreviations

Cal — Calories	Chol — Cholesterol
Prot — Protein	Sod — Sodium
Carbo — Carbohydrates	g — grams
Fiber — Dietary Fiber	mg — milligrams
T Fat — Total Fat	

Nutritional information for these recipes is computed from information derived from many sources, including materials supplied by the United States Department of Agriculture, computer databanks and journals in which the information is assumed to be in the public domain. However, many specialty items, new products and processed foods may not be available from these sources or may vary from the average values used in these profiles. More information on new and/or specific products may be obtained by reading the nutrient labels. Unless otherwise specified, the nutritional profile of these recipes is based on all measurements being level.

If a choice of ingredients has been given, the nutritional profile reflects the first option. If a choice of amounts has been given, the nutritional profile reflects the greater amount.

- **Alcoholic ingredients** have been analyzed for basic ingredients, although cooking causes the evaporation of alcohol, thus decreasing caloric content.
- **Buttermilk, sour cream** and **yogurt** are the types available commercially.
- **Cake mixes** which are prepared using package directions include 3 eggs and ½ cup oil.
- **Chicken**, cooked for boning and chopping, has been roasted; this method yields the lowest caloric values.
- **Cottage cheese** is cream-style with 4.2% creaming mixture. Dry curd cottage cheese has no creaming mixture.
- **Eggs** are all large. To avoid raw eggs that may carry salmonella as in eggnog or 6-week muffin batter, use an equivalent amount of commercial egg substitute.
- **Flour** is unsifted all-purpose flour.
- **Garnishes**, serving suggestions and other optional additions and variations are not included in the profile.
- **Margarine** and **butter** are regular, not whipped or presoftened.
- **Milk** is whole milk, 3.5% butterfat. Lowfat milk is 1% butterfat. Evaporated milk is whole milk with 60% of the water removed.
- **Oil** is any type of vegetable cooking oil. Shortening is hydrogenated vegetable shortening.
- **Salt** and other ingredients to taste as noted in the ingredients have not been included in the nutritional profile.

Pg #	Recipe Title (Approx Per Serving)	Cal	Prot (g)	Carbo (g)	T Fat (g)	% Cal from Fat	Chol (mg)	Fiber (g)	Sod (mg)
13	Apricot Pecan Spread	99	2	6	8	68	16	1	46
13	Baked Brie	296	10	32	15	44	41	0	576
14	Asparagus Roll-Ups	179	6	8	14	69	32	1	398
14	Cheddar Chili Squares	136	9	1	11	71	83	<1	277
15	Cheese Strips	161	5	9	12	65	15	1	208
15	Balsamic Chicken Wings*	168	15	1	11	60	48	<1	48
16	Sea Time Finger Sandwiches	141	2	8	12	73	14	1	171
16	Chicken Wings*	181	17	3	11	56	48	<1	1190
17	Crab Grass	88	9	1	5	54	41	<1	238
17	Green Olives and Ham Canapés	68	5	1	5	62	16	<1	486
18	Ham and Cheese Rolls	190	6	15	12	55	31	1	391
18	Barbecued Appetizer Meatballs	97	6	11	4	32	18	<1	243
19	Spiced Oyster Crackers	109	1	11	7	56	0	<1	277
19	Boiled Peanuts	Nutritional information for this recipe is not available.							
20	Easy Shrimp Butter	173	5	1	17	86	72	<1	179
20	Sun-Dried Tomato Pâté	33	1	5	1	29	0	2	237
21	Sausage Mushrooms	64	3	1	5	76	16	<1	146
21	Tortilla Roll-Ups	57	1	4	4	63	11	<1	108
21	Artichoke Dip	135	3	2	13	84	13	<1	287
22	Baked Beef Dip	150	4	2	14	83	33	<1	376
22	Black-Eyed Pea Dip	74	4	12	1	17	0	5	581
23	Bleu Cheese Dip	82	3	1	8	81	22	<1	241
23	Green Chili and Tomato Dip	48	1	5	3	58	0	1	397
24	Microwave Crab Dip	222	11	2	19	78	97	<1	339
24	Hummus	115	4	12	6	46	0	1	157
25	Salsa Dip	85	1	13	4	37	0	2	450
25	Shoe Peg Corn Dip	263	6	26	16	53	42	2	669
26	Mexican Taco Dip	164	6	6	14	73	25	1	326
26	Spinach Dip	150	2	5	14	82	15	1	262
27	Vidalia Onion Dip*	227	1	33	11	43	8	1	81
27	Champagne Punch	176	<1	20	<1	1	0	<1	22

Pg #	Recipe Title (Approx Per Serving)	Cal	Prot (g)	Carbo (g)	T Fat (g)	% Cal from Fat	Chol (mg)	Fiber (g)	Sod (mg)
28	Christmas Eve Punch	39	<1	10	<1	2	0	<1	8
28	Christmas Eve Eggnog	361	5	21	26	63	241	0	49
29	Kentucky Eggnog Spike	65	0	0	0	0	0	0	<1
29	Sangria	180	<1	18	<1	<1	0	<1	10
30	Blonde Sangria	176	<1	25	<1	<1	0	<1	13
30	Instant Spiced Tea	46	<1	12	<1	<1	0	0	2
31	Beach Cooler	18	<1	4	<1	4	0	1	54
31	Wassail	103	<1	26	<1	1	0	<1	2
35	Chilled Avocado Soup	345	9	12	31	77	37	3	706
35	Gazpacho	119	5	11	8	38	0	2	652
36	French Market Soup	193	13	31	3	12	4	10	430
37	Wharton Cheese Soup	233	11	13	16	61	45	1	1428
37	Firehouse Chili	354	30	19	17	44	84	7	805
38	Great San Luis Green Chile Soup	336	20	17	21	56	66	3	1085
39	Chinese Hot and Sour Soup	215	18	14	11	44	63	3	1296
39	Cucumber Soup	218	8	17	14	55	29	2	1385
40	Great Lakes Corn Chowder	532	9	45	38	61	106	6	570
41	Carrot Vichyssoise	322	7	23	23	64	81	3	1156
41	Crab Bisque	348	21	18	21	55	118	2	1584
42	Jalapeño Potato Soup	282	10	39	10	32	30	2	528
42	Taco Soup	345	24	33	13	35	61	3	1322
43	Tortilla Soup	337	31	13	19	49	89	4	468
44	Tortellini Spinach Soup	252	16	32	7	24	31	2	907
44	Portuguese Vegetable Soup	282	22	20	13	40	50	3	1868
45	Turkey Vegetable Soup	306	21	16	18	52	78	3	573
46	Crenshaw County Camp Stew	234	25	19	6	24	70	2	454
47	French Stew	428	22	37	19	39	61	4	1186
51	Salad with Sugared Almonds and Orange Vinaigrette	460	5	27	39	74	0	4	109
52	Apricot Salad	230	3	32	11	41	1	1	87
52	Tossed Club Salad	454	27	10	35	68	88	2	921
53	Salad with Artichokes and Hearts of Palm	275	8	33	14	43	57	3	777

Pg #	Recipe Title (Approx Per Serving)	Cal	Prot (g)	Carbo (g)	T Fat (g)	% Cal from Fat	Chol (mg)	Fiber (g)	Sod (mg)
54	Cauliflower Salad	574	10	14	55	84	52	2	723
54	Pecan and Chicken Salad	619	31	7	53	75	125	2	1025
55	California Salad	236	13	7	18	67	63	1	575
56	Sesame and Almond Slaw	384	7	22	32	72	0	4	698
56	Summer Coleslaw	184	2	26	10	44	0	2	376
57	Mobile Bay Salad	369	23	4	29	71	113	<1	317
57	Florida Salad	198	3	15	15	65	0	3	152
58	Potato Salad	418	4	43	27	56	16	4	170
58	Artichoke and Rice Salad	170	2	11	14	71	6	3	575
59	Yellow Rice Salad	164	5	32	2	10	0	3	155
59	Wild Rice Salad	428	8	46	24	50	7	3	1265
60	Shrimp Salad	404	12	17	32	71	110	<1	645
60	Spinach Salad	275	6	10	24	77	27	2	415
61	Spinach Salad with Chutney Dressing	297	8	13	25	72	15	4	279
62	Herbed Tomatoes	74	1	5	6	72	0	1	98
62	Cool Tomato Salad	137	3	7	11	71	14	2	331
63	Green Salad with Tarragon Bleu Cheese Dressing	135	4	4	12	76	28	1	298
67	Beer Bread	151	3	27	2	13	5	1	417
67	Banana Bread	228	3	35	9	34	35	1	169
68	Chili Cheese Bread	369	12	31	22	54	38	2	599
68	Grandmother's Famous Cranberry Bread	250	3	51	5	16	28	2	301
69	Poppy Seed Bread	462	5	60	23	44	43	1	255
69	Cuban Bread	137	4	29	<1	3	0	1	334
70	Pumpkin Spice Bread	351	3	39	21	53	47	1	163
70	Spoon Bread	182	8	18	9	43	126	1	372
71	Strawberry Bread	275	3	28	18	56	35	2	134
71	Three-Two-One Bread Plus	157	5	27	2	14	7	1	433
72	Stone-Ground Wheat Bread	215	6	38	5	21	12	5	551
72	Beignets+	203	4	17	14	60	111	<1	134
73	Biscuits	35	1	3	2	54	8	<1	59
73	Priory Biscuits	54	1	8	2	35	5	<1	51

Pg #	Recipe Title (Approx Per Serving)	Cal	Prot (g)	Carbo (g)	T Fat (g)	% Cal from Fat	Chol (mg)	Fiber (g)	Sod (mg)
74	New Orleans-Style French Toast	248	7	42	5	18	79	1	281
74	Monkey Bread	367	5	54	18	41	0	<1	822
75	German Apple Pancakes	416	14	37	25	52	426	3	134
75	Special Popovers	98	4	14	3	25	68	<1	34
76	Cinnamon Rolls	43	1	8	1	21	1	<1	59
77	Overnight Pecan Rolls	253	3	34	12	42	<1	1	343
77	Artichoke Brunch Pie	457	15	21	35	69	146	1	647
78	South-of-the-Border Omelet	365	15	9	32	75	378	1	755
78	Breakfast Sausage Casserole	383	18	11	30	70	234	<1	919
79	Cheesy Sausage Quiche	400	23	12	28	64	260	<1	1068
79	Spinach Pie	345	15	17	25	64	158	2	572
80	Yesterday's Eggs	226	12	7	17	66	188	<1	667
80	Baked Cheesy Apples	375	7	47	19	44	51	2	468
81	Baked Apricots	608	4	92	27	39	50	3	500
81	Rice Pudding	252	6	48	4	15	17	1	63
81	Sunrise Surprise	770	23	145	15	17	4	9	364
85	Landing Catch	799	58	72	29	34	347	3	2118
85	Catch of the Day Salad	354	21	25	20	50	137	2	726
86	Bowtie Salad	399	12	48	18	40	7	2	357
87	Linguine with Tomatoes, Basil and Brie	963	37	100	46	43	82	8	1575
88	Cheesy Italian Macaroni	1329	63	104	73	50	221	3	1983
88	Sea Shell Macaroni Casserole	677	15	56	44	58	66	2	1066
89	Lasagna	612	34	41	35	51	129	4	500
89	Pesto Pizza	Nutritional information for this recipe is not available.							
90	Linguine with Pesto Sauce	555	17	60	27	44	19	2	1865
91	Pasta and Chicken Salad	347	15	34	18	45	46	2	236
91	Rotini and Spinach Salad	715	18	69	41	52	10	4	691
92	Angel Hair Pasta	463	15	73	12	23	3	6	555
93	Red Sauce	157	3	15	9	49	0	4	410
94	Sausage and Spaghetti	387	19	31	22	49	55	3	1048
95	Spaghetti with Chicken and Sausage	1205	63	147	38	28	155	9	950

Pg #	Recipe Title (Approx Per Serving)	Cal	Prot (g)	Carbo (g)	T Fat (g)	% Cal from Fat	Chol (mg)	Fiber (g)	Sod (mg)
95	Seafood Pasta	707	28	62	39	49	128	3	202
96	Japanese Sesame Noodles	210	9	39	3	11	0	2	1666
96	Pasta-Stuffed Zucchini	551	29	29	36	58	87	3	919
97	Filled Noodles	280	20	25	11	35	142	2	120
101	Bacon and Green Bean Bundles	147	2	8	12	74	23	1	281
101	Sesame Broccoli	63	3	7	3	43	0	2	192
102	Broccoli and Rice Casserole	437	22	25	28	58	69	3	1038
102	Carrot Casserole	362	5	47	18	44	106	3	302
103	Creole Black-Eyed Peas and Rice	606	28	82	18	27	35	15	1131
104	Hopping John	383	16	45	15	36	26	7	1149
104	Sautéed Corn with Bacon and Scallions	253	7	32	13	43	8	7	175
105	Baked Onions with Balsamic Vinaigrette	144	1	10	12	70	0	2	214
105	Scalloped Green Peppers	238	14	17	13	49	42	1	626
106	Golden Stuffed Baked Potatoes	202	4	18	13	58	36	2	197
106	Potato Casserole	327	9	29	20	54	21	1	635
107	Spinach Quiche	575	32	22	40	63	205	2	728
107	Squash Casserole with Bacon and Green Chilies	188	10	15	11	49	106	3	573
108	Green Tomato Ratatouille	212	4	20	14	57	0	5	382
108	Tomato Pudding	236	2	33	12	43	31	2	447
109	Cheesy Vegetable Casserole	256	9	15	18	63	23	2	580
109	Zucchini Pancakes	148	7	14	8	46	106	3	307
110	Pot Stickers	61	3	4	4	54	12	<1	74
111	Polenta with Two Cheeses	355	13	32	20	49	55	2	522
111	Cheesy Rice	319	13	26	18	51	101	2	614
112	Curried Rice	142	4	26	2	12	2	1	611
112	Mixed Fruit Chutney (per tablespoon)	55	1	14	<1	5	0	1	81
113	Doctored Dills (24 servings)	104	<1	27	<1	1	0	<1	485
113	Mango Salsa	88	1	23	<1	4	0	3	3
117	Brisket	148	26	2	3	19	96	<1	130
117	Tenderloin with Creamy Horseradish Spread	343	34	4	20	54	122	<1	232
118	London Grill*	205	24	<1	11	51	60	<1	430

Pg #	Recipe Title (Approx Per Serving)	Cal	Prot (g)	Carbo (g)	T Fat (g)	% Cal from Fat	Chol (mg)	Fiber (g)	Sod (mg)
118	Rapid Roast	233	39	0	8	31	92	0	83
119	Bohemian Pot Roast	424	51	50	25	36	246	1	131
120	Rolladen and Rotkohl	526	31	23	36	60	85	5	1148
121	Grilled Flank Steak*	477	25	12	36	68	60	<1	1447
121	Grayton Steaks	611	60	31	26	39	284	2	895
122	London Broil Steak*	469	18	2	43	83	45	<1	430
122	Beef and Noodles	558	49	53	33	42	210	1	832
123	Grilled Venison with Green Peppercorn Sauce*	206	27	<1	9	40	110	<1	443
124	Lemon Veal Piccata	407	23	18	27	60	120	1	744
124	Grilled Pork Tenderloin*	535	21	3	46	78	110	<1	256
125	Spinach Meat Loaf with Tomato Olive Sauce	456	32	14	31	61	152	3	997
126	Sunday Night Skillet Supper	358	16	16	26	65	183	<1	610
126	Stuffed Artichokes	215	13	25	9	34	88	8	859
127	Grilled Butterflied Lamb with Mustard Vinaigrette*	965	92	4	63	59	283	<1	959
131	Broiled Marinated Chicken	328	34	32	8	20	72	9	548
132	Chicken Stack	813	53	56	42	46	163	5	1990
132	Marinated Chicken Breasts	355	40	13	15	40	108	<1	516
133	Chinese Smoked Chicken	462	67	5	17	34	201	<1	2288
133	Chicken Caper	413	43	8	23	50	149	1	1406
134	Chicken Maciel	471	27	29	27	51	128	<1	217
134	Braised Chili Chicken	872	43	10	74	76	149	2	220
135	Company Chicken	347	16	21	23	58	69	2	837
135	Coq au Vin	615	54	15	37	53	213	4	1540
136	Crazy Chicken	790	50	67	36	41	184	3	1119
136	Grilled Lemon and Tarragon Chicken	540	50	1	37	62	213	<1	837
137	King Ranch Casserole	468	37	30	22	43	109	3	1169
137	Hawaiian Chicken	452	33	56	11	21	100	<1	482
138	Keystone Chicken	208	29	6	7	30	83	1	473
138	Lemon Chicken	436	29	2	34	71	171	<1	312
139	Lightly Lemon Chicken	311	31	15	13	39	72	1	394
139	Chicken Pie	531	34	35	28	48	93	4	1497

Pg #	Recipe Title (Approx Per Serving)	Cal	Prot (g)	Carbo (g)	T Fat (g)	% Cal from Fat	Chol (mg)	Fiber (g)	Sod (mg)
140	Miss Pat's Quick Chicken Pie	358	31	22	15	39	80	1	1060
140	Chicken Tetrazzini	359	36	21	14	36	90	2	565
141	Chicken Pontalba	913	47	30	66	65	388	2	989
145	Grilled Fish*	374	41	2	21	50	67	<1	412
145	Corney Grouper+	387	37	49	3	8	127	2	663
146	Smoked King Mackerel	412	33	10	28	59	124	1	576
146	Grilled Salmon Fillet	523	50	3	31	55	158	1	255
147	Grilled Red Snapper with Garlic and Lime	256	25	5	15	54	43	1	54
147	Grilled Tuna*	326	42	19	9	24	67	<1	412
148	Seafood Lasagna	976	66	57	53	49	334	5	1083
149	Crab Claws*	336	14	3	30	79	62	<1	551
149	Best Scalloped Oysters	Nutritional information for this recipe is not available.							
150	Oysters Rockefeller	439	11	12	40	80	142	2	597
150	Cold Bay Scallops	442	12	6	39	79	58	<1	699
151	Barbecued Shrimp	758	46	1	63	75	422	0	1198
151	Curried Barbecued Shrimp	195	17	2	13	60	179	<1	315
152	Cold Boiled Shrimp with Herb Mayonnaise	481	30	3	39	73	297	<1	565
152	Louisiana Heads-on Shrimp	475	32	43	19	36	277	2	1355
153	DeJean's Shrimp Remoulade*	324	32	3	20	56	295	<1	602
153	Shrimp Scampi	1454	35	1	148	90	564	<1	1701
154	Swiss Fondue with Shrimp	844	36	84	40	43	273	4	1521
154	Shrimp with Artichoke Hearts and Feta	623	42	77	16	23	250	4	1039
155	Shrimp with Roasted Red Pepper Sauce	337	39	3	17	45	355	1	452

Pages 159 to 181—Nutritional Profiles for Dessert Recipes are available upon request—but do you really want to know!

Pages 185 to 195—Nutritional Profiles for Children's Recipes are available upon request.

*Nutritional Profile includes entire amount of marinade.

+Nutritional Profile does not include cooking oil.

CONTRIBUTORS

David & Elizabeth Allison
Bob & Shirley Anderson,
  Belvedere
Don & Joan Anderson,
  Ashley
Bill, Barbie, Tiffany, & Natalie
  Borlaug, *Tide's Inn*
Victor Bowman & Carolyn
  Pendleton, *Maiden's
  Chamber/The Conservatory*
Judith Brantley & Benny
  Hyatt, *Dreamweaver*
Fred & Linda Buehler,
  Blue Belle
Bill & Star Burnett
Gordon & Carol Burns,
  Seastar
Joe & Sandy Carey,
  Carey Cottage
Bob & Jan Cirincione,
  Seaquel/Peach Delight
Jeff & Sue Clark, *Mis B'Haven*
Don & Libby Cooper, *Fantasia*
Jim & Judy Crawford, *C'Scape*
John & Pat Curphey,
  Curphey Cottage
Robert & Daryl Davis, *Krier*
Allessandro DeGregori &
  Sarah Hitchcock, *Acadia*
Monti & Debbie Dobson
Joe & Theo Doyle,
  Creole/Coquina
Bill & Lisa Dudney,
  Toasty Sunset
Charles & Sue Dunseth
Mark & Buffy DuPuis
Jim & Sue Gobert,
  Nirvana
David & Jill Hammes (Ruth),
  Flamingo
Tom & Melanie Hansbrough,
  About Time

Earl & Janice Hayford,
  Hayford
Dick & Jo Hepler, *Sandpiper*
Tim & Bonnie Horne,
  Beach Walk
Carl & Sissy Hubbard,
  Postcard/Picture Book
Hal & Suellen Hudson,
  For Keeps/Last Edition
Karen Hutcheson & Dave
  Wannemacher, *Greenpeace*
Carol Irvine
Bill & Emily Jackson
Ed & Linda James,
  Bagby-James
Carl & Connie Johnson,
  Starry Night/Little Dipper
Peter & Marianne Kircher,
  Gulf Manor
Alan & Sheila Klein,
  This Is The Life
Janet & Bruce Lewis,
  Dream Chaser
Robert & Eileen Ligday,
  English Cottage
Ed & Charlene Lilly,
  Adagio/Romance
Lowry & Marla Lomax,
  Peaches 'n Cream
Rex & Connie Lowe
Randy & Linda McCloy
Ray & Janie McLaughlin
Cyndi & Con McMahon,
  Shangri-La
Jerry & Cheri McWilliams
Tony & Pamela Meyers,
  Persimmon
Jeff & Susan Miller, *April 16th*
John & Linda Moore,
  Moore Fun
Steve & Gail Morton,
  Briermor by the Sea

Joe & Betty Mustachio,
  Somewhere in Time
Bob & Lisa Nesbit, *Narnia*
Lisa Newnum-Queen
Becky Norris, *DoLittle*
Louis & Karen Parvey,
  Easter Cottage/Sunrise
Neal & Martha Pedersen,
  *Vista del Mar/Carriage
  House*
John & Carolyn Peterson
Leahmon & Lois Phillips
Gillis Pippen, *Magnolia*
Dale & Robin Prophet,
  Briar Patch
Leigh & Sherwood Robins
Kenneth, Rosemary, & Jessica
  Scoggins, *Tupelo Honey/
  Floridays*
Duane & Terrie Shroyer,
  Southern Splendor
James & Doris Spain,
  Spinnaker
Chris & Lois Truss,
  Melrose/Woodlawn
Corey Walters, *Sundaze*
Geoffrey & Susan Wilder
Brad & Heidi Wilkins,
  Plum Crazy

Restaurants
  Basmati's
  Bud & Alley's
  *Dolphin Inn Bed and
    Breakfast*
  Josephine's Dining Room
  Modica Market
  Shades
  Silver Bucket

COTTAGES

A Summer Place
About Time
Acadia
Adagio
Alcorn Cottage
Allegro
Allison Cottage
American Dream
Anderson Cottage
Anniston
April 16th
Ashley
As You Like It
At Last
Auberge
Avondale
Bagby-James
Beach Walk
Bella Vista
Belvedere
Benedictus
Beside the
   Waterside
Bit-O-Heaven
Bloomsbury
Blue Belle
Blue Moon
Blue Note
Boswell Cottage
Briar Patch
Brickwalk
Bridgeport
Briermor by the Sea
Brigadoon
B's Nest
Burnett Cottage
Callan Cottage
Callaway Cottage
Cape May
Carey Cottage
Caribbean
Carpe Diem
Carriage House
Casa del Mar
Casablanca
Charleston
Chatham
ChelSea
Clark Cottage
Colony
Colors
Compass Rose

Coquina
Coral Cove
Corn Cottage
Crackerbox
Craige Cottage
Crawford Cottage
Creole
C'Scape
Cubbie Hole
Curphey Cottage
Dahlgren Cottage
Dapper's Den
Dargusch Cottage
Daydream Believer
Daysi's Castle
Delor Cottage
DeoGratis
Desire
DoLittle
Dollhouse
Dolphin Inn
Domino
Dove Crest
Dragon's Lair
Dragonette
Dream Catcher
Dream Chaser
Dream On
Dreamsicle
Dreamweaver
Duet
Duffy Cottage
Dune
Dunseth Cottage
DuPuis Cottage
Easter Cottage
Eclipse
Ecstasea
Eden
Elegance
Enchantment
English Cottage
Enon
Eyer Cottage
Fantasia
Fernleigh
Flamingo
Fletcher Cottage
Floridays
For Keeps
Forsythe Cottage
Frascogna Cottage

Frumious
   Bandersnatch
Gadsden
Gatewalk
Gazebo
Getaway II
Giant's Roost
GoodnightMoon
Gorlin Cottage
Grayton One
Grayton Two
Green Cottage
Green Gables
Greenpeace
Guest Cottage
Gulf Manor
Gulfview
Gull Cottage
Haardt Cottage
Hampton
Harvest Home
Hayford
Heavenly Days
Helvie Cottage
His Greenhouse
Hodges Cottage
Home Alone
Honalee
Hoover Cottage
House of Cards
Hurrah!
Idlewild South
Irvine Cottage
Isaacs Cottage
Ivy
Jasmine
Jasper
Jennifer's Castle
Josephine's
Jubilee
Kaleidoscope
Kennedy Cottage
Key West
Kitchens Cottage
Krier
La. House
Last Edition
Latitude
LeBlanc Cottage
Leeward
Lehman Cottage
Leonardo da Bicci

Lewis Cottage
Limehouse
Little Dipper
Little Sandpine
   Lodge
Lonesome Dove
Lost Goggles
Lowe Cottage
Lucas Cottage
Magnolia
Maiden's Chamber
Marietta's Cottage
Marisol
Martha Green
McChesney Cottage
McCollister Cottage
McLaughlin
   Cottage
Mellow Yellow
Melrose
Memories
Midsummer
   Night's Dream
Mirador
Mis B'Haven
Modica Cottage
Moore Fun
Nancy's Fancy
Narnia
Natchez House
Next Wave
Nightshade
Nirvana
Olson Cottage
On the Veranda
Ondine
Orth Cottage
Outer Banks
Overboard!
Park Place
Parvey Cottage
Peach Delight
Peaches 'n Cream
Pelican Perch
Periwinkle
Persimmon
Persuasion
Peterson Cottage
Picture Book
Pitter Patter
Pleasure Principal
Plum Crazy

Portera Cottage
Postcard
Precious
Propinquity
Puglin
Rainbow
RemBach
Renaissance
Rendezvous
Rhett's Revenge
Ricky's
Roanoke
Robin's Nest
Roger's Lighthouse
Romance
Rooftops
Rose Cottage
Ryan's Castle
Sabella Cottage
Salad Days
Sandcastle
Sandi Shore
Sandia
Sandpail
Sandpiper
Savannah Rose
Savannah Sands
Sawyer Cottage
Scott Cottage
Scruggs Cottage
Sea for Two
Sea View
Sealink
Seaquel
Seaspell
Seastar
Seawynds
Serendipity
Shangri-La
Shell Seeker
Sisters Three By
   The Sea
Skinny Dip
Smith Cottage
Somewhere in
   Time
Southern Comfort
Southern Splendor
Spinnaker
Stanziale Cottage
Starry Night
Stillman Cottage

Stringer Cottage
Sundance
Sundaze
Sunnyside Up
Sunrise
Sunrise Wishes
Sunset Dreams
Suntime
Taupelo
Temple Cottage
Thanksgiving
The Beach House
The Conservatory
This Is The Life
Tide's Inn
Tiger Paw
Tilling-on-the-Sea
Time Out
Toasty Sunset
Tommy T
Topisaw
Tower Breeze
Toye
Treetops
Trio
Tropical Holiday
Tupelo Honey
Tupelo Tucker
   Tower
Up On The Roof
Veranda
Villa Whimsey
Vista del Mar
Wakeham Cottage
Waterside
Wayback
Weber Cottage
Wilder Cottage
Windler Cottage
Windswept II
Windward
Woodlawn
Wright By the
   Beach
Zebulon
Zeidman Cottage
Zurn Cottage

INDEX

APPETIZERS. *See* Dips;
Hors d'Oeuvres; Snacks;
Spreads

APPLE
Apple Pecan Cake, 168
Baked Cheesy Apples, 80
French Apple Dessert, 159
German Apple Pancakes, 25

ARTICHOKES
Artichoke and Rice Salad, 58
Artichoke Brunch Pie, 77
Artichoke Dip, 21
Salad with Artichokes and Hearts
of Palm, 53
Shrimp with Artichoke Hearts
and Feta, 154
Stuffed Artichokes, 126

ASPARAGUS
Asparagus Roll-ups, 14
Japanese Sesame
Noodles, 96

BEEF. *See also* Ground Beef; Veal
Baked Beef Dip, 22
Bohemian Pot Roast, 119
Brisket, 117
Crenshaw County Camp
Stew, 46
French Stew, 47
Grayton Steaks, 121
Grilled Flank Steak, 121
London Broil Steak, 122
London Grill, 118
Rapid Roast, 118
Rolladen and Rotkohl, 120
Tenderloin with Creamy
Horseradish Spread, 117

BEVERAGES
Beach Cooler, 31
Blonde Sangria, 30
Champagne Punch, 27
Christmas Eve Eggnog, 28
Christmas Eve Punch, 28
Instant Spiced Tea, 30
Kentucky Eggnog Spike, 29

Sangria, 29
Sunrise Surprise, 81
Wassail, 31

BISCUITS
Biscuits, 73
Priory Biscuits, 73

BLUEBERRY
Deep-dish Blueberry
Cobbler, 159
Lemon Mousse with
Blueberries, 163

BREAD
Beignets, 72
Biscuits, 73
Dolphin Inn Sour Cream
Waffles, 203
German Apple Pancakes, 75
Monkey Bread, 74
New Orleans-style French
Toast, 74
Priory Biscuits, 73
Special Popovers, 75
Spoon Bread, 70

BREAD, LOAVES
Banana Bread, 67
Beer Bread, 67
Chili Cheese Bread, 68
Cuban Bread, 69
Grandmother's Famous
Cranberry Bread, 68
Poppy Seed Bread, 69
Pumpkin Spice Bread, 70
Stone-ground Wheat Bread, 72
Strawberry Bread, 71
Three-Two-One Bread
Plus, 71

BREAD, ROLLS
Cinnamon Rolls, 76
Overnight Pecan Rolls, 77

BROCCOLI
Broccoli and Rice Casserole, 102
Sesame Broccoli, 101

CAKES
Apple Pecan Cake, 168
Cupcake Cones, 189
Fresh Coconut Cake, 169
Hazelnut Cake, 169
Mexican Chocolate Cake, 168
Ooey Gooey Cake, 189

CAKES, POUND
Chocolate Chip Pound
Cake, 170
Fabulous Lemon Pound
Cake, 171
Five-flavor Pound Cake, 170

CANDY
Peanut Butter Fudge, 190
Peanut Butter Honeybees, 190
Quick Graham Cracker
Delights, 191

CHEESECAKES
Amaretto Cheesecake, 166
Cheesecake, 166
Cheesecake with
Raspberries, 167
Praline Cheesecake, 167

CHICKEN
Balsamic Chicken Wings, 15
Braised Chili Chicken, 134
Broiled Marinated
Chicken, 131
Chicken Caper, 133
Chicken Wings, 16
Chicken with Goat Cheese and
Roasted Red Peppers, 207
Chinese Smoked Chicken, 133
Coq au Vin, 135
Crazy Chicken, 136
Crenshaw County Camp
Stew, 46
Great San Luis Green Chile
Soup, 38
Grilled Lemon and Tarragon
Chicken, 136
Hawaiian Chicken, 137
Pasta and Chicken Salad, 91

Pecan and Chicken Salad, 54
Spaghetti with Chicken and
    Sausage, 95
Tortilla Soup, 43
Tossed Club Salad, 52

CHICKEN, BREASTS
Chicken Pontalba, 141
Chicken Stack, 132
Keystone Chicken, 138
Lemon Chicken, 138
Lightly Lemon Chicken, 139
Marinated Chicken
    Breasts, 132

CHICKEN, CASSEROLES
Chicken Maciel, 134
Chicken Tetrazzini, 140
Company Chicken, 135
King Ranch Casserole, 137

CHICKEN, GRILLED
Grilled Lemon and Tarragon
    Chicken, 136
Hawaiian Chicken, 137
Marinated Chicken Breasts, 132

CHICKEN, PIES
Chicken Pie, 139
Miss Pat's Quick Chicken
    Pie, 140

CHILI
Firehouse Chili, 37
Great San Luis Green Chile
    Soup, 38

CHOCOLATE
Almond Chocolate
    Squares, 172
Black Bottom Pie, 176
Brownie Pie, 177
Chocolate Chess Pie, 176
Chocolate Chip Pound
    Cake, 170
Chocolate Icebox Cake, 162
Chocolate Icebox Torte, 161
Chocolate Mousse, 161
Chocolate Pecan Pie, 177
Chocolate Roulade, 211

Clipper Chocolate Chip
    Squares, 173
Clown Face Sundae, 187
Cupcake Cones, 189
Death by Chocolate, 160
Kathryn Hepburn's
    Brownies, 171
Mexican Chocolate Cake, 168

CLAMS
Clam Dip, 23
Seafood Lasagna, 148

COCONUT
Coconut Caramel Pies, 178
Fresh Coconut Cake, 169

COOKIES
Almond Chocolate
    Squares, 172
Carolina Spice Cookies, 175
Clipper Chocolate Chip
    Squares, 173
Dottie L's Cookies, 193
Filled Cookies, 173
Kathryn Hepburn's
    Brownies, 171
Macadamia Nut Tea
    Cookies, 174
Oh Henry Bars, 192
Peanut Butter Cup Cookies, 192
Pecan Sandies, 174
Salted Nut Bars, 175
Snickerdoodles, 193
Stained Glass Cookies, 194
Whoopie Pies, 188

CORN
Great Lakes Corn Chowder, 40
Sautéed Corn with Bacon and
    Scallions, 104
Shoe Peg Corn Dip, 25

CRAB MEAT
Crab Bisque, 41
Crab Claws, 149
Crab Grass, 17
Landing Catch, 85
Microwave Crab Dip, 24
Mobile Bay Salad, 57

Seafood Lasagna, 148
Soft-shell Crabs, 149

CRAFTS
Chocolate Play Dough, 188
Chunky Chalk, 189
Crystal Garden, 192
Ocean-in-a-Bottle, 191
Soap Bubbles, 195
Spicy Sachets, 186
Tissue Paper Art, 187

DESSERTS. *See also* Cakes;
    Cheesecakes
Brazilian Mousse, 160
Bundt Kugel, 162
Buttermilk Strawberry
    Sherbet, 165
Chocolate Icebox Cake, 162
Chocolate Icebox Torte, 161
Chocolate Mousse, 161
Chocolate Roulade, 211
Clown Face Sundae, 187
Death by Chocolate, 160
Deep-dish Blueberry
    Cobbler, 159
Dirt Cake, 185
French Apple Dessert, 159
Fruit Pizza, 186
Homemade Peach Ice
    Cream, 164
Ice Cream Sandwiches, 185
Lemon Ice Cream Trifle, 163
Lemon Mousse with
    Blueberries, 163
Rice Pudding, 81
Russian Creme with Strawberry
    Sauce, 164
Sauce for Fresh Fruit, 165
Whoopie Pies, 188

DIPS
Artichoke Dip, 21
Baked Beef Dip, 22
Black-eyed Pea Dip, 22
Bleu Cheese Dip, 23
Clam Dip, 23
Green Chili and Tomato
    Dip, 23
Hummus, 24

Mexican Taco Dip, 26
Microwave Crab Dip, 24
Pizza Dip, 26
Salsa Dip, 25
Shoe Peg Corn Dip, 25
Spinach Dip, 26
Vidalia Onion Dip, 27

DUMPLINGS
Filled Noodles, 97
Pot Stickers, 110

EGG DISHES
Artichoke Brunch Pie, 77
Breakfast Sausage Casserole, 78
Cheesy Sausage Quiche, 79
South-of-the-Border Omelet, 78
Spinach Pie, 79
Spinach Quiche, 107
Sunday Night Skillet
    Supper, 126
Yesterday's Eggs, 80

FISH
Corney Grouper, 145
Grilled Fish, 145
Grilled Red Snapper with Garlic
    and Lime, 147
Grilled Salmon Fillet, 146
Grilled Tuna, 147
Smoked King Mackerel, 146
Yellowtail Snapper with Fire-
    roasted Tomato
    Tarragon Sauce, 201

FISH, GRILLED
Grilled Fish, 145
Grilled Red Snapper with Garlic
    and Lime, 147
Grilled Salmon Fillet, 146
Grilled Tuna, 147
Smoked King Mackerel, 146

French Market Soup Mix, 36

GROUND BEEF
Barbecued Appetizer
    Meatballs, 18
Beef and Noodles, 122
Filled Noodles, 97

Firehouse Chili, 37
Lasagna, 89
Spinach Meat Loaf with Tomato
    Olive Sauce, 125
Taco Soup, 42

HAM
Chinese Hot and Sour Soup, 39
French Market Soup, 36
Green Olives and Ham
    Canapés, 17
Ham and Cheese Rolls, 18
Hopping John, 104
Portuguese Vegetable
    Soup, 44

HORS D'OEUVRES
Asparagus Roll-ups, 14
Baked Brie, 13
Balsamic Chicken Wings, 15
Barbecued Appetizer
    Meatballs, 18
Cheddar Chili Squares, 14
Cheese Strips, 15
Chicken Wings, 16
Finger Sandwiches, 16
Green Olives and Ham
    Canapés, 17
Ham and Cheese Rolls, 18
Pesto Pizza, 89
Sausage Mushrooms, 21
Tortilla Roll-ups, 21

ICE CREAM
Buttermilk Strawberry
    Sherbet, 165
Homemade Peach Ice
    Cream, 164
LAMB
Baby Lamb Chops with
    Couscous Timbale, 205
Grilled Butterflied Lamb with
    Mustard Vinaigrette, 127

LEMON
Cookie Crust Lemon Pie, 179
Fabulous Lemon Pound
    Cake, 171
Grilled Lemon and Tarragon
    Chicken, 136

Lemon Chicken, 138
Lemon Ice Cream Trifle, 163
Lemon Mousse with
    Blueberries, 163
Lemon Veal Piccata, 124
Lightly Lemon Chicken, 139

MARINADES, 127, 131

MOUSSE
Brazilian Mousse, 160
Chocolate Mousse, 161
Lemon Mousse with
    Blueberries, 163

MUSSELS
Seafood Lasagna, 148

OYSTERS
Best Scalloped Oysters, 149
Oysters Rockefeller, 150

PASTA
Angel Hair Pasta, 92
Bowtie Salad, 86
Catch of the Day Salad, 85
Cheesy Italian Macaroni, 88
Chicken Tetrazzini, 140
Filled Noodles, 97
Japanese Sesame Noodles, 96
Landing Catch, 85
Lasagna, 89
Linguine with Pesto Sauce, 90
Linguine with Tomatoes, Basil
    and Brie, 87
Pasta and Chicken Salad, 91
Pasta-stuffed Zucchini, 96
Portuguese Vegetable
    Soup, 44
Red Sauce, 93
Rotini and Spinach Salad, 91
Sausage and Spaghetti, 94
Seafood Lasagna, 148
Seafood Pasta, 95
Sea Shell Macaroni
    Casserole, 88
Shrimp with Artichoke Hearts
    and Feta, 154
Spaghetti with Chicken and
    Sausage, 95

Tortellini Spinach Soup, 44

PEACH
Homemade Peach Ice
Cream, 164
Melba Pie, 180
Praline Peach Pie, 180
White Peach Pie, 181

PEAS, BLACK-EYED
Black-eyed Pea Dip, 22
Creole Black-eyed Peas and
Rice, 103
Hopping John, 104

PECAN
Apple Pecan Cake, 168
Apricot Pecan Spread, 13
Chocolate Pecan Pie, 177
Overnight Pecan Rolls, 77
Pecan and Chicken
Salad, 54
Pecan Sandies, 174
Southern Pecan Pie, 181

PIES
Black Bottom Pie, 176
Brownie Pie, 177
Chocolate Bar Pie, 195
Chocolate Chess Pie, 176
Chocolate Pecan Pie, 177
Coconut Caramel Pies, 178
Cookie Crust Lemon
Pie, 179
Daddy's Favorite Peanut Butter
Pies, 195
Kahlua Pie, 178
Margarita Pie, 179
Melba Pie, 180
Praline Peach Pie, 180
Sinkhole Cheese Pie, 194
Southern Pecan Pie, 181
White Peach Pie, 181

PIZZA
Pesto Pizza, 89

PORK. *See also* Ham
Crenshaw County Camp
Stew, 46

Creole Black-eyed Peas and
Rice, 103
Great San Luis Green Chile
Soup, 38
Grilled Pork Tenderloin, 124
Pot Stickers, 110

POTATOES
Chicken Pontalba, 141
Golden Stuffed Baked
Potatoes, 106
Jalapeño Potato Soup, 42
Potato Casserole, 106
Potato Salad, 58

PRALINE
Praline Cheesecake, 167
Praline Peach Pie, 180

QUICHE
Cheesy Sausage Quiche, 79
Spinach Quiche, 107

RICE
Artichoke and Rice Salad, 58
Cheesy Rice, 111
Creole Black-eyed Peas and
Rice, 103
Curried Rice, 112
Wild Rice Salad, 59
Yellow Rice Salad, 59

SALADS
Apricot Salad, 52
Artichoke and Rice Salad, 58
Bowtie Salad, 86
California Salad, 55
Catch of the Day Salad, 85
Cauliflower Salad, 54
Cool Tomato Salad, 62
Florida Salad, 57
Green Salad with Tarragon Bleu
Cheese Dressing, 63
Herbed Tomatoes, 62
Linguine with Tomatoes, Basil
and Brie, 87
Mobile Bay Salad, 57
Pasta and Chicken Salad, 91
Pecan and Chicken Salad, 54
Potato Salad, 58

Rotini and Spinach Salad, 91
Salad with Artichokes and
Hearts of Palm, 53
Salad with Sugared Almonds
and Orange Vinaigrette, 51
Sesame and Almond Slaw, 56
Shrimp Salad, 60
Spinach Salad, 60
Spinach Salad with Chutney
Dressing, 61
Summer Coleslaw, 56
Tossed Club Salad, 52
Wild Rice Salad, 59
Yellow Rice Salad, 59

SALADS, DRESSINGS, 53, 55, 86
Chutney Dressing, 61
Creamy Bleu Cheese
Dressing, 53
Orange Vinaigrette, 51
Red Dressing, 61
Tarragon Bleu Cheese
Dressing, 63

SAUCES, 141
Dolphin Inn Fruit Sauce, 203
Fire-roasted Tomato Tarragon
Sauce, 201
Green Peppercorn Sauce, 123
Linguine with Tomatoes, Basil
and Brie, 87
Mustard Vinaigrette, 127
Pesto Sauce, 90
Red Sauce, 93
Roasted Red Pepper Sauce, 155
Sauce for Fresh Fruit, 165
Tomato Olive Sauce, 125

SAUSAGE
Breakfast Sausage Casserole, 78
Cheesy Sausage Quiche, 79
Creole Black-eyed Peas and
Rice, 103
Portuguese Vegetable Soup, 44
Sausage and Spaghetti, 94
Sausage Mushrooms, 21
Spaghetti with Chicken and
Sausage, 95
Spinach Meat Loaf with Tomato
Olive Sauce, 125

Stuffed Artichokes, 126
Sunday Night Skillet
  Supper, 126

SCALLOPS
Cold Bay Scallops, 150
Seafood Lasagna, 148
Seafood Pasta, 95

SHRIMP
Barbecued Shrimp, 151
Catch of the Day Salad, 85
Cold Boiled Shrimp with Herb
  Mayonnaise, 152
Curried Barbecued Shrimp, 151
Curry Shrimp, 199
DeJean's Shrimp Remoulade, 153
Easy Shrimp Butter, 20
Landing Catch, 85
Louisiana Heads On
  Shrimp, 152
Seafood Lasagna, 148
Seafood Pasta, 95
Shrimp and Tomato Bisque, 209
Shrimp Salad, 60
Shrimp Scampi, 153
Shrimp with Artichoke Hearts
  and Feta, 154
Shrimp with Roasted Red
  Pepper Sauce, 155
Swiss Fondue with Shrimp, 154

SIDE DISHES
Baked Apricots, 81
Baked Cheesy Apples, 80
Doctored Dills, 113
Mango Salsa, 113
Mixed Fruit Chutney, 112
Polenta with Two Cheeses, 111
Pot Stickers, 110
Tomato Pudding, 108

SNACKS
Beary Good Snack Mix, 187
Boiled Peanuts, 19

Spiced Oyster Crackers, 19
Sweet Spiced Nuts, 191

SOUPS
Chinese Hot and Sour Soup, 39
Crab Bisque, 41
French Market Soup, 36
Great Lakes Corn Chowder, 40
Great San Luis Green Chile
  Soup, 38
Jalapeño Potato Soup, 42
Portuguese Vegetable Soup, 44
Shrimp and Tomato Bisque, 209
Taco Soup, 42
Tortellini Spinach Soup, 44
Tortilla Soup, 43
Turkey Vegetable Soup, 45
Wharton Cheese Soup, 37

SOUPS, COLD
Carrot Vichyssoise, 41
Chilled Avocado Soup, 35
Cucumber Soup, 39
Gazpacho, 35

SPINACH
Rotini and Spinach Salad, 91
Spinach Dip, 26
Spinach Pie, 79
Spinach Quiche, 107
Spinach Salad, 60
Spinach Salad with Chutney
  Dressing, 61
Tortellini Spinach Soup, 44

SPREADS
Apricot Pecan Spread, 13
Crab Grass, 17
Easy Shrimp Butter, 20
Reuben Spread, 27
Sun-dried Tomato Pâté, 20

STEWS
Crenshaw County Camp
  Stew, 46

Firehouse Chili, 37
French Stew, 47

STRAWBERRY
Buttermilk Strawberry
  Sherbet, 165
Russian Creme with Strawberry
  Sauce, 164
Strawberry Bread, 71

TOMATOES
Cool Tomato Salad, 62
Green Tomato Ratatouille, 108
Herbed Tomatoes, 62
Tomato Pudding, 108

TURKEY
Spinach Pie, 79
Turkey Vegetable Soup, 45

VEAL
Lemon Veal Piccata, 124

VEGETABLES. *See also the*
  Individual Kinds
Bacon and Green Bean
  Bundles, 101
Baked Onions with Balsamic
  Vinaigrette, 105
Carrot Casserole, 102
Cheesy Vegetable Casserole, 109
Green Tomato Ratatouille, 108
Rotkohl, 120
Scalloped Green Peppers, 105
Squash Casserole with Bacon
  and Green Chilies, 107

VENISON
Grilled Venison with Green
  Peppercorn Sauce, 123

ZUCCHINI
Pasta-stuffed Zucchini, 96
Zucchini Pancakes, 109

To order additional copies of

SEASIDE™

Pastels & Pickets

write to:

Seaside Town Council
P.O. Box 4957
Seaside, Florida 32459

Be sure to include Your Name and Complete Address for return mail.

For one copy send:	$22.95
Plus postage and handling	3.50
Total	$26.45

(Note: Florida residents add $1.86 sales tax for a total of $28.31)

For each additional copy up to 10 copies send:	$22.95
Plus postage and handling	1.00
Total	$23.95

(Note: Florida residents add $1.68 sales tax per book for a total of $25.63)

For volume purchases call 1-904-231-1551

Make checks payable to **Seaside Town Council**

Allow three weeks for delivery

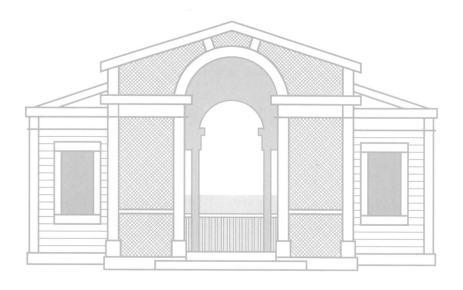

To see a world in a grain of sand
And a heaven in a wildflower:
Hold infinity in the palm of your hand,
And eternity in an hour.

—William Blake